THE PSYCHOLOGY OF ABANDON: BERSERK STYLE IN AMERICAN CULTURE

129

Books by Kirby Farrell:

Cony-Catching (New York: Atheneum, 1971)

Shakespeare's Creation: the Language of Magic and Play
 (Amherst, Mass.: Univ. of Massachusetts Press, 1976)

Play-Death and Heroism in Shakespeare
 (U. North Carolina Press: Chapel Hill, N.C., 1989)

The American Satan (New York: Walker & Co., 1990)

Women in the Renaissance: Selections from English Literary

Renaissance, ed. Kirby Farrell, Elizabeth Hageman, and Arthur F. Kinney
 (Amherst: Univ. of Massachusetts Press, 1990)

Snuff (New York: Walker & Co., 1991)

Post_Traumatic Culture: Injury and Interpretation in the 90s
 (Baltimore: Johns Hopkins Univ. Press, 1998)

Critical Essays on Shakespeare's Richard II, ed. Kirby Farrell
 (New York: G. K. Hall, 1999)

The Mysteries of Elizabeth I, ed. Kirby Farrell and K. Swaim
 (Amherst: Univ. of Massachusetts Press, 2003)

Berserk Style in American Culture (New York: Palgrave Macmillan, 2011)

The Psychology of Abandon (Amherst: Leveller's Press, 2015)

THE PSYCHOLOGY OF ABANDON: BERSERK STYLE IN AMERICAN CULTURE

Kirby Farrell

Published by *Levellers Press*, Amherst, Massachusetts

Printed in the United States of America

ISBN 978-1-937146-72-6

CONTENTS

LIST OF FIGURES

PREFACE

Each of us lives in a magic circle of familiar conventions. As long as we stay inside the circle of what we know—language, customs, and roles—the world is manageable and we feel safe. Most social encounters—"How are you? Fine, and you?"—follow an implicit script. Even in puzzling moments, consciously or not, we may be guided by a conventional scenario that we're trying out in order to test what sort of experience this is, and what might work.

We begin learning the conventions from birth, long before we can remember. They help us form and confirm our interpretation of reality. They feel right. Relying on them, *we* feel right. Even though they are tools and enabling fictions, they feel natural, and habit reinforces them. When something—an accident, a death—shocks us "out" of our routine life, suddenly everyday reality seems enchanted: a dream or a play. We become aware of how much we don't know beyond the circle, and of our strategies for controlling the boundary. Slang pictures someone living "on the edge," "in denial," or "out" of his mind. Some of the territory outside we can explore and study, mapping it as the unconscious, trance, God, the beyond, and the like. The strangeness may bring nervous system arousal and heightened vigilance. Under stress, blinding rage or visionary awareness may take over.

This book significantly revises and updates *Berserk Style in American Culture* (2011), which examined language and ideas that Americans use to think about going out of the magic circle. Experiences of the beyond are shaped by physiology. Paradoxically, they are also structured by what we already know, as when religions imagine God as father, king, and judge. In abandon, you give up or overthrow self-control and go "outside" or "beyond" conventions. If you reach the berserk state, overtaken by rage, you may run amok. If you're "swept away" by erotic abandon, you may relax or violate some inhibitions and see things differently, but you can remember who you were. If you are fired from your job and want vindication or vengeance, you are apt to choose a recognizable role such as plaintiff in a lawsuit or, if sufficiently enraged, perhaps the gunman shooting up the office.

Abandon always has some interpretive context; almost nobody is ever wholly "out of it." For this reason it can be productive to examine the imaginative materials out of which people construct experiences of abandon. In addition, since there are strong incentives to believe that such experiences takes you beyond responsibility and everyday limits, it also makes sense to examine how people mystify the experience.

My approach owes much to *Post-Traumatic Culture* (1998), which explores how cultures used the concept of trauma in the 1890s, when it crystallized in its modern form, and in the Vietnam War era. Trauma overwhelms psychic defenses and disrupts the magic circle of everyday reality, yet its impact is not predictable. Symptoms cluster around depressive and aggressive behaviors. One person may be immobilized, another panicked, while a third may become furiously charged—berserk. Some will recover quickly, while others suffer lasting injury. As the psychiatrists say, much depends on how you are wrapped.

How you're wrapped, in turn, depends partly on your neurological makeup, and partly on how you interpret your experience. How you understand what is happening to you affects your particular symptoms. And since the experience is also an idea about the experience, you can use trauma as an explanatory tool or as a descriptor, as in "a traumatic hurricane." The anguish of post-traumatic stress disorder (PTSD) can be real, but it can also function as an over-the-counter popular rationalization for all sorts of problematic behavior.

Aggressive responses to traumatic stress make headlines as berserk rampage killing in a war zone, in a workplace, or a school. But running amok is a highly adaptable idea. Journalism, for example, uses it to describe excesses or loss of control in all sorts of endeavors, from the playing field to Wall Street and the gaming table.

When the idea of going "beyond" everyday experience becomes readily available in ads, movies, politics, and more, berserk behavior becomes berserk style. Two premises follow and need periodic re-emphasis. As an idea, abandon is radically equivocal and ambivalent. Even berserk fury is horrific in its potential for destruction but alluring as a promise that escape from inhibitions can open up access to extraordinary resources. In Hollywood thrillers, heroes accomplish amazing feats by throwing restraint to the wind and emerging unscathed. The merciless killer is a hero on the battlefield, a "madman" on Main Street. The allure of abandon can be ecstatic as well as sinister.

The second premise is that as a style, berserk abandon can be used for all sorts of ends. The idea of uncontrollable frenzy can be a tool, a role, a means to manage morale or to influence others. It can be personal, conscious or not, and it can be cultural, shared by a group, even contagious.

These premises are tools that the present book uses to examine American culture from the Vietnam War era to the economic crisis that closed the first decade of the new century. In finance and the military, not always for predictable reasons, abandon was significant during those years. Americans relaxed controls on behaviors from sex and gambling to broadcast taboos and marijuana. Technology has escalated mayhem in movies, video games, and Internet content. Unprecedented access to lethal weapons and copycat publicity have made rampage killing a familiar hazard of American life.

The same ambiguities that make berserk style seductively potent in the world outside your window also frustrate tidy explanations, since the behavior is interpretive as well as neurophysiological, cultural as well as individual, and always subject to manipulation. What's more, in the new century the pace of change makes events a moving target. This new edition updates material from the original book, and analyzes in more detail subjects such as sexuality and the interplay of culture and mental illness in rampage killing.

The book's subject is emotionally charged, and its focus on extremes means that it risks misinterpretation. An account of soldiers and policy makers who have run amok in Iraq, for example, cannot do justice to individuals or to the tragic complexities that may overtake them. Likewise, the premise that mafia behavior is widespread in economic life is not an indictment of all businessmen or a Spenglerian disquisition on the decline and fall of American culture. And finally, if the argument appears politically biased, this is primarily because some ideologies have made abandon a preferred tool in their discourse.

Figure 0.1 A Pontiac 2000 Grand AM advertisement

Berserk style takes a variety of historically particular forms in cultures around the world. And given the urgent character of the core ideas, those forms are volatile. In the go-go 1990s, for example, Detroit sold thrilling themes. In a magazine advertisement a new Pontiac tears across a no-man's land spiked by giant saw blades, its windshield and wheels jagged with saw-toothed reflections, its caption defying danger "When the Road Bites, Bite Back" (figure 1). As in action comics, the daredevil motorist could be dashing through enemy lines in a war movie, on a mission, triumphantly invulnerable. The ad is selling not just transportation but survival.

With terrorism and the Bush administration's actual wars in the news, marketers toned down the thrills. But by 2008, ads were pumping adrenaline again, showing a slow-motion fist punching a board, shattering the wood and turning into a new Acura sedan. But the long post-Vietnam recovery and boom was about to crash. A year later, not only was the death-defying Rambo-like Pontiac muscle car gone, the whole Pontiac division had been liquidated by a bankrupt General Motors reorganizing on the lip of a financial precipice.

Still, berserk style does not vanish; it mutates.

It adapts.

It bites back.

ACKNOWLEDGEMENTS

The Psychology of Abandon owes much to the friends who held onto my shirttails as abandon drew me on: Dr. Neil Elgee and the Ernest Becker Foundation, Kay Smith, Steve Helmling, Claire and Bob Hopley and Roberto Carrion. Helena Farrell deserves special thanks for her inspired cover design.

Some materials in this book originally appeared in *Berserk Style in American Culture* (Palgrave Macmillan, 2011). Excerpts from my essay of the same title have been reprinted with the permission of *Cultural Critique* and the University of Minnesota Press. In different forms some of the book's arguments have appeared in *The Interdisciplinary Handbook of Trauma and Culture*, ed. Yochai Ataria, et al (Springer, 2015), "The New Rampage Mentality," in *Truthout*, August 28, 2012: truth-out.org/opinion/item/11148-the-new-rampage-mentality and also in "A Swim in The Nile," my essays for *Psychology Today* online: www.psychologytoday.com/blog/swim-in-denial.

INTRODUCTION

You went berserk...you'll probably be
liable to fits of it all your life.

Rudyard Kipling

"Abandon" is a peculiarly ambivalent word. As a verb, it implies
volition: you renounce or relinquish something; shed inhibitions; flee
from danger; give up control; halt a difficult or dangerous effort.

As a noun, "abandon" denotes a complete lack of inhibition or
restraint, implying recklessness, impulsiveness, wantonness, ecstasy or
ultimate wildness. In this sense, inhibitions may not be holding you
back but rather holding you together, and without them you may
explode into another condition such as ecstasy or fury.

It's the teasing difference between self-control and lost control.
In practice, consciously or not, many behaviors blur the distinction.
Certain mystical traditions seek an experience of ecstatic cosmic abandon through strategic discipline. In combat, enraged and stressed
soldiers may interpret an order as encouragement to run amok, in
berserk abandon, as in the slaughter of farm families at My Lai in the
Vietnam war. If "they abandoned themselves to rage," how conscious
was their action? To what extent was it a function of stress chemistry?
What if we say "rage overwhelmed them"?

Dictionaries define the berserk state as frenzied, violent, or deranged. The original berserker was "a wild Norse warrior of great strength and ferocious courage, who fought on the battlefield with a frenzied fury known as 'the berserker rage'; often a lawless bravo or freebooter." The term may refer to a Norse hero who "never fought in armor but in his *ber sark,* which means 'bearskin' in the Nordic languages. Thus the term berserk became synonymous with reckless courage. During the Saga time in Iceland and in the Scandinavian countries (A.D. 870-1030)...the Berserks, apparently bearing the same name as the legendary warrior, arose as a predatory group of brawlers and killers who disrupted the peace of the Viking community repeatedly."[1] Some sources suggest that the Viking fury was a temporary psychosis induced by eating the mushroom *Amanita muscaria* (Fabing, 239).

The term is not just an antique curiosity. Based on his clinical work with Vietnam War veterans, the psychiatrist Jonathan Shay concludes that in combat today soldiers may experience the same icy rage that Homer describes in *The Iliad,* stripping off armor like the Viking's "bare sark."[2] Pumped up by stress, the berserker's emergency physiology brings reckless courage and indifference to pain. As inhibitions fall away, abandon presents as a different psychic state or identity, so the civilized warrior in the bear sark or shirt acquires the bear's ferocity. Lacking claws and a carapace, humans have long relied on prosthetic weapons and a shell of animal hides or armor. Even today military units and sports teams commonly take the name of a fearsome animal. By sharing the unconstrained potency of wild predators, warriors want to frighten enemies, suppress their own terror, and pump up "fighting spirit"—their willingness to kill without compunction.

In such behaviors emergency physiology combines with creaturely hunger for life to shed peacetime identity. The great leader is the hero who can access this berserk abandon. Since the core motive is the drive for more life—survival—the behavior reaches far beyond the battlefield. In *New Yorker* cartoons, Vikings have become a conventional symbol for violent abandon. In the issue of August 10 & 17, 2009, for example, a personnel manager tells a Viking job applicant that "Your resume is remarkably similar to our C.E.O.'s." In the cartoons as in the Norse Sagas, Viking abandon has a mythic quality that exceeds conventional ideas about violence.

A cartoon Viking is stylized. Survival rage makes the real thing terrifying and chaotic. Shedding protective gear, killing and mutilating without mercy, soldiers may be wildly vicious even while believing that they are restoring "what's right" through revenge or sacrifice; mystically replenishing life by slaughtering enemies; or commanding death itself. In peril, berserkers may feel transported, in touch with uncanny powers and luck.[3] They may feel God or some other supernatural agency guiding them. In that supercharged state, facing death, godlike but also beastlike, they are apt to feel invulnerable, throw off their armor, and attack the threat head on. Even when berserkers survive, Shay concludes, the traumatic outcome "leads to lifelong psychological injury" (20).

Since 1983, when the first workplace rampages among U. S. Postal Service workers gave rise to the coinage "going postal," berserk abandon has been associated with rampage killing. Although taboo obscures the connection, rampaging civilians share many characteristics of berserk soldiers. They are overwhelmingly male, half with military training, and often emulate soldiers in their weapons and dress. The forensic psychiatrist Park Dietz has coined the term "pseudocommando" to categorize killers who plan their massacres around military themes and expect to die in a blaze of glory. As many as half of rampage killers have histories of serious mental health problems: therapy or a hospitalization, prescription psychiatric drugs, a suicide attempt or evidence of psychosis. They may imagine themselves in a race war with biblical dimensions, as the paranoid Colin Ferguson did shooting passengers on a Long Island commuter train (December 7, 1993). In concentrating outrage, they behave as if their foundational sense of "what's right" is threatening to come apart. Most rampage killers have suffered reversals in status and relationships, and seethe over grievances focused on enemies. Under stress and alienated, they face social death, which can be as frightening as real death. The ability to terrify the world is intoxicating for wounded self-esteem.[4]

Although rampages accounted for less than 1% of all homicide deaths from 1980 to 2008, "the attacks "are a matter of great public interest and concern."[5] They are also not peculiar to the U. S., since "the best scientific thinking, in a field that is admittedly understudied, now holds that multiple public murder occurs at a fairly constant level across time and cultures. What some people call 'running amok,' a term first used in Malaysia to describe frenzied, indiscriminate killing, has been observed in many cultures."[6] That conclusion needs to be qualified, since the American civilian's unusual access to firearms, and especially combat-style weapons, makes possible a higher death toll. "More than half of the most deadly mass shootings documented in the past 50 years around the world occurred in the United States, and 73 percent of the killers in the U.S. obtained their weapons legally."[7]

To complicate matters further, most rampage killings show signs of copycat behavior, with killers aware of previous atrocities and competing to outdo them. "In 1995," for example, "as he "set out to mow down a company of soldiers at Fort Bragg with an assault rifle and a semiautomatic pistol," a soldier named Kreutzer "told a friend he knew what the record number of multiple killings was."[8] A comprehensive analysis by researchers at Harvard concludes that "in 2011 the United States entered a new period in which mass shootings are occurring more frequently." Their finding "corroborates the FBI's findings that 'active shooter' incidents have become more frequent."[9]

Berserk episodes, in a word, are a function of our creaturely endowment—how we're built. But as copycat qualities reveal, they are also the outcome of interpretation.

ABANDON AS A BEHAVIOR AND TROPE

Abandon is an action but also an idea about action on the edge of control. "The edge" is of course just a crude metaphor for experience in which autonomic forces overtake conventional self-control. Fight-or-flight physiology may produce the mix of panic or rage spotlighted in the news, but "the edge" can also be—for example—an experience of manic play, drunkenness, or visionary ecstasy. As a result, abandon is far more pervasive than conventional wisdom recognizes. Soldiers and fired employees may go berserk, but so do politicians, cancer cells, and financial markets.[10] Couples may be "head over heels" in love. Abandon implies a clinical category but also a trope that shapes a wide range of personal and cultural fantasies.

As a trope, the term "berserk" is strikingly volatile and ambiguous. It can apply to almost any loss or overthrow of control. In everyday speech, to be berserk is to be carried away or "unhinged." While psychiatry refers to the berserk "state," the term "berserking" responds better to the headlong motion implied, as in to "run" amok, to go "over the edge," "over the top," "off" the deep end, or "out" of your mind." You can "go for broke," "go rogue," or "go ballistic"; "freak" or "flip" out, "lose it," go "haywire" or "fly off the handle" or off your predictable rocker. In love and war "anything goes," with "no holds barred." Slang reveals the violent fantasies implied. In a "winner take all" competition the athlete with the "killer instinct" triumphs. You can be "wildly" successful or "shop till you drop," and spend "like there's no tomorrow." An "explosive" new idea can "blow your mind." At a bar you can drink "car bombs." "Carpe diem" may be genteel poetic convention or an injunction to "throw caution to the winds." Getting "high" can be a chemical shortcut to the berserker's sense of godlike exaltation. So can binge gambling or orgasmic recklessness in an era of AIDS. A good time can be a "blast."

Slang shows how ambivalent we are about berserk abandon. It can be a chaotic disintegration of character, but also it can imply that "letting it all hang out" is a means of getting access to the ground of personality or a more authentic self. The core idea of early psychoanalysis, some religions, and scientology, for example, is abreaction: that unconscious, perhaps traumatic material is obstructing the self and needs to be dispelled. In a related way psychedelic drug culture promised to "expand" or "raise" consciousness, or as Aldous Huxley put it, "open the doors" of perception." The core assumption is that some higher, deeper, truer, "other" reality lies just beyond everyday consciousness, and we can get "in touch" with it.

But again: we are ambivalent about berserk abandon, and for good reason.

Love can denote a vision of divine harmony or a terrifying loss of control. Couples "fall" in love, "head over heels," toward an orgasmic climax associated with surrender, abandon, ecstasy and for Tristan and Iseult, doom. Yet panic or fury can also lead to a climactic "blackout." Mystics and warriors both report feeling "transported," with a conviction of transcendence or access to the beyond. Going "over the edge" can be frightening but also alluring as an access to uncanny power and psychic expansiveness. Facing death, soldiers may charge into enemy fire—and possibly survive. Since a failure of nerve can be fatally paralyzing, such recklessness may be life-saving courage or suicidal folly. For survivors it may have the color of miracle or magic, and make them heroes.

How can we not be of two minds about a behavior as equivocal as abandon? Viking berserkers could be bestial marauders or legendary heroes. If it doesn't get you killed on the battlefield, heedless fury may stun and scatter your enemies. Abandon may culminate in mad folly, or bring triumph and more life—and the symbolic equivalents of more life: loot, sex, land, marble statues, and apotheosis. The ambivalence is vivid in the reaction to crowd disasters such as a stadium or post-Thanksgiving shopping crush. Scientific studies show that such fatal stampedes are caused by miscommunication and the laws

of physics, not by abandon. Yet when a Wal-Mart employee died trying to manage a throng of shoppers in 2008, media voices reacted
with shrill horror. One letter to the New York *Post* condemned "the
animals (you know who you are) who stampeded that poor man at
Wal-Mart on Black Friday. You are a perfect example of the depraved
decadence of society today."[11] The crowd's miscommunication is
a combination of faulty story and nervous system panic. The letter
writer, however, moralizes the disaster, imagining "depraved" shoppers greedy for loot—like frenzied Vikings. In this story consumerist
America is caught in a chokepoint doorway, maddened to abandon.

The letter writer envisions the shoppers carried away by the voice
of greed, deaf to the civilized voice of self-control and cooperation.
It can be useful to think of abandon as a boundary managed by internal debate. Rampage killers play out such a debate when they seethe
for months, persuading themselves to run amok. Stress physiology
intensifies a feedback loop that climaxes in do-or-die action. Alone in
his room at night, Colin Ferguson developed a pseudo-biblical rant
about race war that eventually crowded out reality-testing arguments
and led him to murder commuters on the Long Island Railroad. In
praying obsessively throughout the day, Mohammed Atta, leader of
the 9/11 hijackers, reinforced the voice of cold-blooded rage and
subsumed conventional religious inhibitions. The Columbine killers
ranted online and in diaries. In Newtown Connecticut, Adam Lanza
tabulated his rampage "research" in a spread sheet.

Isolation and secrecy diminish or even dissociate constraining arguments, enabling the mind to fixate on abandon. Societies can also
experience these dynamics. In the 1960s as in the "roaring" twenties,
voices that cried "let it all hang out" assumed that abandon could
liberate personal authenticity and fulfillment that are repressed in everyday life. The ancient Greeks ventriloquized this voice through the
god Dionysus, who presided "not only over wine and theater but
over ecstatic song and dance and 'liberating' madness (as his epithet
eleutherios, 'the Liberator,' suggests."[12] In Christianity, the voice of
the Lord urges you to lose yourself to find yourself (Mat. 10:39). Arrayed against calls to abandon are dialectical voices from Apollo and
Pontius Pilate to the mundane Stop sign on the street corner today.

LOSING TO GAIN

Abandon takes many forms. Hypnosis and the Sufi's trance can induce self-forgetfulness. It can be sublime in Christ's injunction to

lose yourself in order to find yourself, but ridiculous in sales pitches bidding you to "find the new you!" with the swipe of a credit card. The assumption is that extraordinary resources lie within us and just beyond us, accessible if we could only shed the inane inhibitions that hold us back. If we could go "over the edge" or "outside the box," we might experience bliss or an abyss.

The idea that self-loss opens access to superhuman resources is ancient. In *Ion*, for example, Socrates concludes that the poet cannot create "until he has been inspired and put out of his senses, and his mind is no longer in him" (533d). Sinners "surrender" to Jesus to be forgiven and restore their sense of "what's right." In movie theaters the mild-mannered Clark Kent turns into Superman with superhuman powers from the beyond. Wall Street wizards report exceptional profits from "lightning" trading software and derivatives whose algorithms defy plodding analysis. The shared fantasy is that various forms of abandon open up resources that are more authentic than the everyday self.

The faculties associated with abandon—risk, fearlessness, uncanny instinct—have the potency and allure of magic. Athletes try to psych out that magic or invoke it with steroids. Superheroes and Harry Potter gratuitously command it. Fulfilled, the magical connection is the climax of comedy. When it fails or proves vicious, tragedy prevails. Little wonder that efforts to master berserk abandon are at the heart of culture, whether tribal elders are initiating the young through extreme tests, or performers are ritually pumping up backstage. And no wonder popular culture obsesses over the theme. Stevenson's Dr. Jekyll destroys himself attempting to master the berserk Mr. Hyde within him. Ang Lee's film of the Marvel comic *Incredible Hulk* (2003) updates the same struggle. Made susceptible to berserk transformation by radiation poisoning, Bruce Banner (Eric Bana) periodically becomes the Hulk: his eyes glow with alien fury, and his body swells to superhuman proportions. He becomes indomitable but also abominably dangerous. The story is a parable about the risk of self-destruction in the struggle to master heroic autonomy.

Hollywood's *Hulk* openly retails heroic aggrandizement to audiences in a blurb promising viewers "A super powered adrenaline blast" (Peter Hammond). The "adrenaline blast" is of course an advertising fiction: an alluring idea about berserk frenzy. Nobody expects fans to storm out of the theater uprooting telephone poles and throwing cars about. But Insofar as it pumps up morale and sells tickets, the advertiser is using the idea of an adrenaline blast to evoke at a tame distance the uncanny powers associated with abandon. In the process, the advertisement makes the concept's terror enticing and a product for sale.

This is berserk style.

BERSERK STYLE

A story about the experience of berserk abandon is not the same thing as the experience itself. The story represents and interprets the experience. In the blurb for *Incredible Hulk* just mentioned, an advertisement is representing and interpreting a story (movie) that is representing and interpreting in theaters a berserk experience (the Hulk's) that is frankly fictional, from a screenwriter's conception of berserk experience. We need not be mesmerized by the infinite regression. Rather, the crucial point is to see that people *use the idea* of abandon in all sorts of ways, often unwittingly, and the experience and the story about it can be bewilderingly entangled.

In James Toback's documentary film *Tyson* (2009), for example, the champion boxer Mike Tyson uses a version of the Hulk's story to stabilize an explosive personality torn by "extremes" (his word) of violent exaltation and demonic chaos. From childhood terror, humiliation, predatory fury, and prison, Tyson rose to dominate the ring. As he tells it, his powers came from harnessing the fury of berserk abandon, thanks to the boxing skills and warrior ethos—the heroic story—instilled in him by his fatherly trainer Gus D'Amato. In prefight publicity and in the ring, Tyson was able to dramatize a threat of wild force that intimidated opponents and excited fans, yet his focus on the warrior story kept him in control. At his peak he enjoyed the berserker's conviction of godlike invulnerability, with spectacular fame, loot, and sexual conquests as a reward. As time went on, however, the champ increasingly cycled between monstrous appetite—drugs, rape, profligacy, egomania—and collapse. Style proved unable to manage his furies.

After more time in prison Tyson attempted a comeback, trying to relive the story of warrior poise "on the edge." But in a classic plot line, his heart was no longer in it, and in 1987 the story fell apart in his desperate title match with Evander Holyfield. When both fighters began to lose control, Tyson wildly bit off a piece of his antagonist's ear as berserk soldiers may bite or even eat parts of slain enemies. As if fighting for his life in a teenage gang brawl, he ran amok. The abandon thrilled and outraged the boxing world. In the film Tyson takes a penitent, confessional role to come back from failure. He advances a new story created out of family bonds and psychotherapy to substitute for the mirage of uncanny powers.

Tyson himself lived through some berserk moments. But in *Tyson* we are mostly looking at examples of berserk style: "berserk" because some of the recounted actions entail self-abandon, and a "style" insofar as the *idea* of abandon is being used in stories that shape everyday experience. Tyson and his trainer relied on the idea of mastered abandon as a goal in training and as a tool for supporting morale under stress. For fans and advertisers the material functioned as an elixir enhancing excitement, million-dollar purses, and golden glories.

A core premise of this book is that this is a cultural process. Fascination with berserk powers is variously personal and collective, but also crucially conditioned by fantasies that are pervasive if often unacknowledged. Mike Tyson attributes his toxic rage to the humiliation and terror of urban poverty—a "toxic" environment. The Hulk's superhuman force is the product of toxic radiation. Like Tyson's rage, radiation made the nuclear weapons that promised the U. S. godlike dominance after the horrors of World War II, and implied a prosperous future of unlimited cheap power. Once "harnessed," as propaganda used to put it, radiation would be akin to Tyson's fantasy of warrior mastery. The "world champion" was entitled to boast that nobody could beat him. In effect, the relation was reciprocal: the boxer and the country drew on a cluster of fantasy materials signifying supremacy.

Yet like Tyson's career, that magical prospect proved to be painfully equivocal for the nation as challenges to nuclear supremacy proliferated. By the time investment guru Warren Buffett spoke of Wall Street's fabulously profitable, stupefyingly destructive derivatives as "financial weapons of mass destruction, carrying dangers that, while now latent, are potentially lethal" (2002), his allusion to nuclear superiority was meant to evoke menace.

Buffett recognized the berserk quality in Wall Street's behavior. And true to the symbolic logic, the 2008 financial crisis did in fact pose the "mega-catastrophic risk" for the economy that Buffett foretold (March 4, 2003), a tale taken up in later chapters. For now it is enough to note that berserk style operates in intimate personal thought but also in the more abstract reaches of cultural fantasy. And it implies belief. The belief may be woozy, fanatical, or outright magical thinking. Or in countless movies—and in life—it may be a visionary commitment to a seemingly impossible project "worth fighting for." Carried beyond conventional safeguards, the risk is always the sway of delusion. "During the housing bubble," said James Surowiecki tartly in 2009, "the financial sector essentially tried to create reality."[13] More exactly, *as if* "creating reality," berserk style confirms biases and assumptions.

This expanded conception of berserk behavior and style requires an expanded investigation. Psychiatry conceives the berserk state as a pathological response to traumatic stress. The core experience of trauma, says the textbook, is "intense fear, helplessness, loss of control, and threat of annihilation."[14] In combat, berserking is an emergency response to stress physiology. Overtaken by terror and exhaustion, soldiers may charge into enemy fire. They appear carried away or deranged. Fight overcomes flight. "It is plain," says the psychiatrist, "that the berserker's brain and body function are as distant from everyday function as his mental state is from everyday thought and feeling" (91).

In the words of one Vietnam veteran, "I was a fucking animal. When I look back on that stuff, I say, 'That was somebody else did that'" (83). He speaks as if he was out of control, really not there, yet he recognizes his behavior—"that stuff"—clearly enough to reject it as "not me." The behavior is alien but not meaningless. The behavior may be recklessly impulsive or chaotic, yet combat soldiers who have run amok may report a feeling of godlike invulnerability and purposefulness. Some rampage killers make cunning plans and even advertise their exploits. Dr. Shay calls the berserker's cold rage "flaming ice," evoking the contradictory sense of actions coldly willed yet wild. "The true physiological relationship between the burning rage of the berserker and his icy deadness remains uncharted territory" (93).

Where in this uncharted territory is individual responsibility? This is the familiar challenge posed by trauma. Since traumatic injury entails an interpretation of the injury, to what extent is it beyond control? Stress physiology and individual make-up determine behavior, but not in a vacuum. Why does berserk behavior take one particular form and not another? The complication, as witnessed by the law's long struggle to clarify accountability, is that everyday thought shades into self-abandon, richly conditioned by autonomic or unconscious qualities, not least of all denial.

Berserk behavior may be erratic or even suicidally reckless, but that need not rule out some degree of premeditation and strategic awareness. Rampage killings often have a copycat character. "The copycat phenomenon is real," said Andre Simons of the FBI's Behavioral

Analysis Unit. "As more and more notable and tragic events occur, we think we're seeing more compromised, marginalized individuals who are seeking inspiration from those past attacks."[15] In 1995, Timothy McVeigh bombed a federal building in Oklahoma City on the second anniversary of the government's incineration of the Branch Davidian compound in Waco Texas. The Columbine High School killers planned their 1999 rampage to outdo McVeigh on the anniversary of his attack. They called their plan "NBK" after Quentin Tarantino's movie "Natural Born Killers." Almost a decade later, half a world away in Finland, a 22-year-old culinary arts student gunned down ten vocational school students after posting on YouTube video clips of himself dressed in black like a professional assassin in a movie thriller, and revealing his fascination with video clips from the Columbine attack. Adam Lanza, who murdered children and staff at Sandy Hook elementary school (December 2012), studied precedents, especially Columbine, creating a spreadsheet to master the data.

Copycat behavior shows that the *idea* of abandon can be objectified, imitated, and manipulated. What's more, the idea may condition actions. Copycats are aware of precedents as models to be repeated and outdone. Fantasizing about spectacular revenge, copycats are not (yet) physically amok. They may be seething or brooding, on the edge of self-control. They may be aware of their rage and gratified by the prospect of record-breaking sensational violence, even if they have not (yet) decided to act. But they may also be only half-aware, in denial or self-deceived, trying out the possibilities of abandon.

This book treats that mode of being on the edge as a style. The term is appropriate because it connotes casual as well as formal behavior—which is critical, because casualness and routine readily mask denial and manipulation. As a boxer, Mike Tyson could be conscious of living close to the edge while trying to be relaxed about it in his social life. At this distance it is impossible to gauge the quality of his awareness of his potential for rage. If berserk behavior falls along a continuum, then when style predominates, abandon takes on the quality of role-playing. When style is minimal, impulse and emergency physiology are prominent.

In style meanings proliferate. Comedy has traditionally exploited berserk excess in exploding stale pieties for laughs. Even the terminology such as a "punchline" or "gallows humor" reveals the violence lurking in comic imagination. Chaplin, Buster Keaton, Keystone cops, and other comedians systematically made mayhem and reckless physical daring triggers for hilarity. Verbal jokes likewise breach boundaries and turn humdrum reality upside down. When clowns run amok in a slapstick melee, they burlesque berserk aggression. Tamed for the spectators, and especially for children, who are still wrestling with self-control, the freewheeling assaults and harmless pratfalls are an act, conventionalized as style. The clowns break all the rules, triumph over pain and fear, and fascinate everyone.

But impulsive violence may also be ambiguously conditioned by style, since even an action that is "out of control" raises the question: why did the action take this particular form? Who or what "chose" or predisposed it? At a hockey practice a suburban father argues with his son's coach, leaves the arena for a few minutes, and on his return, before bystanders and his own children, beats the smaller man to death.[16] Granted, the father was enraged. But why act it out as a fight to the death? Many of the likely forces shaping the behavior are grounded in routine cultural fantasies. Bizarre as the attack is, it played out the underlying structure of sport as combat. "Body contact" sports are less sublimated than some others, but all draw on a cluster of metaphors for deadly struggle and self-esteem. Even in the dignified Olympics commentators enthuse about athletes "killing," "dominating," "attacking," "defending," and the like. Games may end in "sudden death" overtime. Verbal assault on an umpire is a personal contest and may be surreptitiously regarded as a game or rite. But then, the experience of play is associated with enchantment because it can be all-absorbing.

Assimilated to the headline news topic "sports violence," the hockey murder becomes part of a genre with its own explanatory system: a warning to impassioned fans but also proof that sports is serious, even heroic in its ability to evoke tragic passions as the irate fan defends his son or his team. "Show me your budget, and I'll tell you what you hold most dear. And as long as the NFL's propaganda wing, NFL Films, shows you every brutal takedown in super slo-mo, from nine different angles, and glorifies brutes...we'll know what this league is all about....The actuary tables for NFL players are horrifying. The men who play this game die much younger, on average, than most other groups of men. But out of sight, out of mind. Goodell knows that while the players are in full view, they have to be considered modern gladiators, impervious to normal levels of pain and fatigue." The sports writer is well aware of the role of style as a disguise: "I say this in shuddering admiration of the league's PR skills, so powerful that they have made millions of people believe they cannot live without the three hours of carnage brought to their living rooms."[17]

By extension, sports combat is grounded in a structure of self-esteem. Winners are culture heroes and larger than life. Losers stand for failure, inadequacy, and social death. Identifying with his son, the hockey dad wanted to win. Overridden by the coach—the smaller man invested with authority—the hockey dad very likely felt humiliated or vengeful on behalf of his own imagined rightness. By temporarily leaving the rink, he may have tried to save face or perhaps cool his indignation. Returning to pick up his son, his intentions conditioned by berserk style, he acted out the drive to revenge prominent in many workplace and combat rampages. However deliberately, by grappling with the coach, he was engaging in—staging—a primitive athletic agon, showing his son and the crowd that he could win.

To complicate matters, our capacity for ambivalence means that in the father's eyes the combat could be both a heroic contest and an appalling murder. And still more perplexing: insofar as he "lost" his temper and was "carried away," the hockey dad could claim he was momentarily "beyond" self-control, outside the magic circle of everyday life. In that state, where inhibitions and safeguards fall away, our ancient survival physiology goes into emergency overdrive. We behave like predators—housecats as well as tigers—in the throes of seizing and killing prey.

Did the man intend to murder the coach? The question leads into a maze, with criticism following on a string.

CHAPTER 1

BERSERK STYLE

"Nothing succeeds like excess"

Oscar Wilde

In berserk abandon body and mind interact in an escalating feedback loop. A woman imprisoned for violence against a partner reports that in rage "I cry because there is no other outlet. I get hot and sweaty, clench my fists...I take my glasses off and tell people, 'I'm having a bi-polar moment.' It's my trigger to warn people before I explode... In rage, I'm intense...I'm afraid of myself—I'm going to kill you because you did something to me...I just get relief after rage." Another woman said, "I get red, shake and cry. My legs shake, I'm pacing, I get red. I look for something to hit, and it's a warning to people. I look for an object to destroy." [1]

The way the women interpret the ostensibly irresistible rage is shaping it. One decides that her rage "has no other outlet," but knows it will give her relief. They both warn bystanders and look for things to destroy. In effect, like the fantasy figure the Hulk, they take on the heroic role of publicly trying to master their superhuman wrath. They are both proud of it and afraid of it—and assume others will be as well. Is the nervous system storm real? Yes. Is imagination complicit in it? Also, yes.

The women say they feel as if an alien force intrudes on them. Conventional wisdom unfailingly treats rage as an aberration associated with beasts and gods. The body appears to have a perverse will of its own. But abandon is functional. Diminished conscious control enables emergency physiology to direct behavior—eminently desirable if you encounter a grizzly bear. The crucial question is whether abandon is appropriate. The conventional answer is that in a complex modern society, rage is best switched off. In reality, berserk experience persists all around us. But as history shows, it has also been progressively sublimated, scripted, seeping into remote symbolic areas of culture. If anything, the problem of appropriateness requires more acute interpretation than ever.

In his well-known studies psychologist Dolf Zillman finds escalating anger to be "a sequence of provocations, each triggering an excitatory reaction that dissipates slowly."[2] As Daniel Goleman elaborates, "every successive anger-provoking thought or perception becomes a minitrigger for amygdala-driven surges of catecholamines, each building on the hormonal momentum of those that went before" (61). The eventual eruption of unreasoning rage entails a high level of excitation that "fosters an illusion of power and invulnerability" (62)—core symptoms of the berserk state. This physiology, with the help of illusion, makes rage a process.

Berserk dynamic is seductive in part because it is self-intoxicating and contagious. As in mania, the conviction of purpose may grow stronger even as the behavior becomes more erratic and unrealistic. In a treacherous paradox, greater momentum appears to stabilize resolve, whether as obsession or as fatalism. The effect is like pedaling faster on a bicycle. Greater speed increases the bike's gyroscopic stability and momentum, but also the danger. The bike becomes more committed to its trajectory, but emergency steering and stopping become harder to control. In combat, a soldier may feel this as fate or God directing him.

In the experience of abandon, short of a blackout, imagination interprets physiology, and self-awareness complicates the loss of control. And no matter how idiopathic the disturbance, culture affects the interpretation. Rampage killers and warriors often explain their fury as a defense of what they believe is right, or as revenge. For the women inmates above, rage is "a bi-polar moment" or a "trigger" because "you did something to me." The example shows the need to feel right to be physiological as well as cognitive. Understandably, since it is more than "just" an idea, it is associated with the beyond inhabited by gods, demons, and heroes. Several women in the prison study compared rage to a supernatural force. One said, "It's more than anger. It felt like an evil spirit was in me." Another drew on the familiar ideation of religious hysteria: "My hands shake, my jaw clenches together. It's like the devil is crawling up my back. It's a horrible experience. I hate when I feel like that."

The inmate "just get[s] relief after rage." She looks for explosive aggression to discharges her agitation like a relief valve in a steam boiler. Incarceration, with its strict psychic confines, pressurizes personality. Anticipating a furious discharge may raise internal tension even as the idea of a safety valve soothes it. It is impossible to say whether an alternative calming or relaxation regimen would relieve her agitation. The use of violence as a relief valve can be self-reinforcing if the anticipated episode of abandon brings rewards such as feelings of dominance and self-respect. If so, the woman is using berserk fury like a drug to manage morale.

With the body in emergency mode, behavior can feel as if it is beyond control and nevertheless be a role. In *Drunken Comportment,* Craig MacAndrew and Robert B. Edgerton describe an encounter with a tribesman in Kenya who interrupted a rampage to greet the visitor, then resumed his "drunken rage" and the berserk interpretive frame.[3] In colonial Indonesia, the syndrome of running amok "essentially disappeared" when the Dutch administration insisted that berserkers no longer be killed but instead taken into custody and sentenced to lifetime penal servitude.[4] With no suicidal blaze of glory to discharge rage and preempt second thoughts, potential assailants chose to be more strategic about their heroic desperation.

Conventional wisdom forces experience into one category or another, for simplicity's sake or in denial. But inhibitions are not a simple on-off switch, all or nothing. Under extreme conditions people do black out or dissociate, but more likely some form of role-playing or doublethink will complicate awareness.

THE USES OF ABANDON

Once style conditions emergency physiology, imagination radically complicates the possible outcomes. You can pretend, disguise, or deny berserk abandon. You can project it onto others, or use it to punish them. In fact, people use abandon or the idea of abandon for countless ends. As a style, berserk intensity can become a powerful tool, and enticing. In the popular mind it is a weapon, the rage that obliterates threats and enemies. But that intensity can also be treated as a catalyst, dissolving inhibitions, overriding worries, and enabling change, as civilians often discover in wartime. Like a forbidden steroid, it can tap reserves of energy and confidence. The rush of arousal can shake off uncertainty and inner conflict, and the result can be heroic selflessness as well as sadistic fury or the folly of "go for broke" gambling or a drug binge.

Culture is continually assimilating and taming abandon to make use of its energy or to defuse it. Where "going postal" initially signified horrific workplace murders, now it is also a mailing business franchise, "Goin' Postal: Your Friendly Neighborhood Shipping Center." Consider the way fight and flight combine in an advertisement for luxury SUV's that ran at the time of the Columbine slaughter (figure 1.1). A street of identical suburban houses sports an army tank in each driveway, its cannon pointed at an invisible neighborhood off the page. In one driveway sits a Lexus SUV, and the caption promises that a smart consumer can combine security, lethal threat display, and elite, stylish comfort. The neighbors are allies or enemies, and driving is war.

Figure 1.1 A Lexus SUV advertisement

An article in *The Atlantic* reported in 1998 that road rage is largely a media myth created by journalistic hype feeding on itself.[5] Allusions to apocalypse and berserk frenzy stand out in Michael Fumento's quotations from the Associated Press ("ROAD WARRIORS...TURN

FREEWAYS INTO FREE-FOR-ALLS"), *Newsweek* ("ROAD RAGE: WE'RE DRIVEN TO DESTRUCTION"), the *San Francisco Examiner* ("TWO-THIRDS OF ALL AUTO DEATHS BLAMED ON STRESSED-OUT, AGGRESSIVE DRIVERS"), the Albany *Times Union* ("SEETHING MOTORIST MAKES CARS WEAPONS"), and a study released by the American Automobile Association Foundation for Traffic Safety ("What used to be just two people screaming at each other is now one person losing it and pulling the trigger").

In these examples berserk style is used to manage morale. It gives humdrum highway frustration thrilling significance even as it reinforces cautionary self-control. In road rage headlines the driver is an incipient psychopath related to tabloid monsters such as the office rampage killer. In the supposedly environmentally friendly *National Geographic* magazine (August 2014), a Toyota advertisement titled "Keep It Wild" pumps up drivers to "Push yourself. Over rocks, over snow, over mud, over sand. Into the heart of no-man's land. 4Runner and its available Multi-terrain Select are made to take thrill-seekers like you across all kinds of off-road to untamed places where you can keep it wild." Nature is "no-man's land," a battlefield; you are using an elite machine ("Select") to access the wild in yourself as well as nature.

In "shock jock" attack broadcasting, rant makes berserk style a naively explicit genre. The manipulation of outrage serves transparent partisan politics, but it also functions as a technology for managing morale. As the host pumps up indignation at the scapegoat du jour, audiences can use the dose of outrage as a stimulant to counter boredom, anxiety, or depression. It can be self-medicating behavior, mildly addictive, using anger as some people use coffee, alcohol, or drugs, to stimulate, soothe, or impose order on inner life. In practice the broadcast content is secondary, as it is in supermarket tabloids whose headlines screech exciting improbabilities.

When the use of abandon becomes obvious and dull, style has to escalate. In the movies the conventions of berserk abandon are continually evolving, pushing hyperbole, violating taboos, searching out new avenues to arousal. This year's over the top sensation is next year's routine brawl. Today the fistfights and decorous bullet wounds of classic crime and cowboy sagas have given way to exploded bodies, crime lab evisceration, and in a film such as Roland Emmerich's *Independence Day* (1996), urban cataclysm.

When use becomes especially sophisticated, style can make it possible to scoff at our fascination with violence while indulging it. In a Toyota advertisement from the spring of 2005, we are in the control booth at an indoor laboratory test track. Two young boys urge the lab technician to crash one car after another into a wall while a voiceover sums up the safety features of each model. The crashes delight the kids, and the ad climaxes when they beg, "Come on, Bob. Do another one." Bob replies, "There are no more." The kids then deliver the enthusiastic punch line, "What about your car?" The more destruction the kids see, the more they want. This is the subtext of the sales pitch in the voiceover, that the Toyota "has everything kids want." How much is enough? The escalation would take the violence outside the lab and smash up "Bob's" car. The advertisement uses berserk style to sell safety by reminding us of our childlike appetite for violence and inviting us to enjoy it vicariously.

The Toyota advertisement illustrates some basic features of abandon. Cars represent personal desirable autonomy. The assumption is that everyone wants maximum independence, but safety too. The adult mind (Bob) is crash-testing the limits of safety. The kids' version of autonomy appears as delight in the power of destruction, and the process is self-intoxicating for them. The more you smash, the more smash-ups you demand. This is a comic version of the release anticipated by the woman inmate described above. If we think of the scenario as an intrapsychic experience, Bob is resisting the urge to regress when he refuses to give in to the kids' plea to destroy his autonomy (his own car). The scenario illustrates the way excitement feeds on itself, looking for "blow-off" relief. This is a pattern many rampage killers cultivate.

But the lure of catharsis is everywhere in culture. The experience can be ecstatic as well as maddening and chaotic. For lovers, berserk style is an aphrodisiac. As in bungee jumping, they "fall" in love. For them, the environment is saturated in erotic cues. In supermarket muzak the singer' wails "I will love you forever." And as in Renaissance wordplay on "dying" as sexual climax, erotic desire from time immemorial has joined orgasm to self-abandonment. From Romeo and Juliet and Wagnerian love-death to the enveloping obsession of Oshima's *In the Realm of the Senses* (1976) and the orgiastic, alcoholic self-destruction in Mike Figgis's *Leaving Las Vegas* (1995), erotic passion has been associated with reckless orgasmic apotheosis and doom. As lovers try to lose themselves, drugs, alcohol, potions, and poisons become markers for the internal experience of fatal abandon. As the perils of the AIDS epidemic emerged in the 1980s, survival ecstasy intensified the allure of risky promiscuity in some areas of gay culture.[6] As in warfare, death can give risky sex an incomparable larger-than-life urgency. In all its varieties sexual abandon can be calculated—a sort of erotic bungee jump into the arms of death—but it is also akin to religious rituals that seek to relinquish or dissolve the self in order to induce a conviction of renewal and the divine.

"THEY WANTED A FUCKING HERO"

At this point the uses of abandon enter a zone of paradox and perversity where criticism struggles to keep a clear head amid dissolving preconceptions. A simple example are rock concerts whose promise of liberation and creativity climaxes with stoned audiences, ear-splitting amplifiers, and musicians smashing their instruments as The Who did in the 1960s until that became a worn out gimmick. At the famous Altamount Speedway concert (December 6, 1969) the Rolling Stones played through a set unaware that in the surrounding mayhem a fan high on methamphetamine had drawn a pistol in a skirmish with a Hell's Angel and been stabbed to death.

In *Hated*, Todd Philips' 1993 documentary about the marginal punk rocker GG Allin and the Murder Junkies, the camera catches Allin acting out suicidal abandon onstage. His performances were symbolic rampage killing. Naked, defecating and hurling excrement, chairs, and the microphone stand, Allin assaulted audiences, tacitly inviting violent retaliation. In one melee with fans he suffered a broken arm. Toward the end of his short career he repeatedly vowed to kill himself onstage, and in 1993 did die of a drug overdose. Allin seems trapped in compulsive, fixated behavior characteristic of mental illness. Yet the performer, fans, and rival musicians all monotonously interpreted his behavior in crude ideological terms as a struggle for freedom. Even on a network television talkshow no one challenged Allin's boasts that he represented total freedom.

Allin and his fans grew up in the psychic aftermath of the 1960s and the Vietnam War. His rant about total freedom at all costs can be seen as a grotesque mutation of Cold War and counter-culture ideologies and the dead-end excitement of rock subculture. Allin's berserk tantrums combined infantile grandiosity with suicidal recklessness. "My mind is a machine gun," he tells the film maker, "my body the bullets and the audience is the target." Apparently high on drugs, he claims he wants "to conquer the world—not to entertain but to annihilate." "My rifle is human," says the Marine Rifle Creed, "we will become part of each other." The paranoid Jared Loughner, who ran amok in Tucson believing he was saving the nation from a conspiracy (January 8, 2011), had himself tattooed with bullets.

The fantasy of becoming a weapon empowers the self as conventional reality is disintegrating. It confirms the urge to be heroic and pump up self-esteem to counter fear and depression. Allin's tattoo, "Life Sucks," resonates with the malevolent depression and ecstatic violence that Dylan Klebold conjured up in his journal while planning the Columbine High School massacre. For Jared Loughner, law, money, even language itself were falling into psychotic chaos.

The drive toward ecstasy and blackout is always potentially suicidal. What keeps it alluring, especially in the arts, is the fantasy of play-death. Once the curtain falls, Romeo and Juliet will jump to their feet and be applauded back to life. Jihadists imagine death as a paradise and a divine pat on the back. The Columbine killers looked forward to "a better place" substantiated by worldwide notoriety. They saw themselves not annihilated, but promoted.

Everyday commercial entertainment flirts with these materials in developing ambivalence toward vampires. Beginning with Anne Rice's sagas, vampires became intensely personal and dramatized the romance of abandon. Like berserkers, they act out survival rage, preying on others. They operate in a zone of play-death, beyond daylight reality, enjoying superhuman qualities. Vampires stop short of annihilation, transforming rather annihilating their victims and themselves. In the popular revision represented by Stephanie Meyer's *Twilight* (2005) and Alan Ball's HBO series *True Blood* (2008), vampire eros is about sharing liberating transgression and the dream of undying abandon. Vampires are "like the supernatural version of rock'n'roll bad boys," says Ball. "They have special powers, they're forever young and they don't play by the rules. No wonder so many people have sexual fantasies about them."[7]

These behaviors raise nagging questions. If berserkers "put on" their fury as warriors once did bear or jaguar skins, to what extent are they role-playing? Is berserk fury a technic for inducing acute physiological arousal akin to ceremonies such as a war dance that sharpen fighting spirits and turn warriors into weapons? We think of rage as autonomic: a bizarre interruption of everyday serenity, something that happens to someone under stress. But the Norse warriors deliberately shed inhibitions, pumping up morale and muscle. Warrior frenzy was also a tactic and a tool—berserk style.

Warrior abandon has always aroused acute ambivalence. After the capture of Antioch in 1098 during the First Crusade, the daughter of the Byzantine emperor reported that the Franks "have no military discipline or strategic skills." In battle "a raging fury seizes their hearts and they become implacable, common soldiers and leaders alike. They hurl themselves with invincible impetus into the midst of the enemy ranks as soon as the latter give a little ground." The Emir Ousama-ibn-Munquidh summed up the ambivalence: "Anyone who knows anything about the Franks looks on them as beasts, outdoing all others in courage and warlike spirit, just as animals are superior when it comes to strength and aggression."[8] The warriors' abandon was a cultural practice, a style that felt natural to them. It served as a tool akin to "shock and awe" today. Intimidating propaganda can also be a motivational technique and one solution to problems of competition and hierarchy within a group of high-strung and well-armed males. Such abandon is a window on questions underlying all creativity and atrocity: how do we sort out heroic and vicious motivation? symbolic and neurophysiological components? Is there an identifiable threshold or "edge" marking off the berserk state?

The psychiatrist Jonathan Shay acknowledges the equivocal god-like or beastlike ambiguity that makes the berserk state fascinating: "A soldier who routs the enemy single-handedly is often in the grip of a special state of mind, body and social disconnection at the time of his memorable deeds. Such men, often regarded by commanders as 'the best,' have been honored as heroes.... the word *berserk* is the most precise term available to describe the behavior." He acknowledges "the ambiguous borderline between heroism and a blood-crazed, berserk state in which abuse after abuse is committed" (77).

That "borderline" is treacherous. Recall the hockey dad who murdered his son's coach. A psychiatrist might classify him as a "sadistic borderline personality" or an "explosive psychopath": someone calm enough to cope with daily life most of the time, though subject to sudden episodes of hostility.[9] But of course this terminology is just a label, and a self-evident label at that. It is safe to say that the "borderline" father saw himself as a hero defending his son, his own self-esteem, and justice, or attacking the coach as a rival, bad father. He may have identified so closely with his son—the "victimized" child in himself—that he felt as if he was suffering the son's unjust defeat, perhaps in the way that some abortion opponents so closely identify with the unborn that they call themselves "survivors" and have bombed clinics and murdered doctors. Claiming self-defense and that the death was accidental, the hockey dad was convicted of involuntary manslaughter: a judgment allowing for diminished responsibility.

Fury readily preempts responsibility—hence the design of Dante's Hell. Once beyond cultural controls, abandon is self-intoxicating and more autonomic. As one Vietnam veteran described a crisis in combat, "I just went crazy....I lost all my mercy. I felt a drastic change after that. I just couldn't get enough. I built up such hate. I couldn't do enough damage....Got worse as time went by. I really loved fucking killing, couldn't get enough. For every one that I killed I felt better. Made some of the hurt went away" (Shay 78). Based on his clinical work with veterans, Shay calls the berserk state "ruinous," concluding that it usually leads to the soldier's maiming or death in battle, and to lifelong psychological and physiological injury if he survives (98).

This view is based on painful evidence and not to be gainsaid. Its limitation is the core problem of berserk style. The borderline between heroism and berserk frenzy is not only ambiguous, as Shay says, but insolubly ambivalent. We fear the berserk state as a kind of madness; but we also honor its awe-inspiring powers. Deeds may be disgusting yet charged with heroic meaning on the battlefield under the pressure of death. The Vietnam veteran quoted at the outset bitterly recollects that "I became a fucking animal. I started putting fucking heads on poles. Leaving fucking notes for the motherfuckers. Digging up fucking graves. I didn't give a fuck anymore. Y'know, I wanted—They wanted a fucking hero, so I gave it to them. They wanted fucking body count, so I gave them body count. I hope they're fucking happy. But they don't have to live with it. I do" (83). The man feels he was out of control, icily indifferent—"I didn't give a fuck anymore"—yet he "couldn't get enough" and was also guided by what "they" wanted: by the values and feelings of his culture, by the demands of home no less than of his superiors. "They" are tacitly a voice in his head shaping his behavior. Being starkly ambivalent about what "they" demand of him, he is agonizingly alienated now about the culture—the home—he had been prepared to die for.

After the defeat in Vietnam, Hollywood briefly allowed on screen "the unpredictable, violent psychotic vet of films like *Taxi Driver* (1976), *Tracks* (1977), *Rolling Thunder* (1977), and *Who'll Stop the Rain* (1978)."[10] By the 1980s, berserk style made the war more euphemistic. In Ted Kotcheff's *First Blood* (1982), the Vietnam vet John Rambo (Sylvester Stallone) runs amok after police in a small town abuse him. His one-man war against police injustice escalates to a fiery climax yet is scripted to harm no one. Rambo is a traumatized renegade yet also an omnipotent adolescent hero: *Don't mess with me, I can destroy your entire town.*

In the *Rambo* films, berserk style projects stylized mayhem. But in the competition to arouse audiences, as Mark Crispin Miller points out, "The empathic function of today's screen violence has changed the character of movie heroics."[11] In films such as *Bullitt* (1968) and *The French Connection* (1971), even graphic violence was "muted by a deep ambivalence that shadowed even the most righteous-seeming acts of vengeance, and...therefore suppressed the (male) viewer's urge to join in kicking. Now, by contrast, screen violence primarily invites the viewer—man or woman—to enjoy the *feel* of killing, beating, mutilating....There is no point to Rambo's long climactic rage, or Cobra's, or Chuck Norris's, other than its open invitation to *become him* at that moment—to ape that sneer of hate, to feel what it feels to stand there tensed up with the Uzi....Stallone's Cobra gets a charge out of being *exactly* like the psychopaths he chases, just as we are meant to feel *exactly* like him" (210-11).

The berserk warrior may be both a revered hero and a crazed killer, and the film implicitly casts the audience in a similarly equivocal role. Viewers can "enjoy the feel of killing" because they are guided away from critical awareness. Frenzy has become a tool, a usable role. "Putting on" the warrior's bearskin, so to speak, is a style. As a result, berserk style can be an innocuous facsimile of action or a way of mediating or sublimating action.

The veterans' psychiatrist understandably protects the idea of a healthy norm and emphasizes the "ruinous" effects of the berserk state. "If a soldier survives the berserk state, it imparts emotional deadness and vulnerability to explosive rage to his psychology and a permanent hyperarousal to his physiology—hallmarks of post-traumatic stress disorder in combat veterans" (98). But combat frenzy is the most extreme form of the syndrome, since the soldier is fighting for his life. Framed as style, the berserk is less extreme. It is more likely to hold in suspension the potential for survival rage that is built into us.

CREATURELY MOTIVES

Conventional wisdom thinks of abandon as regression from conscious self-control to a state associated with animals, children, and barbarians. When emergency physiology takes over, behavior more clearly reveals the creaturely motives—the underlying instincts to perpetuate life—that shape us. Our survival reflexes are especially complex because as Ernest Becker says, "to live a whole lifetime with the fate of death haunting one's dreams and even the most sun-filled days" creates "an impossible situation for an animal to be in. I believe that those who speculate that a full apprehension of man's condition would drive him insane are right, quite literally right."[12]

In this view, thanks to symbolic faculties, our conception of reality can be vastly expanded and yet always conditioned by denial. Life is expansive. Creatures grow larger into maturity, and shrink into death. We "shrink" from threats or "stand up" to them. The hero is a "big man" with monumental immortality, whereas the loser is a "nobody" subject to social death.[13] We are programmed to grow through appetites for food and fertility: that is, hunting and foraging, mating and child-rearing. The meanings are built into us. God promises Abraham infinite progeny. Great conquerors have had great harems, and insatiably "swallow" new territories. Violence, mating, and feeding combine in combat, since the victor gains access to more fertility and food through rape, slavery, and the plunder of resources. Killing enemies, the warrior assumes their vitality and prowess. Yet no matter how good it feels, expansion can never be an ultimate solution, since sooner or later it ends in death. Exterminate all rivals and the survivor would be a lone, doomed big shot. Too many offspring and the tribe starves, or impatient sons murder an aging father.

We have evolved as radically conflicted beings. We kiss to make love with the same mouth that bites to feed and destroy. The part of us that speaks is also a weapon. We are not *given* life: on the contrary, we live by corralling, slaughtering, chewing, digesting, and excreting other lives, plundering their nutrients and fortifying ourselves to search for more life to consume. Ordinarily culture harmonizes or buries these radical conflicts. We celebrate good table manners, say, yet eating is not a chosen pastime: like breathing and mating, it is a compulsion. If we fail to satisfy the compulsion to kill and feed, we die. The hungry baby's tantrum is an alarm going off.

In this perspective "frenzied fury," the Oxford English Dictionary's (OED's) definition of the berserk state, resembles a "feeding frenzy" in the animal world. And this is the motive that applies to the OED's secondary example of the berserker: "a lawless bravo or freebooter." After all, Norse "warriors" were also plunderers, exacting "tribute," taking slaves, and sometimes stealing land to settle on. Like other voracious raiders of history, they fed on the vitality of others. The Vikings were impressive predators. They fascinate us like dinosaurs, whose epoch, says Becker, "is an epic food orgy with king-size actors who convey unmistakably what organisms are dedicated to."[14]

Still, we are also symbolic animals. More than extinction, we fear extinction with insignificance. We want our lives to matter. The wish to be heroic is also the wish not to be nothing: the expansive wish to be bigger than death. Karen Horney and Becker both see as tragic the temptation to falsify the self through inflated claims on the world.[15] Since we begin life as helpless infants and know we will die, we grow up fearing and hating our vulnerability and direct that animus toward scapegoats and enemies. We love godlike parents and sacred symbols. Research shows that we respond viscerally to immortality symbols such as the flag and the cross.[16] In a crisis we will kill for them. As long as we believe, our lives feel purposeful: we feel *right*.[17] We emulate "big shot" heroes. Through transference, we want to share their powers and importance, but we also dread and hate the possibility of our failure or their rejection of us.

The clever animal that digests other creatures into foul-smelling excrement is able to repudiate its creaturely origins by using "the Purist Hatbox," the Kohler Corporation's toilet in the shape of a hatbox that "aims to bring the throne to your home into the 21st Century,"[18] offering you regal elevation above your animal mortality. Toilet behavior tames the shame and inadequacy presented by excrement. The reflex of this denial is scatological rage: the use of "shit" as an all-purpose insult and marker for nemesis, and the hatred of "assholes." It underlies the combat berserker's mutilation and desecration of the bodies of enemies.

Since the body represents creaturely filth and death, in warfare and at home, again and again, rage breaks out as an effort to defy or deny the connection. One day after a military officer killed thirteen people at Fort Hood, Jason Rodriguez opened fire at the engineering firm that had let him go two years before. He was divorced, in debt, with past indications of mental disturbance. As if colleagues had killed him two years before, he rose from social death with guns blazing, "Because they left me to rot."[19] The man was expressing the anguish of being cut off and feeling himself left to putrefy.

To be cut off—rejected, stripped of identity—is to be cut off from the symbolic security of society. Money, for example, signifies autonomy. A supermarket is a storehouse of symbolic vitality and immortality that includes plants and animals shrink-wrapped and labeled to screen out awareness of the killing that brought them to the shelves.

The market's brightly lit, aesthetic displays, trustworthy cash register, and cornucopia of immortality markers—vitamins, cleaning agents, beauty magazines, meat, and the like—assure us that life is plentiful, under control, and enduringly meaningful. Aisles of pills enable us to "fight" infections. "Consumer" choice supplants killer instinct. Splitting off guilt and butchering prey in an offstage factory, we can forget that we are meat eating meat.

Excrement is both a creaturely and symbolic phenomenon. Like the concept of beauty, its significance is conditioned by sensory perceptions. They contribute to our sense of what is right. From birth we develop a vision of reality that includes rules and values, but also a sense of what is natural and trustworthy, and what works. It begins to form before we can even remember, continually develops, partly conscious and partly shaped by our creaturely endowment: the way we're built. Not only is it the basis of self-esteem, it makes the world and our place in it seem natural and secure. This sense of rightness is foundational, the closest thing we have to a ground of personality. It supports the conviction that our lives have lasting meaning and that we matter.

At the same time, we readily forget that the self is not a thing, but action that ceases when the neurochemical conditions of conscousness lapse in sleep. From infancy, the self comes into being and feels secure through the attention of others. The desire to be heroic is critical for self-esteem because heroism holds the attention of other people and therefore substantiates the self. Attention makes us feel real and meaningful. Celebrity culture dreams of a spotlight and attention that not only confirms, but magnifies, the self. Hence the immortality and boundless godlike powers attributed to rock, movie, sports, and other "stars."

And hence the rampage of addiction or abuse that often overtakes stars when their sense of identity and what's right becomes disoriented or conflicted by overwhelming attention. The rampage may try to force new coherence on the personality in trouble, and compel attention from others that can bring shaken identity into focus again. As in a child's tantrum, the "breakdown" or outburst is an emergency response to conflict or overwhelming pressure.

Attention substantiates us when it is positive: agreement, praise, or love. This is the profound context of Otto Rank's conclusion that "Every conflict over truth is in the last analysis just the same old struggle over...immortality." As Becker elaborates in *Escape from Evil*, "No wonder men go into a rage about fine points of belief: if your adversary wins the argument about truth, you die. Your immortality system has been shown to be fallible, your life becomes fallible" (64). It deepens the insight to add that the issue is not *truth* alone, but a relationship in which someone uses attention not to substantiate another, but to undermine their reality: in effect, to kill.

The crucial premise is this: when identity and the sense of what's right goes out of phase with others, we feel threatened by chaos and all the varieties of failure, futility, and decay that signal death. In response we may lash out, abandoning the troubled self and attempting to enforce a superior sense of right beyond boundaries, through do-or-die violence. This paradoxical fusion of explosive abandon and "what's right" seems counter-intuitive when applied to a berserker slaughtering innocents, especially children. By extension, the paradox applies as well to the suicidal end of rampages in which what's right, when turned to frenzied violence, brings coherence that is also a tragically illusory dead end.

These paradoxes require analysis to be open to creaturely motives as well as to the familiar signs that mark everyday life. In this spirit, here are several clusters of language and fantasy in which creaturely and everyday cultural motives interact. One cluster of signs originates in the hunt, since we have to kill in order to live. Throughout history hunters have had to manage conflicted and violent creaturely motives. Evolving cultural controls helped hunters to master fear, greed, and hunger pangs, especially in the supercharged, dangerous moments when the prey fights for its life and triggers the conclusive burst of ferocity. Early hunters had to learn to summon, and then calm, the "killer instinct." In sharing out the kill afterward they had to develop heroic roles as providers that could tame greed.

In warfare, hunters prey on other humans and their resources. As warriors, providing more life for the group, they came to dominate the group and its fertility. In this way predation has been an important adaptive strategy in human evolution, "providing benefits for genetic fitness (passing on one's genes) in forager, pastoral, and urban societies, and its enjoyment is a 'culturally elaborated' manifestation of the initial predatory adaptation."[20] The hunt has mythic status for Americans, in solitary exploits, in the binge-killing of plains buffalo, and by extension in the Indian-war writing of New England Puritans.[21]

These themes persist today. "As part of an instruction course named 'Combat Hunter,' the Marines have brought in 'big-game hunters' to school their snipers in the better use of 'optics.' According to a September 2007 article by Grace Jean in *National Defense Magazine*, '[T]he lab conducted a war game with Marines, African game hunters and inner city police officers to search for ways to improve training.' The program included a 15-minute CD titled 'Every Marine a Hunter.'"[22] A Marine team forms a hunting pack, ritualized at the end of briefings when "Marines put their hands together and shout, 'Kill!'"[23]

Themes of fertility and harvest cluster around the hunt and warfare. Warriors and raiders harvest life, slaughtering rival males, enslaving women and children, hauling off food, livestock, and valuables—the adversary's "livelihood." The potency of the victor shimmers in the king's scepter, which originated as the hunter's club and the warrior's mace, but also in prodigious harems. In subsuming their rivals' women, warriors acted out a godlike power to propagate more life: creating more children or slaves to extend a master's will. The trope of the hunt is luridly visible in erotic obsessions such as stalking, rape, and domestic violence. Lust can be understood as hunting as a fixation in which the act supersedes the goal. Even when the hunter-warrior role is disguised, as in racist lynching, the mob acts to strengthen its feeling of dominance—its self-feeling—through the pursuit, torture, and death of a scapegoat, mutilating his body and especially his genitals, supposedly to protect "our" women and children.

By extension, the cluster includes abandon in food practices and in related phenomena such as drugs, and especially psychotropic drugs. Binge consumption can be an attempt to invest celebrations, personal status, or the body with significance. In feasting or gluttony, abandon entails excess in a hunt for memorable pleasure. In the god Dionysius the ancients gave the perverse possibilities of extravagant drink and drugs a mythic character. The violence and revelry associated with the god have never abated. In postwar America, counter culture voices promoted psychotropic drugs with the idea of transport. In Timothy Leary's catechism, "Turn on, tune in, drop out," abandon is a paradoxically disciplined psychic quest. The sense of pilgrimmage in altered states shades into a third cluster of markers for berserk style, associated with religion.

As a primary tool for relating the everyday world to ultimate concerns, religions have traditionally emphasized conceptual boundaries. Shamanism entails personal transformation and quest-journeys with characteristics of the hunt. Attempts to reach an altered state and a spiritual realm often imply abandon, as in experiences of trance, transport, and rapture. Since religions usually address the terrors of death, evil, and ambivalence, they are always susceptible to panic and distortion. From the First Crusade through the schismatic massacres of the early modern period, Christian Europe was intermittently amok, vanquishing enemies of Christ in an effort to stabilize group identity and convictions of what's right. In the U.S., the varieties of religious experience continue to proliferate and recombine. Berserk style facilitated the seventeenth century New England witch panic and the sectarian furies that plagued, among others, Joseph Smith's Mormons.

The dilemma is that in ministering to a fallen world, religion always risks inflaming guilt, self-doubt, and death anxiety—or messianic self-aggrandizement. Since 9/11, the berserk style commanding global attention has been jihadist fanaticism, which has evolved a merciless logic easily warped to serve expedient ends. "Killer groups engaging in groupthink have an illusion of invulnerability and moral righteousness that leads to excessive risk-taking.... Genocides, viewed this way, constitute a virulent form of social hysteria, one with a hapless target group for extreme aggression."[24]

It needs to be said that creaturely motives operate in scale as well as in individual lives. As Canetti demonstrated, individuals readily merge their identity with an enfolding group.[25] Religious terrorism, for example, is invariably expansive. Its "appetite" for converts and slain enemies is the familiar creaturely compulsion to organismic expansion that registers everywhere in history as survival greed. Groups fight to the death over food and mates and territory, including claims to the beyond. As a species we are built to reproduce, with no reliable means of managing runaway overpopulation. UN population conferences usually wind up with pledges of self-restraint, paranoid glances at fertile rivals, and more babies. Proponents of sustainable development warn that reckless exploitation of resources threatens to make the planet uninhabitable. The impact is especially forbidding because current economic systems are based on debt and boundless expansion, by warfare if necessary.

Greed seems natural when markets assume that more is always better. The prejudice is built into us. As Becker puts the question, "Whoever gets enough life?" The question leads to everyday "Faustian economics" which, says Wendell Berry, is "not only prodigal extravagance but also an assumed limitlessness," as if we are gods, open to the beyond, and not creatures who must live in a finite world.[26]

Whether it leads to rescue or calamity, abandon puts the self at risk. Culture celebrates heroes because they are willing to sacrifice a safe conventional identity in pursuit of great deeds and more life. The cost of failure is extinction. Venerable heroes are "larger than life," symbolically immortal. Those who survive are generative rescuers: "the father of his country," the deified Roman emperor, a transcendent saint or a frankly mythic hero such as Hercules or the warrior Cú Chulainn. Heroic self-sacrifice counters the temptation to survival greed. In 2007, for instance, the Carnegie Hero Fund Commission selected recent heroes who had been able to "run into burning buildings and cars," "fight off men with knives and snapping dogs," and "go after people hanging off cliffs." The deeds "must be done by a 'civilian who knowingly risks his or her own life to an extraordinary degree while saving or attempting to save the life of another person.' To underscore the point, three winners died while saving someone else."[27]

Heroism always needs renewal. Not only do circumstances change, but no mortal hero is able to live up to our dreams. As women's roles have changed, traditional verities appear stereotyped. The search for new forms may revealingly expose the creaturely limits that shape all humankind. Where women were once idealized as models of harmony and nurture, for example, Hollywood now makes many heroines as violent as men. The script writers send the glamorous Uma Thurman on a "vengeful rampage" to *Kill Bill* (2003), "the worldly father figure of a pack of crack assassins." In *Salt* (2010), Angelina Jolie is a spy and an unstoppable supercharged killer. Steig Larsson's best-selling Lisbeth Salander is viciously persecuted but more than equal to her tormenters. Once established as berserk style, the role of romantic avenger is endlessly adaptable, as in 2008, when the attractive vice presidential nominee Sarah Palin quipped, "You know what they say is the difference between hockey mums and a pit bull?" she joked. "Lipstick." Pit bulls are known for frenzied killing, and the candidate deliberately chose to play underdog and attack dog in a media atmosphere in which unstoppable rage can be a virtue. By the end of the campaign, Secret Service agents revealed, "Sarah Palin's attacks on Barack Obama's patriotism provoked a spike in death threats against the future president."[28]

IN THE FUNHOUSE OF STYLE

Close at hand, predatory threat and heroic force appear to be discrete categories, morally distinct and easy to recognize. Like the hard-boiled detective, analysis should be able to follow the money, count the corpses, and hand over malefactors to the law. But in berserk style, the two categories may blur in paradox and hallucination.

Mediated by style, motives can be incalculable. Threat display, for example, often uses berserk style in its effort to intimidate an adversary. Since adversaries may counter with their own threats, what ensues is a contest of illusions, inescapably theatrical. A major theme of *New Yorker* cartoons, however, is the boss who rules the office through sly threats, and the underling trapped in the nightmarish force field of devious threats, with no way to fight back, and no one to fight back against, even though the deep threat is death. In the news, when ISIS terrorists in Iraq behead an American journalist, as they did James Foley (August 21, 2014), the murder is obscene and the journalist irrelevant to them, but the terrorists calculate that suppressed panic will take the horrific propaganda around the globe.

Berserk potential is most deceptive when the cues and interpretive categories deform in the funhouse mirrors of cultural expectations. In a society where the once-taboo expletives "fuck" and "fuck you" may be shocking or banal, even "fighting words" can be chimerical. In his America Online profile, amid a rant about obnoxious people on the street, Eric Harris, one of the Columbine killers, snarled, "'Kill 'em AALL!!!' (27). Given his slangy spelling and the permissive atmosphere online, this could be merely self-consciously comic bravado in adolescent male culture fizzing with smartass exaggeration. It could also be that in the fun house of the Internet, Harris was experimenting with threat display, testing limits and reactions, and yet as time would prove, he meant what he said.

Conventional wisdom seems to recognize a connection between violence in media and behavior on Main Street, but for all practical purposes the topic remains mystified. The public is divided and conflicted about the effects of violence and the costs of cultural controls, even as researchers such as Jonathan Friedman demonstrate that the causality is anything but straightforward.[29] Since the Vietnam era broadcasting taboos have been relaxed, so that displays of corpses and grisly wounds today are provocative to a degree unimaginable a generation ago. Even nature documentaries stress berserk style in their preference for sharks and other predators, poisonous insects and snakes, and battles over mating. These themes play to our creaturely concerns rather than put the natural world in perspective.

Rant media, one of the landmark developments in post-Vietnam broadcasting, frequently pits the host against a guest in head-butting competition for alpha status—like a nature documentary. Rant's partisan content has been permissible since the Reagan administration abolished the FCC's impartiality doctrine in 1987.[30] Some shock jocks try to choreograph interviews to produce a climax of outrage that "puts down" opponents. The host and audience take the roles of police or warriors hunting down enemies. In a June 10, 2008 show, Michael Reagan urged his audience to kill Christian antiwar activists who were trying to persuade troops in Iraq to oppose the war. "Take them out and shoot them.... You call them traitors, that's what they are, and you shoot them dead. I'll pay for the bullet." A week later, Reagan apologized on the air,[31] as if it was a fault in etiquette, not an incitement to murder.

The theatricalization of rage—I'm fed up, I won't take it anymore— creates a vicarious voice for a nation that ambivalently celebrates the virtues of self-reliance under stress, even as poverty forces reliance on government relief accompanied by anxiety about dependency. Such conflicts help to explain how attack media can function as a vehicle for self-medication. Playing at fury to rouse morale, the shows counter depressive feelings with a pick-me-up of stimulating anger like caffeine or alcohol, turning flight into fight. Rage in the airwaves can legitimize unassuaged grievances and extend membership in a "Savage nation" of angry fellow citizens bent on hunting down and figuratively lynching enemies. The host's familiar disembodied voice models heroic indignation that can transmute helplessness and gloom into a mirage of righteousness and mastery.

Still, it is useful to remember that satire—the fusion of criticism and laughter—originated as cursing, in the belief that language charged with magical power can injure or kill enemies.[32] To defuse its curse, entertainment bills satire as comedy. Where a curse destroys its object, humor deflates. When coworkers give a hostile and unstable employee a nickname such as "Crazy Pat," they are relying on humor to ease their anxiety and preserve the group's solidarity and tolerance. At the same time the nickname has a satiric edge likely to be sensed and resented by the insecure, paranoid Pat, whose belligerence is after all a form of threat display. When Johnny Paycheck sings "Take this job and shove it" as a number one hit on the charts, the world seems to be validating workplace hostility. And when Crazy Pat is finally fired, shoots three coworkers, calmly surrenders to police, and finds himself on death row, criminal madness has become a storm of meanings.

The security consultant Gavin de Becker argues that with a general theory of human needs, anyone can predict aggression by seeing things through the eyes of the threatening person.[33] While he over-states the possibilities of do-it-yourself psychiatry, he is encouraging the imaginative sympathy that makes critical awareness effective in the theater of social life. Yes, he says, danger can be deceptive, but people too often ignore their own self-protective anxiety and premonitions. Anxiety has evolved as a protective mechanism. But our propensity for denial keeps us from responding to the vital signals anxiety sends. What's more, he sees that culture can foster denial. Fear should be "a mere servant of intuition" and not chronic, numbing background noise (277)—"saturation violence." In an atmosphere of anxiety it is easy to be distracted and cowed. Fear "says something might happen. If it does happen, we stop fearing it and start to respond to it, manage it, surrender to it, whereas when real danger leaps out, fear will gal-vanize action" (283). By amplifying danger or reward, berserk style can move worry toward action. The drawback is that berserk style is likely to be indiscriminate.

In this psychic zone where motivation is furiously concentrated, contingency could hardly be more volatile. The heroic striving that converts death-anxiety into creative energy also makes humans spec-tacular predators. Ideas about abandon are easiest to isolate when behavior is most out of control. Yet the behavior is incremental, and appetite is always probing. "The shark does not have dexterity, guile, deceit, cleverness, or disguise," says deBecker. "It also does not have our brutality, for man does things to man that sharks could not dream of doing" (283). When imagination can use the *idea* of abandon even while acting it out, style camouflages behavior. Style may present a storm of ironies and implications. Where creaturely and cultural mo-tives intersect in the narratives and signs around us, analysis has to look for ambivalence, conflict, and incongruity. Criticism can ask what kinds of work the ideation is doing.

As style, for example, berserk abandon can be a technique for con-verting flight to fight. It can be the crucial catalyst in rabble-rousing or in leadership claims. The rhetorical process of "getting psyched" or "pumping up" can itself be a kind of abandon, especially in an age of industrial entertainment, ubiquitous advertising, and spin. Since today's shocking violence is tomorrow's cliché, there is always pressure for more extreme feats of imagination. When asked about Osama Bin Laden during a debate among presidential candidates in May 2007, one senator vowed: "[W]e will do whatever is necessary. We will track him down. We will bring him to justice. We will fol-low him to the gates of Hell." To outdo his competitors in a show of resolve, the candidate was making a berserk vow, something like: *My rage is cosmic. It knows no bounds.* But as his vows inflated toward their eschatological showdown at the infernal portal, the senator stopped and suddenly smiled beatifically—and sheepishly—into the camera. The incongruity stirred The Daily Show's satirical correspondent, "standing outside the gates of Hell waiting for the senator's limousine to arrive," to comment that the senator's rhetoric had to be "over the top," since the president "has raised the bar on hollow threats" so high (May 7, 2007).[34]

In different ways the satirists' and the senator's smiles acknowledged that berserk rage can be a theatrical gesture intended to dramatize superhuman strength and reassure followers. But the smiles also conveyed an embarrassed awareness of acting out an absurd style for strategic ends. Before the cameras the speaker tried to project and appeal to towering rage, but his sensible smile broke the spell. The question in such a situation is whether such a failed bluff will lead to greater prudence or to more brazen risk-taking.

When supercharged motives act on an overdetermined world, the signals can boggle the mind. Modernity expands the scale of things and strains the limits of imagination, but it also provides science and other tools for coping. When those tools fail or come to serve panic and hatred as in industrial warfare, force runs wild. Globalization is one sign of modernity's change of scale, as is globalization's handmaiden, the Internet. With ubiquitous electronic communication, the horrors of civil war in Syria are at your fingertips; terrorists can burn a prisoner alive for propaganda and be guaranteed global exposure. Closer to home, a 14-year old eighth grader in Olympia Washington sent a nude cellphone photo of herself to a new boyfriend, he passed it on to her ex-girlfriend, whose jealousy sent the photo viral on the Internet. Petty anger ("If you think this girl is a whore, then text this to all your friends") turned into berserk rage for order that came to involve handcuffs and court.[35]

A HISTORICAL SKETCH

The chapters that follow explore the psychology of abandon and berserk style in the decades between the Vietnam war and the watershed first decade of the new century. They begin with an analysis of moral aggression in vigilantism, lynching, and rampage killing, followed by investigations of abandon in post war American military culture, finance, economic crime, and apocalyptic religion. Readers hot on the trail of abandon may want to skip ahead at this point. For others, this chapter closes with a sketch of abandon in American history. It will come as no surprise, I think, that a sketch cannot account for the uses of berserk style in the rambunctious and sometimes atrocious American past. A good place to begin might be Richard Slotkin's *Regeneration through Violence* (1973).

Since cultures as well as individuals develop particular techniques for coping with boundary behavior, history can be seen as a succession of strategies for managing berserk style. As such, etiquette and civility are evolving technologies akin to formal institutions such as law and religion. Cross-cultural evidence shows that berserk behavior occurs around the globe. It takes a bewildering variety of forms and sometimes appears in clusters or waves.

Many groups, including Native American tribes, have cultivated heroic abandon as a function of warrior morale. In the Huron and Iroquois rite described by the Jesuit Francis Parkman and others, the tribe assembled in the long house to torture to death a captive who was expected to sing warrior songs and prove his courage.[36] Killers and victim cooperated in a ritual that bonded the group and acted out the power to withstand suffering and terror. Neurologically the rite converted flight to fight, mastering death-anxiety by controlling death itself through the warrior code.

In the New World early settlers plunged into a tantalizing, terrifying beyond, with desperate ambition and mortality to match. Many such as Ralegh were avid for treasure and glory. The first New Englanders were escaping exasperating constraints back home, absurdly conflicted in their appetite for life: self-aggrandizing and sometimes rapacious servants of God propagating a familiar Old World order and yet given to frontier improvisation and revolution. Benjamin Tompsons's two poems about King Philip's War. *New-Englands Crisis* (1676) and *New-Englands Tears* (1677) envision the founders' arcadia ruined by greed and barbarism. In imagery of conflagration, cannibalism, and slaughter the poems report the Great Swamp Fight against the Indians as a nightmare of psychic violence[37] that would persist in the outbreaks of witch panic to come.[38]

As prosperity dismantled the Puritans' ideological stockade, the settlers found themselves not in a New Jerusalem but amid feverish expansion. Gradually the forerunners who labored over a divine compact became merchants and helped draft a federal constitution meant to stabilize boundaries. Later generations cherished neighborliness and private property while taking Native American lands and lives, and fighting to the death over secession and slavery. The Civil War typified the way events outran cultural expectations, both in the scale of its horrors and in its traumatic aftermath, including nearly a century of lynch mob horrors.

Practically speaking, the west took its modern form in several frenzied decades of land rush and gold rush. Reckless courage and Colt's "Peacemaker" acquired mythic status in the triumphalism that flavored the berserk style of pulp novels, Hollywood westerns, and today's grittier television series *Deadwood*. As finance and industry stampeded across the continent, the pace of development, like the desperate exertions that settled the frontier, demanded levels of stress and stamina that by today's standards were continually testing the edge of self-control and social death.[39]

In 1850 *Moby Dick* set sail out of Herman Melville's inkwell, depicting imaginations literally "at sea." The novel never had the sensational influence of, say, Buffalo Bill's or P. T. Barnum's showcases of super-reality. All conventional reality, Ahab famously declaims, is "but pasteboard masks," behind which is the "outrageous strength" and "inscrutable malice" of the white whale that has maimed him. The captain commands, begs, bribes, and seduces his crew to "strike through" the "unreasoning mask" and kill the beast. "That inscrutable thing is chiefly what I hate; and...I will wreak that hate upon him."[40]

The obsession with penetrating the pasteboard mask of reality is a response to the realization that everything is constructed of parts—and that even selves are composed of "parts": masks and roles. The novel's sly prefatory matter satirizes natural history. Like the rendering of a whale, scientific anatomy destroys the thing it plumbs. To Ishmael, the whale "shadows forth the heartless voids and immensities of the universe, and thus stabs us from behind with the thought of annihilation." Ahab expresses the shock humans feel at the discovery of the insoluble violence of the universe that lies behind the consoling masks of culture. After all, Ahab has been hunting—warring against—the beast to revenge his lost limb and the recognition of death. His howl resounds in the nineteenth century's reaction to Darwin and the scientific vision of consciousness caught up in a planetary struggle of predators and prey: a shock still resonating in the distress of "creationist" religious groups today. Ahab's frenzy has not dissipated. Despite growing ecological alarm, survival greed continues to dispatch fleets of factory Pequods to sweep the planet's oceans, so voraciously that once-teeming fisheries have suffered alarming depletion[41] and the idea of population crash has begun to haunt the sleep of public reason.

On the hunt, Ahab scans the horizon of modernity, recognizing that conventional reality is a pasteboard enabling fiction, but also locked into a traditional cosmology in which some devilish agency lurks behind appearances. The novel puts to sea, as it were, because in the culture ashore what's right is deceptive. Out of sight of land, fixated on a lost limb and the death-awareness it signifies, the reasoning mind may well find that symbolic immortality—and reason itself—is a mask. And more to the harpoon's point, as Ahab's wrath illustrates, "inscrutable malice" is a fatal, even suicidal problem in sailors, not simply in cosmic whales. Ahab recognizes creaturely motives such as survival rage but denies that they invest us—and *are* us. The outcome is the familiar cluster of berserk characteristics: the godlike and beastlike alienation ("at sea"), slaughter and cutting up of wild "enemies," and recklessness culminating in the symbolic apocalypse that tears apart the ship and leaves Ishmael clinging to a coffin on an imponderable ocean.

Victorian respectability and industrial discipline sought to tame abandon, but Americans pursued Melville's phantom through a desperate civil war, becoming a militarized and corporatized nation operating today on a global scale.

A study of berserk style is bound to be incomplete, as I discovered when events kept outrunning drafts of this book. Too sweeping a scope yields a panoramic blur; an acute squint misses crucial connections. Moral aggression and rampage killers' distortions of what's right are the focus of the next chapter, "Rage for Order." The role of berserk style in post-Vietnam military and economic developments is the subject of the subsequent chapters. "The Living End," considers the implications of abandon in religious thought and doomsday fantasies.

CHAPTER 2

RAGE FOR ORDER

No wonder men go into a rage about fine points of belief: if your adversary wins the argument about truth, you die. Your immortality system has been shown to be fallible, your life becomes fallible.

Ernest Becker, *Escape from Evil*

If you "go into a rage about fine points of belief," you are defending your sense of what's right and punishing someone else for being wrong. What appears to be a contest over truth is conditioned by fight-or-flight neurophysiology. The need to feel right is built into us, and foundational for identity. It enables an ephemeral creature with a volatile imagination to feel at home in an overwhelming world. Operationally, it confirms our sensory perceptions and interpretations of reality, but it also supports the conviction that our lives have lasting meaning and that we matter. Lose that conviction and self-esteem suffers. Losing an argument, you lose "face" and your sense of self is injured. Rage may follow, or suicidal despair. We moralize about what's right, that is, to preserve our place in life and fend off social death.

Honor and Respectability can be whips to punish or defeat others, and to confirm our worth. In this way moral aggression is a weapon of psychological warfare. It can rationalize feelings of victimization and thirst for revenge. In mental illness, individuals may grasp at a distorted form of what's right in an effort to preserve their sanity. But again: the self is not a thing but an event needing to be socially substantiated. So a grave threat to what's right can unbalance anyone. The terror of annihilation can undo your sense of what's right, and reciprocally, chaos in your sense of what's right can tear you to pieces.

This chapter explores the way berserk style conditions moral aggression. At the edge of control, outrage makes a flexible weapon. In a competitive society where what's right is always contested and status is unstable, outrage can be war conducted by other means, as in the century of lynching that followed the Civil War. As vigilantism, moral aggression can be atrocious and contagious. For people primed to feel personal indignation, outrage can seethe beneath outward calm,[1] fueling explosive fury, justified in the world's eyes or not.

As Homer's *Iliad* and Greek tragedy witness, moral aggression can be treacherous, since it justifies taboo violence and risks starting a vindictive cycle. Comic book superheroes and rant broadcasting remind us that vengeance is easily confused with justice. For the U.S., the righteous anticommunist invasion of Vietnam undermined the heroic self-esteem earned in World War II.[2] By 1968, protesters were chanting, "Hey hey, LBJ, how many kids did you kill today?" To choke off dissent at Berkeley in 1970, then Governor Reagan sent in military helicopters to tear gas students. Evoking the war against Hitler, he vowed: "If it takes a bloodbath, let's get it over with. No more appeasement!"[3] A few days later, in May 1970, the Ohio National Guard shot four Kent State University students, and later that month at Jackson State College police killed another two students. By 1971, the Pentagon Papers were exposing Washington's long history of deceptive and confused motives for the war.

In the debate over the war and the counter-culture, positions polarized, hardening fantasies of vigilante justice as a last defense against chaos. In John G. Avildsen's movie *Joe* (1970), an affluent New Yorker searches for his daughter with a factory worker. In an echo of the My Lai rampage, the pair massacre a commune of "wasted" hippie "peaceniks," the father tragically killing his daughter and driving home the film's moral ambivalence. In *Death Wish* (1974) and its four sequels, vigilante justice emerged as berserk style and stereotype. In James Wan's *Death Sentence* (2007), the cops were still feckless, so another father (Kevin Bacon) loses nearly his entire family to gang members and slaughters them all. The rampage ends in derealized moral exhaustion, with the nearly dead vigilante gazing at his chirpy family singing in a home video, at the edge of life, in a cloud of ironies.

EROS AMOK

Since one theme of witchcraft terrors imagines dried-up older women enjoying the Devil's icy member, you might say that sexual panic has plagued American culture from its Puritan beginnings. In the 1980s and 1990s, a popular delusion that excited tabloid media and some clinicians supposed a cult of Satanists, like a witches' coven, to be victimizing children. In some variants, the cult used mind-control to program children to become murderers as adults.[4] Before it subsided, the craze touched other countries and compromised some psychiatrists.

After the perceived excesses of the 1960s, many Americans found ideas about abandon sinister. The panic over satanic ritual abuse appeared during an upsurge in anxiety about child abuse and abduction. Unwittingly coached, children reported improbably or even impossible abuses by child care personnel and others. Andrew Jarecki's *Capturing the Friedmans* (2003) documents one such case. Media and even milk carton advertisements inflamed hysteria about an epidemic of child kidnapping that turned out to be an urban legend. Just as long-simmering underclass frustration had overreacted with urban riots to the Great Society "war on poverty," so feminist efforts to redress inequality, domestic violence, and rape unexpectedly contributed to an acute sensitivity to sexual abuse. Eventually that sensitivity played a role in the exposure of sexual abuse among Catholic clergy a few years later (c. 2002).

Nobody disputes the reality of sexual abuse. The problem is that that predation and helpless innocence, combined with secrecy and questionable evidence, can generate hysteria. For some therapists and clients, the fear of sexual violation came to be a universal explanation of psychological distress. The developing moral panic interacted with a cluster of ideas centered on "multiple personality disorder" (M.P.D.) and "recovered memory"—phenomena reminiscent of the spectral evidence seized upon in witchcraft panics.[5] The idea of a satanic cult drew on hoary pulp fiction clichés about white slavery, conspiracy, and wealthy criminal masterminds, as well as cult scandals from the counter-culture decades.

Pressured by alarmed parents and police, some children began reporting sensational sexual assaults that entangled innocent day care
providers and fathers in the criminal justice system. "The recovered
memory movement readily embraced the idea of male violence, particularly that of repressed C.S.A. [child sexual abuse] at the hands
of fathers, step-fathers, and other male authority figures. Women
(overwhelmingly white and middle class) who sought counseling for
alcohol and drug problems, depression, eating disorders, and a variety of other conditions were told by their therapists that they were
abuse victims because they showed the 'symptoms' of C.S.A., despite
the fact that most had no conscious memories of such childhood
violence. Many were encouraged to 'abreact,' or recover and relive
the repressed memories, and to join ongoing incest survivor self-help
groups to aid in their 'recovery.'"[8] In a classic case former police officer Clyde Ray Spencer spent twenty years in prison after a conviction for sexually molesting his son and daughter. He was released
in 2009 when his children testified that the abuse never happened.[7]
Belatedly the children recognized that their divorced mother had apparently used berserk style as a weapon against her ex-husband. Only
when psychological research and the courts reasserted evidentiary
standards, barring recovered memory as testimony, did the epidemic
abate.

The policeman's imprisonment is a telling parable of berserk style
in a complex historical moment. The real suffering of women and
children was badly served by popular self-help books such as *The
Courage to Heal*, whose authors advised readers that "If you think
you were sexually abused and your life shows the symptoms, then you
were." In their view non-specific and subjective complaints of anxiety,
depression, and their somatized effects qualify as symptoms. The authors go on to incite self-intoxicating rage: it is "A little like priming
the pump, you can do things that will get your anger started. Then,
once you get the hang of it, it'll begin to flow on its own.... Many
survivors have strong feelings of wanting to get back at the people
who hurt them so terribly. You may dream or murder or castration.
It can be pleasurable to fantasize such scenes in vivid detail. Wanting
revenge is a natural impulse, a sane response. Let yourself imagine it
to your heart's content."[8] Such prose legitimized sadistic abandon as
righteous retribution for imagined sexual abandon. The payoff, predictably, gets the woman victim in touch with superhuman resources:
"Imagine all women healed—and all that energy no longer used for

mere survival but made available for…freeing political prisoners, ending the arms race" (129).

This advice ignores the self-intoxicating, self-destructive dangers of rage, which is after all the reason Christianity advocates mercy and forgiveness. But the advice also ignored the actual experience of victims, which as psychologist Susan A. Clancy has reported, usually does not involve violent injury, however reprehensible the violation.[9] As in so many other incarnations of the berserk trope, convictions of victimization have perverse consequences: "a newer 'third wave' of feminism has produced scathing critiques about feminist theory and practice that is rooted in the concept of victimization…. Requiring women to assume the role of the 'victim,' a person who is perpetually in recovery, has been criticized for being disempowering as well as being a suppression of women's rights to sexual, psychological, and economic freedom. Nonetheless, 'victim feminism,' as it has been dubbed, was an integral part of the recovery culture that emerged in the 1980s" (Robbins).

In the new century, Internet aggression among the young has regularly focused on sexual themes. The Internet has chat rooms dedicated to outrage, where anonymity and instant gratification make fury seductive.[10] Sharing the indignation of others, depressive feelings convert to anger (flight to fight), enabling ranters to boost their morale. The danger, needless to say, is that venting anger can be self-intoxicating, especially when amplified in a group, and leading toward a berserk climax.

Headline stories have described posses of students ganging up to bully a classmate to the point of suicide. Parents pressure the young to "grow up," "shape up," and be successful, but adult encouragement masks an implicit threat of social death for losers. And adults, too, are bullied by bosses and other authorities. It's a system, and treacherous when people goad each other with impossible photoshopped ideals. Bullies act out this dark side of adult expectations. Overreacting to adult (parental) demands, they deflect the demands onto a scapegoat, rejecting or "disinheriting" the inadequate child. Driving out the loser, bullies imagine more approval for themselves. By contrast, the scapegoat acts out the fears, helplessness, and self-hatred that the bullies want to expel from themselves. In this dangerous atmosphere, bullies bond like soldiers, enjoying the thrill of escape and survival. And social media arms them with "smart weapons." Safe behind a social network screen, one kid can tell another to die, exploding the "enemy's" self-esteem, as in the suicide of Rebecca Sedwick. Rebecca "had been terrorized for more than a year by girls who used to be her friends....She tried to get away, but Rebecca couldn't escape their hateful words relayed across social media: 'You should die,' someone told the 12-year-old. 'Why don't you go kill yourself?' On Sept. 9 [2013], Rebecca did just that—jumping to her death from a tower at an abandoned cement plant near her home in Lakeland."[11]

Sex combines with rant in "sexting." In sexual and romantic competition, girls have sent nude photos of themselves to doubtful boyfriends. When such taboo photos go viral, rival classmates accuse the offender of being a slut or "ho," in some cases shaming them into suicide.[12] Students are acting out identity "issues," as conventional wisdom has it, but they are also using moral panic to police one another, as adults might, and to compete for status. In the process they reflect the conflicts of a culture that uses sexual desire in consumer marketing, making it a status tool and fashion accessory, and disapproves of the Internet pornography that it enjoys. As photoshopped ideals collide with social realities, sexting reflects our creaturely ambivalence about the body. In moments when sexuality is not enchanting, bodies look more or less alike, among billions on the planet. In this context topless photos advertise sexual maturation, but they can also be a quixotic gift of intimacy and a bid for recognition that can make the giver feel significant.

As berserk style, then, sexting can be a search for something special in yourself and in another that is worth loving, and an equally reckless urge to punish that search. Interestingly, E. L. James's best-selling soft-porn romance *Fifty Shades of Grey* (2012) can be understood as an effort to reconcile the conflicted motives in sexting. In the novels' Seattle, a virginal college student named Anastasia Steele (Ana) discovers exceptional sexual pleasure and eventually idealized romantic devotion in a rich, handsome young man named Christian Grey. Their relationship is based on a contract in which Ana agrees to become Christian's "submissive," willing to be beaten, spanked, and tied up, to lower her eyes in his presence, and to let him dictate her sleep, food and dress.

Nominally the novel dramatizes the partners' search for extraordinary sexual fulfillment. In bondage (BDSM) sex, pain and submission overthrow everyday self-protective inhibitions. They excite hypervigilance and sensitivity, making you more acutely aware of your body and your partner with the whip. *Fifty Shades* walks readers through the sex play in a sort of "self-help eroticism." [13] It introduces and explains techniques of pleasure the way *Cosmo* does. And it manages to wink at you while sounding breathlessly earnest. This pain is really "pain," a technique, and comes with "safe words" to disguise the reality that the thrill of losing control is always under control—in particular, under Ana's control. So the contract here is really a script that's thrilling because you pretend to cut loose and let it all hang out. It uses a taste of pain to strip off the swaddling wrap of habit that keeps us safe and half-asleep in our everyday lives.

Similarly, the quest for identity only plays at self-discovery. Christian has been abused as a child, but Ana's love heals him. And while Ana is emphatically ordinary, vulnerable to self-doubt, Christian's choice of Ana allows her to become "a feminine Horatio Alger" (53). The plot implies equality by making the self-improving Ana also a Galatea shaped by Christian's Pygmalion.

For women readers, Ana's ordinariness "strengthens the fantasy power of the narrative, because it makes her similar to all women who secretly dread not being unique or outstanding enough" (53). Insofar as Ana is seeking validation in sex, her "submissive" contract is akin to the nude photos sexted by adolescent girls. Like the contract, the photos use berserk style risk and taboos to enhance the emotions and the singularity—the significance—of the wished-for validation. The gestures also resemble berserk dynamics in combining godlike and beastlike qualities in the wished-for ecstasy of being chosen for love, and "slutty" bodily transgression.

In the novel, and until photos go viral, the berserk quality promises ecstatic play. Ana's self-exposure is particularly tame because her contract insures mutual privacy. In painful news stories, the bid for ecstasy triggers envious punishment: a threat of social death. *Fifty Shades,* however, internalizes the conflict, as would be appropriate for adult women readers, and berserk style makes that drama of character possible. Ana's role as "submissive" plays out the conflicted feelings of a child. She loves and hates the surrogate parent Christian telling her what to eat and wear while offering her sexual bliss. This turns out to be the crucial work BDSM is doing in the story. Being spanked and bossed, Ana can enjoy having the guilty and self-hating side of her ambivalence punished. In part, the guilt is the feeling of inadequacy that comes from being merely ordinary when the world—and romance—calls for heroic ideals. And in part, the guilt is a way of thinking about the usual human resentment at being bossed: which is bound to happen at some point in all relationships.

For balance, again, Christian also undergoes punishment, but in the continuing pain of his traumatic childhood. Presumably BDSM allows him to magically undo his sense of helplessness by "dominating" Ana and converting pain to pleasure in sex. And there is another dimension to his role, too. As Janice Radway has shown, drawing on Nancy Chodorow's theory of women's development, romance fiction invests its otherwise manly hero with maternal qualities that comfort and relieve the loneliness of women readers.[14] By the third book of the trilogy, Christian is as utterly devoted to his idealized wife Ana as a "submissive" child would love to be, even as he is also fulfilling the role of surrogate—but no longer controlling—mother for her.

In a time when attitudes toward sex are gratefully relaxed and roles are less prescribed, you might expect that this freedom to explore would make for more grown-up insight. But in *Fifty Shades* the plot gratuitously gives the sex partners a happy ending. Nobody has to put up with suffering, hilarity, and hard work to wise up. The contract is a basic tool of good business sense, but it also skirts the hassle of dealing with living personalities. And in consumer capitalism, sex and wish-fulfillment are marketing strategies that flatteringly insist it's all about *You, wonderful You.*

Fifty Shades, then, tries to reconcile "the conflicting imperatives of autonomy and attachment" (70) in a 21st century society in which mating rituals and gender roles have become much less clear. The characters cope by substituting a sexual contract that uses bondage to create bonds and spells out every move. What appears to self-abandon turns out to be a playful loosening of inhibitions, so that the partners, by now lovers, can enjoy intimacy that romance assumes was in them all along. The plot equips their eventual marriage with sex toys and a locked room for pleasure, but the couple's child and their repeated pledges of love suggest that ecstatic taboo will no longer be enough. The consolation is that outgrowing play-bondage is a dream of overcoming the moral aggression pervasive in American culture, a dream as touching as it is unrealistic.

PUNISHMENT AMOK

As part of the turn against the tumultuous abandon of the 1960s, Washington initiated anti-drug policies that headlines called a "war on drugs." The programs associated drugs with urban minorities and the oppositional experimentation of the young, but had only a minor effect on incarceration. In 1981, while celebrating individual freedom, President Reagan vowed that "We're taking down the surrender flag that has flown over so many drug efforts; we're running up a battle flag."[15] In the post-Vietnam slump, the "battle" targeted depressed inner cities and the stranded cohort of young black males in need of jobs. Over time, as in real war, the combat would produce berserk excesses. In the 1980s rates of imprisonment rose sharply. By 2007, berserk style had grossly distorted policy. As Marc Mauer and Ryan S. King reported in "A Twenty-Five Year Quagmire: the War on Drugs and Its Impact on American Society," the demand for punishment mushroomed. The number of drug offenders incarcerated since 1980 had increased 1100 percent, the majority—sixty percent—with "no history of violence or high-level drug-selling activity."[16]

Still, drugs were only part of the prosecutorial boom. "Around 1975...the United States became radically more punitive. In thirty-five years, the incarceration rate ballooned [from 100] to over 700 per 100,000, far outstripping all other countries."[17] The data point to a slow-motion criminal justice rampage. In part it was a response to economic distress following the Vietnam guns-and-butter binge and the dashed hopes of the war on poverty. By the 1980s middle-class families needed two breadwinners and journalism was discovering homelessness and "latchkey kids."

Anxiety about family contributed to the moral panic that kept the prison system expanding. Almost as soon as the last helicopter fled Saigon, *Time* magazine was targeting youth crime as the new enemy: "How can such sadistic acts—expressions of what moral philosophers would call sheer evil—be explained satisfactorily by poverty and deprivation? What is it in our society that produces mindless rage?"[18] The cliché "mindless rage" blocked any curiosity about motivation.

By the 1990s economic blight had magnified the alarm. In the decade of the Los Angeles riots (1992) the riot zone lost 50,000 jobs. "In the vacuum, youthful rage exploded again in gang warfare." In this atmosphere all parties resorted to berserk style to account for carnage and the failure of public policy. Tom Hayden warned that "We need to find alternatives to the 'embedded sense of self-hate' that propels so many inner-city youth to lash out in killing sprees." By contrast, "conservatives such as William Bennett and James Q. Wilson began attaching the label of 'super-predator' to all the [potential killers]. Their notion seemed to be that a fixed percentage of kids were natural-born killers who just couldn't be helped by better schools or jobs—a neo-Darwinian philosophy that fit neatly with the de-industrialization and budget cuts that swept across inner cities like chain saws through old-growth forests." In turn, "The super-predator thesis justified the most massive prison expansion in American history, with its epicenter in California, where there were about 150,000 inmates in any given year, two-thirds of them reputed gang members."[19]

In some cities with poor black neighborhoods, murder rates do reach levels drastically higher than the rest of the country. "According to FBI data, between 2002 and 2012 Chicago lost more than 5,000 people to homicide—that's nearly three times the number of Americans killed in action in Afghanistan."[20] Philadelphia, among others, also saw a disproportionate number of murders. Given the neighborhoods' levels of traumatic stress and the prevalence of weapons, the comparison to a war zone is apt.

No less tragically, white bias about black criminality qualifies as berserk. "The standard assumption that criminals are black and blacks are criminals is so prevalent that in one study, 60 percent of viewers who viewed a crime story with no picture of the perpetrator falsely recalled seeing one, and of those, 70 percent believed he was African American. When we think about crime, we 'see black,' even when it's not present at all."[21]

As more urban black men went to prison, "bad boy" or "gangsta" role-playing became a calculated product of industrial entertainment, celebrating themes of kamikaze defiance, surreal glitz, and sexual dominance. Like Prohibition era gangster epics, the rap phenomenon was richly ambivalent: socially aware yet also regressive and reactionary. The performer Biggie Smalls (Christopher Wallace) sold "ready to Die" (1994) to become a celebrity, and was murdered two weeks before his release of "Life After Death" (1997) at age 24.

At the start of the 21st century, with less than 5 percent of the world's population, the U. S. had almost a quarter of the world's prisoners: a record-breaking product of the rage for order.[22] "Americans "are locked up for crimes—from writing bad checks to using drugs—that would rarely produce prison sentences in other countries. And in particular they are kept incarcerated far longer than prisoners in other nations." What is more, the criminal justice system has corralled a disproportionate number of black men, women, and immigrants. Statistics show no upsurge in crime to explain the phenomenon. "Criminologists and legal scholars in other industrialized nations say they are mystified and appalled by the number and length of American prison sentences."[23] Cable "reality TV" shows about life inside prisons reflect the change in policy from rehabilitation to brute confinement.

Michael J. Moore's film "The Legacy" (1999) records some of the ways in which the will to punish pushed toward "zero tolerance": the obliteration of the criminal. The film centers on two parents who lost daughters in brutal murders and took leading roles in the frenzied process that led to passage of California's draconian Three Strikes law. In 1992, during what began as a minor mugging, two recently released ex-convicts murdered college student Kimberly Reynolds in a flash of cold rage—the berserker's "flaming ice." The heavily armed killer later died in a firefight with police tantamount to a combat rampage.

In reaction to his daughter's death at the hands of repeat offenders, Mike Reynolds, a Fresno wedding photographer, began organizing a push for the "Three Strikes and You're Out" initiative (Proposition 184). [24] The witty allusion to baseball trivializes the law's overkill, which mandates prison terms of 25 years to life for a third felony conviction, even though the third strike could be shoplifting, a forged check, or some other non-violent offense.

At first legislators found Three Strikes simplistic and counterproductive, and Reynolds' campaign stalled. A year later, however, an ex-con abducted and killed 12-year-old Polly Klaas. The public anguish and outrage reached around the globe, amplified by inflammatory media coverage. In time police arrested the feral-looking repeat offender Richard Allen Davis, and the public outcry attracted politicians and new financial support, and turned Reynolds' flagging campaign into a crusade.

Early in the referendum process critics foresaw the danger of overkill: "Data clearly shows that counties that vigorously and strictly enforce the 'Three Strikes' law did not experience a decline in any crime category relative to more lenient counties." [25] In fact a majority of "Three Strikes" sentences have been for non-violent offenses, and the cost to the state has proved crippling. Nevertheless, the public anguish over the appalling murder of Polly Klaas enabled Reynolds to step up his campaign. As the Proposition 184 initiative became a hot button issue, Michael Huffington and other political figures appropriated some of its energy. The National Rifle Association, the prison guards' union, contractors, and other parties contributed funds; a corporation loaned a plane; and talk radio shock jocks scapegoated skeptical lawmakers and inflamed "the court of public opinion."

The Three Strikes movement took on characteristics of moral panic. The public mind judged Polly Klaas's murderer a "monster," and he came to stand for all repeat offenders menacing or not. "Our" survival—the posterity embodied in vulnerable young women—depended on locking up threat forever. So intense was the paroxysm that attempts to tame the Three Strikes bill's excesses failed. [26]

Moore's film movingly captures personalities as they used style to manage extremes. The bill's co-sponsor, California politician Bill Jones, brashly vowed that the goal is "zero" crime," to be paid for, if necessary, by stripped down education and zero quality of life for prisoners. Before the cameras, Mike Reynolds presented himself not as a grieving father, but as a humble citizen overcoming arrogant politicians. Looking back as the "father" of the law, now depicted on the Three Strikes website as a rescuer of untold potential victims, he makes self-effacing gestures.

But more complex post-traumatic motives show in Reynolds's demeanor. He has no curiosity about "those animals" or their motives, and makes no distinctions about levels of threat. He admires the radio shock jocks whose vituperation whipped up public fury. "Those guys are a couple of chainsaws!" he exults, evoking the annihilation of all opposition. In his zeal to punish, Reynolds began to treat government itself as culpable in the murders, as if "the authorities" can eliminate all risk from life. At one point, like a terrorist, he brags that Three Strikes supporters phoning legislators in Sacramento "melted" the switchboard and brought government to a halt.

The media "chainsaws" inflamed—and prospered from—the public's anguish. The issue perfectly suited the theater of righteousness and retribution that talk media had been perfecting for a decade or more. Like supermarket gossip tabloids, the shock jocks operate in a zone of half-knowledge, screening out inconvenient inhibitions and complexities in order to intensify "the money shot"—the knockout put-down. Rupert Murdoch's Fox network is famous for the stagey indignation of pundits such as Bill O'Reilly, who in 2005 "had one of his tantrums and told would-be terrorists to 'go ahead' and blow [gay San Francisco] off the map."[27] O'Reilly's widely broadcast threat display is of course itself a form of terrorism, acting to cow some people and pump up others.

When Governor Wilson signed the Three Strikes bill and handed Mike Reynolds the ceremonial pen, Reynolds brandished it before the cameras and declared: "This pen, with this bill, is like the .357 magnum of pens. This is the toughest, hardest crime bill not only California has proposed but the entire country has ever seen." He was wielding a symbolic equivalent of the weapon that killed his daughter, and the pen reveals the pressure of rage. Although Reynolds' conviction of power arguably helped him cope with traumatic loss, his fantasy of merciless punishment mirrors the killers' cold rage—the berserk state's "flaming ice."

The injured father wanted total revenge, even at the cost of unjust prison sentences. His fantasy aligns him with the vigilante fathers who run amok in movies such as Michael Winner's *Death Wish* (1974) after attacks on wives or daughters, or with soldiers who slaughtered "enemy" civilians in Iraq to avenge dead comrades. Reynolds sees the pen—prison—not primarily as protection from harm, but as a vindictive weapon to kill all the "animals." Since a Three Strikes conviction mandates a de facto life sentence, the law does impose social death. In this sense Reynolds is reenacting the original murder of his daughter, but this time armed with a legislative pistol and personally taking the lives of a potentially endless mob of killers. Accordingly, he imagines himself a special target of wrath. At a traffic light, he says, a criminal "could recognize me as that Three Strikes guy, and I'm gone."

After wrestling with his own anger and grief, Marc Klaas, Polly's father, came to see the overkill in Proposition 184. Although he joined others campaigning against the referendum, it passed by an overwhelming margin. Even so, the imaginative sympathy he was able to feel for those caught in the Three Strikes dragnet enabled him to empathize with Mike Reynolds' suffering, rage, and relentlessness.

In March 2003 a politically conservative Supreme Court upheld the convictions of two Three Strikes prisoners serving virtual life sentences for stealing golf clubs from a country club and videotapes from two convenience stores. The justices reversed a federal appeals court that had declared the 50-year sentence "grossly disproportionate," violating the Eighth Amendment's ban against cruel and unusual punishment.

"Free market" ideology imagined that privatization and technology could make punishment cheaper. In many states inmates became commodities managed for profit by companies such as the Corrections Corporation of America. Overcrowding, inadequate medical care, and the overuse of solitary confinement are demonstrably damaging to prisoners. Five states spend as much on corrections as on higher education, and in California's prisons job training and education were cut virtually to nothing. During the prison population explosion since the 1980s, says Jeanne Woodford, the warden of San Quentin, "The violence went out of control.... And then the programs started going away. I was there during an 18-month lockdown. It was unbelievably horrific."[28] The nominal recidivism rate of the 1980s shot up to 70 percent. Says one analyst: "there are large numbers of people behind bars who could be supervised in the community safely and effectively at a much lower cost—while also paying taxes, paying restitution to their victims and paying child support."[29]

The folly of the system crystallized opposition. In a "scathing" order (2009), federal judges ordered the state of California to reduce its overcrowded prison population because that was "the only way to change what they called an unconstitutional prison health care system that causes one unnecessary death a week."[30] In November 2012, California voters passed Proposition 36, which "would alter California's "Three Strikes" law by imposing a life sentence only when the crime committed is a serious violent crime. Some offenders with two prior serious or violent felony convictions who are currently serving life sentences for many nonserious, non-violent felony convictions could be resentenced to shorter prison terms."[31]

WANTED DEAD OR ALIVE

As berserk style exaggerates the violence and insecurity in everyday life, it also stimulates fantasies of obliterating threat. Broadcasters try to frame threat in ways that excite feelings of mastery while euphemizing the wish to kill. Since 1989 the "reality" television show COPS, for example, has followed police into the incoherent, squalid world at the bottom of society. The camera watches local police subdue a "group of people who are permanently down on their luck for a variety of reasons: momentarily or chronically dysfunctional, inveterate 'outsiders' and misfits…weak of character and prone to the worst kind of judgment. When encountered, most are under the influence of drugs or alcohol." They include incompetent petty criminals, immigrants and mentally ill as well as homeless people, "But since the concept of homelessness has no place in the universe of COPS, these individuals are simply part of the population who are endlessly and violently out of control and in trouble with the law." They inhabit "a world of nothing but brawls, bars, hookers, mental breakdowns, and outbursts. It is difficult to comprehend any of it in any human or social terms."[32]

In each episode of COPS, that is, berserk style frames life at the bottom as alien and beyond help, which absolves the viewer of any responsibility. The camera especially lingers on "a person going more and more out of control, in ways that are painful to watch. Often the person will be wildly, violently rebellious and hysterical. Unkempt, often barely clothed, and surrounded by filth and chaos, he or she is allowed to gyrate and gesticulate as the cops show saint-like restraint." They are "tabloid criminals...marked as subhuman and different than 'normal' Americans like the police" (264).

These episodes imply a policy of triage, with the poor and unfit a surplus population to be culled periodically. As agents of eugenics, the police remove undesirable characters and characteristics from society. Jail, then, acts to sterilize unwanted males. In some states, with transparent echoes of apartheid, this amounts to the castration and social death of a whole generation of young black males. In this way incarceration can be said to shade off into capital punishment.

The death penalty itself is beset with contradictions.[33] Black males are disproportionately convicted of capital crimes, while the rich and well-connected are virtually never put to death. The American south has the highest murder rate and also carries out the most executions. Since 1973, 140 people have been exonerated and freed from death row. The danger of executing innocent people led Governor George Ryan to impose a moratorium in Illinois after 13 people on death row were exonerated (January 31, 2000). Some prosecutors have dismissed DNA and other evidence and fought—no other word will do—findings of innocence.

Moral aggression directs the storm of motives that leads police regularly to kill unarmed young black men. Berserk style governs many of the incidents. Like soldiers in Vietnam or Iraq, officers policing poor black neighborhoods have a contradictory charge, to protect but also control an ambiguously alien population that may prove friendly or hostile in any encounter. In raids and stops, police can apply force with the impunity that soldiers enjoy.[34] Racism and alienation create hair-trigger panic. Studies show that whites exaggerate the association of black males with crime. Police kill 21 times more young black males than whites.[35] Officers who associate blacks with animals are inclined to expect rampage behavior and to overreact. Like soldiers amok, police officers predictably claim they feared for their lives when shooting, and the law just as predictably declines to punish them.[36]

Hair-trigger policing reached the headlines against a background of growing public alarm about rampage killers and a contentious debate about gun regulation. A week after the Sandy Hook school rampage (December 14, 2012), the NRA's Wayne LaPierre channeled public fears into moral aggression: "The only thing that stops a bad guy with a gun is a good guy with a gun." He elaborated: "our society is populated by an unknown number of genuine monsters—people so deranged, so evil, so possessed by voices and driven by demons that no sane person can possibly ever comprehend them. They walk among us every day. And does anybody really believe that the next Adam Lanza isn't planning his attack on a school he's already identified at this very moment?"[37]

The speech imagined an invincible hero quicker on the draw than a "monster." The NRA envisions a paramilitary society, with everyone "carrying" and armed guards in every school. Guns promise to restore injured self-confidence and invincibility. However, if anyone may be armed, with unclear intentions, the danger invites hair-trigger reflexes and adrenalized passions. And if everyone is armed, then marginally stable people will be even more likely to have access to weapons and jobs as guards. It goes without saying that this fantasy requires a world without accidents and fatal misidentifications.

Two months after LaPierre's press conference, George Zimmerman, a neighborhood watch volunteer in a gated community in Florida, spotted an unarmed black teenager wearing a hoodie. Zimmerman assumed he was a housebreaker (February 26, 2013). Trailing Trayvon Martin in the dark, Zimmerman never imagined that the innocent, alarmed "suspect" might see *him* as a predator and react with comparable abandon. When Martin preemptively jumped Zimmerman, dominating him in the scuffle, the pseudo-policeman panicked and shot him to death. A jury declined to convict Zimmerman.

The absurd death played out clashing cultural fantasies. Zimmerman emulated the lone detective-hero, but instead of saving "his" neighborhood, he became a bigoted big shot and killed one of the neighbors he was supposed to protect. Martin too was acting out a cultural fantasy: the young black rebel fighting to survive racist mean streets. He had flirted with the hip-hop bad boy role, suspended from school several times, and once challenged by cops over suspicious jewelry found in his backpack. He had no police record, and these details are innocuous, yet they suggest the ambiguities of outlaw self-reliance and streetwise toughness in adolescent male culture—and the corresponding readiness of officialdom to profile minority males.

Ironically, Zimmerman was more of a "bad boy" than Martin. In 2005, he was in trouble for assaulting a cop, and his ex-fiancee took out a restraining order against him. As moral watchdog, in a recorded call to police, he growls about "fucking punks" and "these assholes, they always get away." This is not the wise voice of the law. You might conclude that Zimmerman used moral aggression to keep himself better under control. He seems to have imagined that law means enforcement, not investigation and mediation. So this is a story about fantasies of heroic mastery and a failure of civility—and the law—to control moral aggression and the allure of abandon.

A year later, in racially tense Ferguson Missouri, cultural fantasies collided when a white police officer named Darren Wilson killed unarmed, black, 18-year-old Michael Brown. A Justice Department investigation eventually concluded that Wilson fired in justifiable self-defense. But by then, weeks of turbulent protests had put a spotlight on a national pattern of police killings of unarmed black males.

In his cruiser officer that morning (August 9, 2014), Wilson heard a radio report of a theft of cigarillos from a local market. Moments later he stopped Brown and a sidekick, Dorian Johnson, walking in the middle of the street, slowing traffic. According to Johnson, Wilson ordered them to "Get the fuck on the sidewalk." Brown shot back: "Fuck what you have to say."[38] Startled by the defiance, Wilson noticed cigarillos in Brown's hand and concluded these were the thieves. When Wilson tried to detain Brown, they grappled. "And when I grabbed him," Wilson reported, "the only way I can describe it is I felt like a five-year-old holding onto Hulk Hogan. That's just how big he felt and how small I felt just from grasping his arm."[39]

With Brown punching him, Wilson felt trapped in the cruiser. When he drew his pistol and threatened to shoot, Brown taunted him. They struggled and Wilson fired two shots, grazing Brown's hand. Now Brown backed away. He "had the most intense aggressive face," Wilson said. "The only way I can describe it, it looks like a demon, that's how angry he looked." Initially witnesses depicted Brown as an innocent victim, his hands up to surrender. But in Wilson's account, which the Justice Department corroborated, Brown charged the officer.

To Wilson, "it looked like [Brown] was almost bulking up to run through the shots, like it was making him mad that I'm shooting at him. And the face that he had was looking straight through me, like I wasn't even there, I wasn't even anything in his way. I shoot a series of shots." "I don't know how many I shot, I just know I shot it."

In fact Wilson emptied his pistol at the suspect. This overkill stopped "the demon."

It was a moment of berserk abandon. As in combat, emergency physiology overtook strategic thinking. For whatever reasons, Michael Brown was on the edge of abandon from the moment of the theft, through his macho threat display with the officer, and his fatal charge into gunfire. Michael Brown was already large (6'4", 290 pounds), and perhaps pumped up by the earlier theft. Police rely on a badge and gun to overawe others. You and the officer both know he can kill you. In the instant of abandon, both men misread the signals. Brown assumed the threat was a bluff. Wilson, humiliated and imagining superhuman rage (the Hulk), felt like a helpless "five-year-old." When Brown charged, as if to dominate him again, Wilson saw it in macho body-building terms: Brown was "bulking up to run through the shots" and "like he was going to run right through me." Wilson then emptied his pistol's 12-bullet clip in a spasm of overkill.[40]

The NRA insists that training would guarantee the safety of an armed paramilitary society. But police, whose professionalism should prove the point, have been tragically susceptible to impulse and misjudgment. Officer Wilson's perception of Michael Brown as a "demon" or the Hulk echoes the NRA's cartoonish vision of a society menaced by "monsters."

In Ohio a 911 call sent officers to gun down a rampage killer who turned out to be 12-year-old, black Tamir Rice playing with a toy gun in an empty playground (November 23, 2014). In a Beavercreek Walmart, Ronald Ritchie called in a prank alarm to a 911 dispatcher, and based on Ritchie's lies, police killed John Crawford III, a 22-year-old black father, as he talked on his cellphone while holding a fake gun from the merchandise rack. Neither Ritchie nor the incautious officer were held responsible.

Berserk style is insidious because it requires us to look beyond the dramatic moment. In 2008, for example, police training in Ohio changed: "Suddenly 'officers are empowered to engage the active threat upon arrival,' without waiting for backup. [Recall Zimmerman and Wilson springing into action.] It cites FBI studies showing that an active shooter event normally last 3-4 minutes, but 'average time per kill/injury is 15 seconds.' Clearly, officers have to act fast."[41] Accordingly, a Beavercreek Ohio police training presentation focuses alarm on rampage killings, which are terrifying but rare. The instruction warns that "the faster we can neutralize [shoot] the suspect the less time he / she will have to harm innocent persons." It concludes with an emotional photo of a teacher leading tots to safety at Sandy Hook school. To make sure you get the message, the power point presents a test situation:

"An Active Threat is in a building with the person I love the most. I want Law Enforcement to: 1/ Wait outside for more

officers. Or 2/ Enter the building and find the threat as fast as possible. What would you want?"

The question *"What would you want?"* is a macho taunt. *Are you man enough to save the person you love most?* The officer is urged to fear a monster, but also himself. The psychological manipulation in this training has echoes in the clashes that killed Trayvon Martin and Michael Brown. It contributes to a culture in which police shoot first and ask questions later. As the next chapter observes, it also plays a role in military culture and ideas about torture.

Berserk style registers in the absurd mismatch between deadly force and trivial or fancied offenses. Michael Brown died for a fistful of cigars. With a chokehold, Staten Island police killed Eric Garner, a large frail black man, for selling loose "untaxed" cigarettes (July 17, 2014). Trayvon Martin paid with his life for wearing a hoodie. Tamir Rice and John Crawford died holding toy guns. The deadly absurdity shows up in the spike of gun sales after a rampage, and in news stories about rattled homeowners who have shot lost motorists ringing a doorbell, and Alzheimer's sufferers wandering in the night. With particularly cruel absurdity, Ismaaiyl Abdullah Brinsley murdered two random New York City police officers (December 20, 2014), then committed suicide in the subway, believing he was revenging black men such as Michael Brown and heroically redeeming his own painful failures.

THE VIGILANTE TRANCE

The "emotional power of imagining killing and death" and its use "for political and cultural purposes" describes berserk style. One such use of the death penalty is to intimidate "them" and reassure "us" (threat display), but another is to deviously denigrate target groups, since executions will reinforce racist beliefs that minorities are criminals. As in other forms of berserk style, this kind of moral aggression can mystify the urge to violence.

As post-9/11 unity unraveled along with the wars in Afghanistan and Iraq, the 2008 financial crisis and a new, mixed-race president sharpened the national mood. Insecurity about money and jobs influenced anxiety about crime and fantasies about social collapse, with flight sometimes converting to fight, and fear to outrage.

Although in January 2009 the FBI reported that crime had declined, "nearly a third of Americans surveyed in the Rasmussen poll say crime has increased in their neighborhoods, and 72 percent say

it's very likely that crime will grow in the near-term.... The fears are
in some cases taking on a Y2K-like fervor, forecasting total social
meltdown. In times such as these, Americans have always reached for
their guns, says David Kopel, research director for the Independence
Institute, a free-market-oriented think tank....Modern fears are fu-
eled by the prospect of an apocalyptic economic failure. Gun-toting
rage for order predictably wears a Revolutionary War tri-corner hat
and invokes the Constitution. 'The logic is simple,' says Tom Lee, a
member of the Virginia Citizen Militia, which traces its roots to the
Revolutionary War. 'People are seeing a looming economic collapse
that will lead to a prolonged and possibly worsening breakdown of
law and order and, eventually, a We-the-People vs. armed-govern-
ment-enforcers scenario.'"[42]

"We the people" here are rhetorical phantoms, a means for Tom
Lee to pump up his heroic self-image and his cause. Militia groups
have generally been racist. Tom Lee imagines imposing vigilante law
and order and potentially fighting off or replacing the U.S. Government. His reference to a "worsening breakdown" implies that he sees
a collapse currently underway. His anxiety resonates in the dystopian
police state of Orwell's *1984* and its offspring, Ridley Scott's *Blade
Runner* (1982), Paul Verhoeven's *Robocop* (1987), and Andy Wa-
chowski's *The Matrix* (1999).

Kentucky pastor Ken Pagano told "his flock to bring handguns
to church in what he said was an effort to promote safe gun ownership." Conflating survival dread with patriotism and placing more
faith in guns than in God, the pastor boasted that "If it were not for
a deep-seated belief in the right to bear arms, this country would not
be here today" (BBC News, July 13, 2009). His rationale imagines
that individual gun owners have rescued the nation from death, drawing on Christianity to give the vigilante mentality a righteous frame..

White power, Islamic terrorists, and other radical groups aspire
to take the law into their own hands. Mafias too operate as a private
legal system, adjudicating disputes and interpreting local codes. A
godfather caricatures judge and jury, particularly when mafias resort
to the death penalty, as in the nickname of Albert Anastasia, "the
Lord High Executioner" of Murder Incorporated. In *The Sopranos*,
whether they are punishing an allegedly abusive girl's soccer coach,
a closeted gay, or a traitor, the mobsters obsess about "honor" and
hair-trigger vengeance.

These different groups share an assumption that vigilante violence
can hold together a world and a personal sense of what is right that

are coming apart. What warrants attention is the way causality is mystified. The breakdown "out there" and in the self is nebulous, and so is the particular violence embraced to counter it. The NRA's Wayne La Pierre contends that "The only thing that stops a bad guy with a gun is a good guy with a gun,"[43] a formula which reduces the principals to abstract forces with no inner life meeting in a magical transaction that destroys evil.

Just this ideation clusters around cyber "soldiers" such as Hollywood's Terminator and the military's "smart weapons" and drones. They are selfless warriors, though their motive energy is dissociated, coming from an invisible command station. When they kill innocents by mistake, as U.S. Predator drones have done, they become symbols of mystified authority run amok. In *Robocop* a policing cyborg goes haywire. As the robots become increasingly superhuman, controls become treacherously critical. The U.S. military is developing "self-governing, armed robots that could find and destroy targets on their own," says Ronald Arkin in a study commissioned by the Army. "The pressure of an increasing battlefield tempo is forcing autonomy further and further toward the point of robots making that final, lethal decision," he predicted. "The time available to make the decision to shoot or not to shoot is becoming too short for remote humans to make intelligent informed decisions."[44]

The military-industrial rhetoric naturalizes berserk style. The study's abstractions take dubious premises for granted, including the promise of control over a level of volition ordinarily beyond us. In traditional societies this has been a religious or magical behavior. When movies today project superhuman qualities onto machinery, the effect is ultimately psychological. In *Terminator*, say, Skynet caricatures a parent judge or God that threatens to punish our human inadequacy. At the same time, it fits the pulp fiction idea of an alien global tyranny. In the aftermath of the 9/11 attacks, some took the terrorists to be alien, machine-like assassins from a globe-girdling tyrannical Islam.

Whatever we name this imaginative syndrome, it figures in a range of behaviors. In historical pogroms, witch-hunts, and the Holocaust, evil and rage against evil act with trancelike determination. Fantasies about vampires dramatize the same dreamlike aggression. In the 1980s and 1990s, Satanic cults supposedly could program victims to forget and later remember instructions to kill. Fascination with the metallic, indestructible Terminator is akin to the public fear of an epidemic of autism. In the popular mind, the autistic personality is uncanny, unable to relate to others, and prone to repetitive mechanical behavior: a characterization that overlaps with ideas about cyborgs and the alienated berserker.

The HBO series *Dexter* explored this cluster of associations. Dexter Morgan (Michael C. Hall) is a crime lab technician by day, and by night a vigilante serial killer of criminals who have evaded the law. Supposedly Dexter is autistic. Adopted, he learned from his stepfather, a Miami cop, to mimic enough social skills to mask his lack of ordinary human feelings. Though his emotional life is all studied play-acting, the sentimental kicker is that in crucial ways he is more sensitive than ordinary people.

Dexter operates a conventional detective. Like Sherlock Holmes, he acts out the fantasy that freed from empathy, the mind can penetrate the masks of ordinary life. And like Holmes in his reckless cocaine addiction and obsession with crime, Dexter is a creature of berserk style, compulsively risking his life to "execute" lawbreakers by pseudo-surgical vivisection in a clinically tidy version of the psychopath's secret torture chamber and the police forensic lab. In his words, "I'm a very neat monster." The series advertises forbidden fantasies with deadpan irony and a wink. Viewers are of course exposed to sadistic feelings that its hero supposedly cannot feel. In this way the show resembles the thrillingly vicious "24," in which torture is also assumed to be unquestionably righteous.

The first serial killer Dexter unmasks turns out to be his long-lost brother, a split-off evil alter ego also psychologically damaged in childhood. In the final episode, Dexter euthanizes his hospitalized foster sister Debra and then sends himself into punishing lonely exile. These themes project a puritanical, paranoid, and demon-infested society. Although the show feints at intimacies, "what's right" turns out to be a murderous obsession with killing. The story plays out the sadistic reactions to death-anxiety in crime shows in which bodies are visibly mutilated or "scientifically" dissected in a forensic lab, as if to locate and extract death itself.[45] Like a vampire, Dexter lives for blood, on the edge of ordinary experience, at home in neither life nor death.

Dexter's America is a nation of theatrical surfaces and crass procedures. The script assumes that everyone is tacitly autistic, faking authentic feeling: but only the "genuinely" autistic can see it. Catching a teenage killer, Dexter tells him: "I'm a lot like you...I'm empty. But I found a way to make it feel less bottomless. Pretend. You pretend the feelings are there for the world. For the people around you. Who knows. Maybe one day they will be." This is the core dread in modernity: the discovery that the self is finally ungrounded and therefore free—and also forced—to spin a sustaining web of fictions that can function as family and "family" do in mafia.

In this light Dexter's emotionless vigilante rampage represents a resort to pseudo-judicial murder to ground the self. His mission is a euphemized form of authoritarianism. The core fantasy is that in dismembering live criminals, Dexter strips away their denial, forcing them to face the full horror of their evil and imminent death. Likewise, the narrative cuts through the viewers' denial. The berserk assumption is that there is some uncanny truth beyond or beneath our civilized inhibitions. The problem is that each discovered evil is gratuitous in the end: a plot device—not tragic or a vehicle for moral insight, or even uncanny. The plot cuts into the heart of evil only to keep finding tabloid melodrama or anatomical mechanism. Dexter disposes of body parts from a powerboat named "Slice of Life." The show's jokey tone ("He's Got a Way with Murder") insists that in the end evil is dissociated and trivial. In this respect the scripts flirt with abandon, manipulating it for maximum—but safe—effect on viewers.

The trancelike, depersonalized aggression of a cyborg or the fictional Dexter captures the cold-blooded quality of the berserk state. But we need to keep in mind that the berserk state is an outcome of stress and emergency physiology. Even when showing icy composure, rampage killers are usually in severe turmoil. Organic mental illness and efforts to cope can be unaccountable drivers of behavior. But what Ernest Becker says of the schizophrenic can apply to anybody under extreme stress: "He has to contrive extra-ingenious and extra-desperate ways of living in the world that will keep him from being torn apart by experience, since he is already almost apart."[46]

Dexter's "executions" dramatize the terror of being "torn apart" mentally as well as physically. His vigilante dissections recall the fascination with Jack the Ripper's disembowelment of women in the 1890s; Dr. Frankenstein's monstrous surgeries; anatomists' experiments upon the cadavers of criminals moralized in Hogarth's ghastly *The Reward of Cruelty;* drawing and quartering; and a history of illicit practices going back to the middle ages.[47] The dissection of immobilized victims also euphemizes Jeffrey Dahmer's attempts to turn his victims into living dead "zombies" with injections before satisfying his fetishism for body parts.

The horror comes in part from the anatomist's fascination of taking apart the living body in an effort to discover or master death.

And in one sense "autism" is a metaphor for the desensitization that comes of repeatedly anatomizing bodies. But the horror springs as well from the terror that the self may come apart under stress: that the foundational sense of what's right may disintegrate and we may lose control as in dying.

The berserk state can have the trancelike quality of psychosis, and rampage violence can be an "extra-desperate" way of coping with a self being torn apart. In 1995, 56 year old James Davis returned to the Union Butterfield tool company in Asheville, N.C., where he had been fired two days earlier for fighting. Firing 50 rounds from a semiautomatic rifle and pistol, he killed three employees. Witnesses reported that he "walked with calm determination [and afterward] lit a cigarette and quietly surrendered to police."[48]

Davis apparently set out to get revenge for the termination two days earlier. But a closer look reveals an ungrounded personality that had long been using a combative posture to make "fighting for his life" a story that could give him coherence. Co-workers had nicknamed him Psycho, because he "repeatedly picked fights at the tool warehouse...and had often told colleagues that if he were ever fired, he would return to kill his bosses. He had seen combat in Vietnam and been hospitalized with schizophrenia after the war. He lived alone, and co-workers knew he owned a .44 Magnum with a scope and had practiced firing it in his basement."[49]

Needless to say, Davis had strong incentives to believe that he was not responsible for his actions. But the dissociated quality of his account is compatible with other accounts of the berserk state. From death row he wrote that "I was calm. I was no longer me. Like someone else in my brain took over." He "went from tunnel vision to total blackout. When I got my vision and my mind back, I looked and seen what had happened. I did not know who I was. In the end, I self-destructed."[50] He focuses on the climax, not on the years he had spent in the grip of pugnacity.

To hold himself together, Davis organized his life around battling threat. In themes (conflict, defiance, revenge) and practice (gun-use) he focused on mastering violent abandon. The compulsion to pick fights acts out a need to dominate threat. To interpret his experience, however, Davis seized on Jekyll-and-Hyde ideas about dissociative states that have been influential in movies such as *The Manchurian Candidate* (1962, 2004) and demonic possession thrillers. The blackout has long been a favorite plot device of screenwriters. "I was no longer me. Like someone else in my brain took over." However responsible for his actions he may have been, Davis felt—and needed to believe that he felt—"carried away." Concluding that "I self-destructed," he was describing the sort of "disintegrative personal experience which rendered the self instinctively meaningless" that overtook soldiers in World War I. Since he had willed his belongings to a relative before setting out on his rampage, Davis must have sensed the likelihood of a fatal outcome. It may be that for him, the idea of a blackout expressed a suicidal wish to put an end to his inner turmoil.

Whatever its motive energy, abandon challenges the integrity of the self. In running amok, the aggression against others can also be an effort to master threats to the self: threats that may be the internal symptoms of illness, but also be objective—the threat of losing his job alarmed James Davis enough to make him warn his co-workers that "If they ever decide to fire me, I'll take two or three of them with me." This bravado emulates war movies and westerns in which the beleaguered hero faces overwhelming odds and seeks to magnify the self that is about to be nothing.

James Davis's rampage shows the paradoxical blend of calm self-control and derangement characteristic of berserk abandon. I emphasize the trancelike quality of his experience because our need to think in terms of conventional motives distracts from the creaturely vulnerability of the self. Interpretations of the Columbine High School killers, for example, initially focused on bullying and adolescent friction, and the FBI attributed their rampage to "a messianic-grade superiority complex." Many of these adduced motives make sense. But as with Davis, these themes are suspended, as it were, in extra-desperate efforts to keep the self from being torn apart.

Murdering helpless classmates, Eric Harris and Dylan Klebold exhibited a lack of feeling that was close to what Shay calls the berserker's "flaming ice" and *Dexter* treats as autism. In pumping up to the fatal climax, the pair revealed more of their inner lives. The FBI's psychological assessment found Harris a psychopath: grandiose, cold, and homicidal. His journal opened explosively: "I hate the f—ing world." On his web site the rant was self-intoxicating:

"YOU KNOW WHAT I HATE!!!? Cuuuuuuuuhntryyyyyyyyyy music!!!…

"YOU KNOW WHAT I HATE!!!? People who say that wrestling is real!!…

"YOU KNOW WHAT I HATE!!!? People who use the same word over and over again!…Read a f—in book or two, increase your vo-cab-u-lary f*ck*ng idiots."

"YOU KNOW WHAT I HATE!!!? STUPID PEOPLE!!!
Why must so many people be so stupid!!?...YOU KNOW
WHAT I HATE!!!?

The tantrum keeps going, line after line. As the FBI's psychologist recognized, "He is disgusted with the morons around him. These are not the rantings of an angry young man, picked on by jocks until he's not going to take it anymore. These are the rantings of someone with a messianic-grade superiority complex, out to punish the entire human race for its appalling inferiority."[51] With its self-conscious, show-off, shock-jock hyperbole, the rant is berserk style, but also explosive moral aggression.

That said, this hate is also so universal, so disproportionate and unrealistic that, like Iago's motiveless malignity, it seems uncanny and empty. This "hate" comes across as a drive seeking a story that can give it coherence. As an expression of "what's right," it comes out of the core of identity, yet its indiscriminateness makes it something like a spasm. Outwardly Harris was a regular kid. But he took pleasure in lying, and in private moments he projected infantile vainglory, feelings of persecution, and a rage to punish. In a typical passage under "Society" he growls that "I live in Denver and god damnit I would like to kill almost all of its residents. [Expletive] people with their rich snobby attitude thinkin they are all high and mighty and can just come up and tell me what to do and then people I see in the streets lying their [expletive] asses off about themselves." Under "Philosophy" he declaimed: "My belief is that if I say something, it goes. I am the law, and if you don't like it, you die. If I don't like you or I don't like what you want me to do, you die....I'll just go to some downtown area in some big ass city and blow up and shoot everything I can. Feel no remorse, no sense of shame."[52] In his America Online profile, Harris allegedly snarled, "'Kill 'em AALL!!!'"

When hatred becomes exterminatory, it ceases to be meaningful hate. The FBI psychologist concluded that Harris was "out to punish the entire human race for its appalling inferiority." The rage to punish might carry the politician's cry of "zero tolerance" to its deadly conclusion, but it sweeps past personal or cultural passions.

Like Dexter, Harris hid a "real" self that despised a world of offenders whose inner lives were totally foreign to him. Like the suicidal 9/11 terrorists, Harris's "enemies" were people who think "they are all high and mighty"—like God. But in his fantasy *he* is God: "I am the law, and if you don't like it, you die. If I don't like you or I don't like what you want me to do, you die." But again, this is pure negation: the "law," the ideal has no content, no application anywhere.

It may be significant that Harris took the drug Luvox, which is licensed for treatment of obsessive-compulsive disorder and in the same family as Prozac. Luvox is often prescribed to treat depression and obsessive thoughts. Did the drug fail to bring equilibrium to a disturbed mind? Many an adolescent male and Hollywood script has shared Harris's fantasies about warrior heroism, monstrous power, persecutory feelings, and invincible rightness, but not everyone acts on them. Wishing to be a Marine (he was turned down because of his drug prescription), Harris was oblivious to his conflicting desires to defend "his" society and to "'Kill 'em AALL!!!'"

Like cultists ritualizing their beliefs, Harris and Klebold pumped each other up day after day with competitive, sensational plans about weapons and enemies. As the son of a career Air Force officer, Harris "thought about war, fantasized about war and wrote about war. He was an angry teenager rebel planning disciplined military revenge with the most destructive weapons he could command. He was thrilled when he heard, one morning in philosophy class, that the United States was about to bomb Yugoslavia. Rebecca Heins, who sat next to him, remembers Harris saying, 'I hope we do go to war, I'll be the first one there.' He wanted to be in the front lines, he said. He wanted, as he put it, to 'shoot everyone,' Heins recalls."[53]

The combat soldier, again, is a slave to command and yet also commands godlike power over life and death. Likewise Harris and Klebold were at once adolescent small-fry and haughty dictators dispensing death at the snap of a finger. "The killers, in fact, laughed at petty school shooters. They bragged about dwarfing the carnage of the Oklahoma City bombing.... Klebold boasted on video about inflicting 'the most deaths in U.S. history.' Columbine was intended not primarily as a shooting at all, but as a bombing on a massive scale. If they hadn't been so bad at wiring the timers, the propane bombs they set in the cafeteria would have wiped out 600 people.... The climax would be captured on live television. It wasn't just "fame" they were after—[FBI] Agent Fuselier bristles at that trivializing term— they were gunning for devastating infamy on the historical scale of an Attila the Hun. Their vision was to create a nightmare so devastating and apocalyptic that the entire world would shudder at their power" (Cullen).

The seeds of this desire to play God are in everyday culture. During the attack, one of the killers reportedly asked a cornered student named Cassie Bernall if she believed in God. When she said she did, he shot her. This story became headline news. Her pastor vowed that "Cassie died a martyr's death. She went to the martyr's hall of fame." "She has graduated," he told mourners, "while the rest of us still have tests ahead of us."

What is troubling about this reaction is its association of a tragic death with sports (the "hall of fame") and school bureaucracy ("tests ahead of us"). This is the language of boosterism, echoed by *Time* (May 31, 1999) when it did a follow-up article about the murders as an inspiration to teen evangelicals, titling it "A Surge of Teen Spirit" in a play on team spirit. This sort of cheerleading turns religion and a grave community injury into a special achievement. Indirectly it contributes to the berserk style in its glib celebration of death as a heroic and useful blaze of glory.

Time approvingly quotes "sixth grader Susan Teran" in Wichita, Kansas, who "has reached a personal decision…based on the example of her new hero," the "Christian victim" Cassie Bernall. 'If there was a shooter in my school,' declares the 12-year-old gravely, 'I'd volunteer to sacrifice my life. I'd say, 'Don't shoot my friends, shoot me,' because I know where I'll go when I die.'" The unrecognized, nightmarish irony is that in his video ramblings just before the rampage, Dylan Klebold allegedly voiced a similar fantasy: "It's a half hour before Judgment Day. I didn't like life very much. Just now I'm going to a better place than here." Yet more ironical is that both Susan Teran's and Klebold's convictions about death echo Justice Scalia's boast that "for the believing Christian, death is no big deal."

These voices too are naively caught up in fantasies of competitive righteousness and a "hall of fame" like the ancient pagan Valhalla. Their narcissism uncannily echoes that of the murderers, who also dreamed of performing an "immortal" story for awestruck audiences. "Directors will be fighting over this story," Dylan Klebold boasted in his video diary. He was avid for the approval of parent-like directors who would "fight"—compete—to validate the killers' importance.

Even planned, a rampage has an explosive quality reflecting inner turmoil. Some killers believe they act to revenge or set right specific grievances. But hatred and other motives usually have the character of "hate." They are stories that make action possible, but they are inadequate to explain it. Even when they act in a spasm of blind rage, rampage killers are trying either to rationalize or annihilate chaos threatening them. One reason for fascination with the Columbine killers is that their hatred has that uncanny character. In asking "Do you believe in God?" before murdering a fellow student, they were mocking conventional immortality consolations, as if to destroy as a sham everyday reality itself. In this light their dream of glorious infamy is a desperate reflection of American celebrity culture and of the infantile need for recognition to feel real. Their "hate" suggests that the deepest fear is of the nothingness of the self, and that destruction is the only way of having an effect on a phony world.

COMING APART

Among the copycats who studied the Columbine massacre was 20 year old Adam Lanza, who ran amok among school children in Newtown CT. His behavior calls for attention in part because accounts of the massacre related the cold-blooded rage associated with cyborgs and autism to Adam's clinically diagnosed autism.

We have enough evidence to make out the rough outlines of Adam's motivation. Despite a relatively happy childhood, he had trouble processing experience. "A doctor diagnosed sensory-integration disorder, and Adam underwent speech therapy and occupational therapy in kindergarten and first grade. Teachers were told to watch for seizures." That he did not speak until he was three and "always understood many more words than he could muster" [54] is symptomatic of cognitive difficulties that led to a feeling of being overwhelmed, trapped in an incoherent body, unable to respond effectively to life. This helps to explain why in fifth grade he said he "did not think highly of himself and believed that everyone else in the world deserved more than he did." [55] This despair may have reflected the child's and the family's anxieties over his disabilities, and also his awareness that he was not fitting in.

In fifth grade, Adam and another boy "wrote a story called 'The Big Book of Granny,' in which an old woman with a gun in her cane kills wantonly. In the third chapter, Granny and her son want to taxidermy a boy for their mantelpiece. In another chapter, a character called Dora the Berserker says, 'I like hurting people....Especially children'" (Solomon, 38). The story suggests that Adam felt pressured to live up to mainstream expectations. Like Granny, Adam's mother Nancy was experienced with guns. Since she was determined to help her son succeed despite his disabilities, it makes sense that Adam identified with the "trophy" boy mummified for Granny's mantelpiece, and felt pressured into a lifeless ideal. Already he was aware of the word "berserker." The book was likely a complaint the child couldn't put into words.

Though he could be voluble when happy and had "a sharp sense of humor" (Solomon, 38), Adam began to lose his equilibrium in adolescence. Noisy, crowded corridors between classes at school upset him. "Many people with autism speak in a flat tone, and avoiding eye contact is common, too, because trying to interpret sounds and faces at the same time is overwhelming" (Solomon, 39). In seventh grade, the child who felt undeserving and fantasized about a mummified trophy boy on a mantel was fantasizing about warfare. A teacher described Adam as "intelligent but not normal, with anti-social issues. He was quiet, barely spoke and did not want to participate in anything. His writing assignments obsessed about battles, destruction and war, far more than others his age. The level of violence in the writing was disturbing. At the same time, when asked to write a poem, he was able to write a beautiful one and presented it in public" (SAR, 34). Like Eric Harris and Dylan Klebold at Columbine, Adam could mask his anger, even as he was identifying with warfare that on paper at least made him a force to be reckoned with.

By the time he was diagnosed with Asperger's Syndrome in 2005, at age 13, Adam "was described as presenting with significant social impairments and extreme anxiety. It was also noted that he lacked empathy and had very rigid thought processes."[56] Additional diagnoses included emotional and/or Pervasive Developmental Disorder (PDD) spectrum behaviors and Obsessive Compulsive Disorder (OCD), which became progressively disabling (SAR, 35). He suffered panic attacks so severe that one day as he started eighth grade, his mother took him to a hospital emergency room, telling doctors he was wracked by anxiety.[57]

Reflecting, his father now says that "It was crystal clear something was wrong." He added that "The social awkwardness, the uncomfortable anxiety, unable to sleep, stress, unable to concentrate, having a hard time learning, the awkward walk, reduced eye contact. You could see the changes occurring" (Solomon, 38).

After Adam's initial success taking college courses at age 16, the pressures became too much for him. Like many teenagers, he compensated for buffeted self-esteem with unrealistic ambitions that tormented him when reality fell short. At a time when he was cutting classes and failing courses, his mother reported, "I have the feeling when he said he would rather be homeless than to take any more tests, he really meant it" (Solomon, 42). To be homeless, abandoned, forgotten is social death, and Adam's threat suggests he was imagining a kind of play-death that would allow him to be at once in and out of the world. Time would show the suicidal character of his despair to be more than adolescent bravado.

By 2010, when high school students ordinarily graduate, Adam was seriously isolated, prone to "meltdowns," and also developing "his private obsession with killing. He started editing Wikipedia entries on well-known mass murderers," although there were still no outward signs of violence (Solomon, 41). He announced that he was going to enlist in the military when he turned eighteen, planning to join the elite Army Rangers yet subject to prolonged weeping fits that proved the futility of his wishes.

On the threshold of adulthood, Adam was at home neither in society nor in his own mind. A few of the materials he left behind—music, comedy videos, and videos of him dancing to DDR (the Dance Dance Revolution video game)—imply a healthy outlook. Most cluster around his obsessions: firearms, the military, politics, suicide, and mass murder. He spent up to ten hours at a stretch at a local theater whose lobby had a larger version of the dance game. (SAR, 26) The perseverance at dance could be evidence that part of him resisted the drive to isolation and violence, although the dance game is solitary and may signal the awkward adolescent's dream of commanding admiration as much as any sociable inclination.

Caught between impossible social fulfillment and fantasies of impressive violence, Adam looked to the prestige and legitimate violence of the soldier as a compromise. His admired uncle had been an army Ranger; his mother gave him guns and trained him to shoot. By definition, soldiers magnify human force and fight for a heroic, gut conviction of "what's right," which offered Adam a means of validating his "very rigid thought processes" and mastering his inner turmoil. To the soldier, what Adam's father described as "the arrogance that Aspies [Asperger's syndrome] can have" (Solomon, 39) is command and dominance. The tragedy is that in military guise, arrogance can also become a "messianic-grade superiority complex such as Eric Harris demonstrated, and for Adam, the wish to enlist would eventually harden into the role that the forensic psychiatrist Park Dietz has called the "pseudocommando"—the rampage killer.[58] Whatever its cause, even the most desperate rage follows one model rather than another, and warrior ideation is a powerful determinant of the direction violence will take.

The State Attorney concluded "that the shooter had significant mental health issues that affected his ability to live a normal life and to interact with others, even those to whom he should have been close. As an adult he did not recognize or help himself deal with those issues" (SAR, 3). Though conventional wisdom depends on it as a black box to contain what we cannot understand, the cliché "mental health issues" explains nothing. Like "pseudocommando," "autism," and "adult," it names a mystery in hopes of taming it—which is how imagination routinely copes with a world that is always beyond our control. In this instance, the black box makes Adam akin to a rogue cyborg.

"As an adult," says the report, "he did not recognize or help himself deal with those issues." Yet we know that Adam felt trapped in himself, and tried to make sense of his mental condition. To one of his few acquaintances in his last years, he "indicated that he had an interest in mass murders and serial killing. They never spent a lot of time discussing them, but it would be a topic of conversation. (SAR, 47n).... Other topics of discussion included human nature, perception, judgment, morality, lack of control, prejudice, empathy, suicide, mental illness, existential crisis, urban exploration of abandoned areas, hiking and cookies" (SAR 32). The topics center on anxiety about alienation and feeling ungrounded as well as explicit rampage themes of suicide and mass murder. As Adam withdrew from social experience, his fantasy of "urban exploration of abandoned areas" suggests an unconscious but healthy concern for the abandoned parts of his personality and anxieties about the ground of personality aroused by his withdrawal. In a treatment session at the Yale Child Study Center at the time of the autism diagnosis (2005-2006), Adam "would ask [the clinician] about schizophrenia and obsessive compulsive disorders but would never elaborate about whether he was experiencing any of the symptoms" (Griffin, Dec. 28, 2013).[59]

In this perspective the "autistic adult" was afraid of being overwhelmed not only from the outside, but also from within. This is the terror of losing a coherent self.

Suicide offers an escape, but arouses the terror of annihilation, which is the root of traumatic stress. Traumatic events "generally involve threats to life or bodily integrity, or a close personal encounter with violence and death. They confront human beings with the extremities of helplessness and terror, and evoke the responses of catastrophe." *The Comprehensive Textbook of Psychiatry* defines the core experience as "intense fear, helplessness, loss of control, and threat of annihilation."[60] Death anxiety is ubiquitous in the background of everyday denial. It becomes traumatic when shock or stress exposes the inescapable threat of annihilation.

Given the pressure of that threat, Adam was not only role-playing a "pseudo"-soldier, he was actually experiencing the sort of do-or-die psychic emergency that triggers a soldier's berserk outbreak. In his last months he stayed in his bedroom, in disembodied internet chat, with black trash bags over the windows, researching rampage killings. In effect, he was immersing himself in a subculture that substantiated —made "real"—his obsessions. Investigators found "Three photographs of what appear to be a dead human, covered in blood and wrapped in plastic; The book *Amish Grace: How Forgiveness Transcended Tragedy*...by Donald B. Kraybill, et al;...Two videos showing suicide by gunshot; Commercial movies depicting mass shootings; The computer game titled 'School Shooting' where the player controls a character who enters a school and shoots at students; Screen shots (172) of the online game 'Combat Arms'; Images of the shooter holding a handgun to his head; Images of the shooter holding a rifle to his head; Five-second video (dramatization) depicting children being shot; Images of shooter with a rifle, shotgun and numerous magazines in his pockets; Documents on weapons and magazine capacity; A document showing the prerequisites for a mass murder spreadsheet; A spreadsheet listing mass murders by name and information about the incident; Large amount of materials on firearms; amount of materials relating to Columbine shootings and documents on mass murders" (SAR, 26).

Brooding over these themes, rehearsing possible plans, Adam must have had moments of relief and terrifying doubt. Binge killing promises to command spectacular attention, but it also reveals the futile nothingness of the self. The warrior can only exist in fantasy, in secret, until the instant of open fury. Just as the wannabe Army Ranger suffered weeping fits, at times the warrior assassin must have seemed to Adam a frightening illusion. Hence the urge to collect more and more rampage materials, and the hours spent testing his resolve and forming up the reality of the warrior role. The compulsive hoarding in effect papers over an abyss.

Despite his individual disabilities, Adam's rampage fits a familiar pattern.[61] The killer seethes, caught between self-aggrandizement and self-destruction, wanting to settle scores, building toward an outburst. The force behind that seething is a form of obsessive moral aggression, an attempt to aggrandize a self shrunk to insignificance by fear and injury. The self, again, is not a thing, but a social process. To fail "in the world's eyes" is to lose the confirmation that comes from the attention of others. Feeling himself conflicted, coming apart, Adam shut out the world to concentrate on substantiating himself through his obsession with larger-than-life violence. The lack of realism in this project shows in its conflation of fantastic triumph with suicide.

For Adam, what's right crystallized in the murder—the execution—of his mother Nancy. His mother gave him conflicted messages, urging him toward mainstream achievement even as she indulged his dependency and his retreat from reality. She seems to have emphasized her own tough-minded independence.[62] In teaching Adam to shoot and keeping guns in an unlocked case, she believed she was encouraging his self-confidence and independence, not tempting him to take desperate measures to keep himself together. Yet in the end she was unable or unwilling to stand up to his bullying and moods, overlooking the role-playing in their relationship. "The mother took care of all the shooter's needs" (SAR, 30). As Adam became more unstable, she was making his care the central purpose in her life: a heroic project in otherwise mundane suburban affluence.

Mother and son were both trapped in their conflicts. The mother who had had to rescue him from panic attacks in school "did the shooter's laundry on a daily basis as the shooter often changed clothing during the day. She was not allowed in the shooter's room, however, even to clean. No one was allowed in his room" (SAR, 30). His demands implied that he was the dominant figure, even as they confirmed his childlike neediness. He exaggerated his difficulties with coordination, for example, to elicit his mother's help. The element of role-playing came out when his father told her that Adam "had to pause to retie his shoes on a hike. Nancy responded in astonishment, 'He tied his own shoes?'" (Solomon, 41).

As his personality constricted, Adam needed his mother more than ever, yet the would-be warrior hated his dependency.[63] She regularly reminded him of the need to make his way in the world; and she could not relieve his anxiety and depression.[64] Adam "disliked birthdays, Christmas and holidays. He would not allow his mother to put up a Christmas tree. The mother explained it by saying that the shooter had no emotions or feelings. Adam's judgment was equally aggressive: "A person who knew the shooter in 2011 and 2012 said the shooter described his relationship with his mother as strained because the shooter said her behavior was not rational" (SAR 30).

Like Kip Kinkel, who murdered his parents and high school students in Oregon (May 20, 1998), Adam turned against the family that mediated his painful connection to the social world. As his father observed, "With hindsight, I know Adam would have killed me in a heartbeat, if he'd had the chance. I don't question that for a minute. The reason he shot Nancy four times was one for each of us: one for Nancy; one for him; one for [his brother] Ryan; one for me" (Solomon, 43).

Why did the rampage target Sandy Hook schoolchildren? The answer probably overlaps with Adam's rage toward his family. The murders of enviable "trophy" children punished parents whose trophy children "Granny" had stuffed in Adam's fifth grade story, even as the killing acted out envy. But there is another, ambivalent dimension to his motivation to consider. Among Adam's effects were "Materials regarding the topic of pedophilia and advocating for rights for pedophiles (not child pornography)" (SAR 26). Since his father remembers Adam being happy as a child at Sandy Hook (Solomon, 37), an attraction to children would be a logical expression of memories of an idealized lost happiness. By extension, it may be that, having decided on suicide, Adam wanted to kill that memory too. In this respect, the murders were probably in part Adam's effort to fulfill and suppress what he recognized as taboo pedophilia in himself. Like the materials justifying pedophilia, his behavior was striking out at strong adult social taboos. And finally, more strategically, the wannabe soldier who wept could attack children and be sure they would not fight back and humiliate him. He had no need to fear children or feel inadequate around them.

A consideration of Adam's motives needs to take account of his mental state as well. The cold-blooded fury in Adam and the Columbine killers resembles the "icy" rage in soldiers who run amok under traumatic stress (Shay, 35-37). The paradox is crucial. Adam and the Columbine killers were systematic about running amok; they knew what they were doing. But both rampages had a copycat dimension. Harris and Klebold code-named their rampage "NBK," after the movie *Natural Born Killers*. Like a parable, the film and the acronym condensed all the irrationality and complicated logistics of their plan into a more manageable form. Likewise, Adam had his spreadsheet, his library of precedents, and his hours of rapt study. Seeking to outdo earlier atrocities, all three murderers were pumping themselves up for maximum impact in a heroic competition. As berserk style, this mentality preconditions decisions at each stage, so that the action, requiring minimal further thought, is already promoting abandon.

It might seem implausible to link murderous civilians with soldiers under fire, but the military fatigues and weapons—the role of pseudocommando—projects another reality for the civilian killers even as it diminishes the guilt and doubt that could inhibit their aggression. They seethe and then kill for revenge or justice or some other form of what's right. But just as "combat trauma destroys the capacity for social trust,"[65] so rampage mentality concentrates emergency physiology and thinking on aggression against others and the troubled self. No matter how fanatically moral or arrogant their motives, the killers are violating foundational taboos, and those who survive may report that they "blacked out" or were "beside themselves," wondering what had "possessed" them.

Like soldiers under fire, rampage killers feel trapped, unable to retreat, knowing that they face police bullets, execution, or the living death of prison. In his mental state Adam Lanza saw the social world ahead (school, career, relationships) as a "dead" end as well; he felt trapped by the world's, his family's, and his own expectations for him. In Vietnam, many soldiers felt that a cynical war betrayed the conviction of "what's right" that they needed to justify their sacrifices and the damage they'd caused. In the name of survival and moral aggression, some retaliated by assassinating sleeping officers through "fragging" (murder by fragmentation grenade) as Adam murdered his mother. In Adam's eyes, his body, his family, women, doctors, schools, and the social world had all failed him.

Pumping up for their attack, Harris and Klebold gloated in anticipation of their "godlike revenge." Like a lynch mob, they were gripped by vigilante conviction. As in the battlefield berserk state, they were insatiable in their ambitions for destruction, and were willing to be consumed by it. For Adam, pumping up took much more effort. He left behind images of himself holding a gun to his head: the godlike soldier executing the futile young man. At the same time the image demonstrates his magical thinking, since it acknowledges his suicidal end even as it compels a beholder's attention, as if that attention, like the spotlight of global infamy to come at Sandy Hook, keeps him from really dying.

There are too many clinical variables in Adam Lanza's history to attribute his rampage solely to Asperger's syndrome. Much of his suffering and alienation reflect the stress of ordinary American adolescence on a particularly vulnerable individual. We can label clusters of symptoms, but their etiology remains uncertain. Berserk style flourishes in this gap, providing interpretations and models for behavior, and channeling logic to transform psychic distress into lethal force.

RAMPAGE PANIC

The Sandy Hook massacre shook the nation. In effect, Adam Lanza shifted his inner torment to the public. The NRA's Wayne LaPierre presented a hysterical vision of American society "populated by an unknown number of genuine monsters—people so deranged, so evil, so possessed by voices and driven by demons that no sane person can possibly ever comprehend them.[66] The inflammatory nature of the speech was less disturbing than the silence that accepted its perversity. Although the speech was tacitly a paid advertisement for the firearms industry, it also replicates the do-or-die urgency of a rampage. LaPierre imagines nebulous demonic enemies that justify a hair-trigger mentality. By implication, it's reasonable to promote unrestricted gun ownership, even to susceptible people, because if necessary, the good man with a gun can always kill them. As in rampage mentality, the vision imagines resolving turmoil by pulling a magic trigger.

Less far-fetched than the NRA vision, but therefore more sinister, is the Ohio police training mentioned earlier, which frames berserk style in the era of the global policeman. Again: "One slide asked what the trainees would do in case of an active threat in a building 'with the one I love the most:' Wait for backup, 'or enter the building and engage the suspect as soon as possible.' Then came a photo of a teacher leading tiny children to safety at Sandy Hook in December, 2012."[67]

The photograph of a teacher rescuing "tiny children" at Sandy Hook directly uses Adam Lanza's rampage to prepare heroic police to kill on sight. The police training material seeks to take a heroic stance toward recent mayhem, but in its inability to assess risk realistically, what stands out is the inadvertent mirroring of rampage killing. The premise is that a squeeze of a trigger can destroy chaos and evil, and the presentation seeks to force heroic action.

After buying his first pistol, rampage killer Elliot O. Rodger exulted that he "felt a new sense of power." and demanded, "Who's the alpha male now?"[68] Adam Lanza killed children trying to feel that berserk alpha mastery. Confronting Michael Brown, officer Wilson felt like "a five-year-old" and turned to a pistol to reclaim his alpha police status. The good guy destroys demonic "monsters," which is

what Elliot Rodger vowed to do before running amok in Isla Vista
California: "Humanity is a disgusting, wretched, depraved species. If
I had it in my power I would stop at nothing to reduce every single
one of you to mountains of skulls and rivers of blood and rightfully
so" (Medina). Just as Rodger's vow to "stop at nothing" culminated
in suicide, so NRA rhetoric urges a righteous fight to the death. Attacking gun-control at the annual convention in 2000, NRA president Charlton Heston roused the audience to a standing ovation by
waving a replica of a musket above his head and paraphrasing an NRA
bumper sticker: "I'll give you my gun when you take it from my cold,
dead hands." However you qualify it, the cry exults at the prospect
the idea of leaving this life in violent triumph.

CHAPTER 3

AT WAR WITH STYLE

Just about no mission is impossible for the United States military.

Michael Barone[1]

My rifle is human…We will become part of each other…
Before God, I swear this creed. My rifle and myself are the
defenders of my country. We are the masters of our enemy.
WE ARE THE SAVIORS OF MY LIFE. So be it, until
victory is America's and there is no enemy, but peace.

The Marine Rifle Creed

You've killed. You've taken life. What I found, though,
is that you feel the shock and weight of it only when you
kill an enemy for the first time, when you move from
zero to one. Once you've crossed that line, there is little
difference in killing 10 or 20 or 30 more after that.

Capt. Shannon R. Meehan

The proverbial berserker is the warrior. As a creaturely motive, war
acts out radical appetite for more life. Although usually formulated as
self-defense and a last resort, war is also a thrilling hunt for justice and

trophies. Victory means more life—freedom, land, sex, slaves, and tribute—but also the joyous conviction of survival and self-worth. War is a technic for harvesting life that can be "planted"—buried in a grave but also sown like a seed—in order to produce more life, as in the Nazi philosophy of blood and soil.[2] Holding the fate of the defeated in their hands, the victors enjoy living proof that they have mastered death. War demolishes limits and burns off humdrum frustration in the fire of heroic purpose: survival registers as rebirth.

The risk of course is that the harvest will be ashes. Defeat exposes the futility of war as an immortality fantasy. But even victory can be dangerous. Once aroused to emergency levels, appetite and fear may be self-intoxicating. Victory brings with it a fear of falling. Like alpha males among our primate cousins, a dominant nation may expend much of its energy policing real and imaginary rivals. Instead of ending, World War II actually persisted as the Cold War and the string of inclusive wars from Korea through today's open-ended "war on terror."

Every culture has to regulate the production of warfare. For victors, that means trying to freeze the moment of glory. Whoever gets enough? On Trajan's column legions march heavenward cutting down enemies in eternal triumph. After civil slaughter the massively serene Abraham Lincoln gazes out of a Greek temple at an America pacified for all time. A 2006 Acorn catalog advertised a framed photograph of the B-29 Enola Gay, "hand-signed" by its pilot, whose atomic bomb "saved countless American lives." The memento turns the annihilated city into a home decoration affirming aging veterans' heroic pride and enshrining symbolic immortality bought by suffering and mass death. Compared to scalp-displays and skull racks, which keep dead enemies personally embodied in the present, the photograph uses style to domesticate and abstract aggression, even as it keeps the experience of killing and survival joy ambiguously alive.

SHOCK AND AWE

In 2003, under a "Mission Accomplished" banner on a warship ironically named for Abraham Lincoln, a new president dressed in a "Top Gun" flight suit took the role of modern conqueror trying to freeze an apparent moment of triumph after the invasion of Iraq. Yet the story was couched in berserk style and already out of control. The carrier landing was also a public relations trick since the president had actually been a passenger in the navy jet, and the carrier was about to dock anyway. Even if taken at face value, the "mission accomplished" story depended on a "magic bullet" scenario in which "the successful invasion and American-sponsored reconstruction of Iraq would lead to the collapse of all the surrounding dictatorial regimes."[3] Like Lincoln, the Top Gun president would free the slaves.

Reality did not respond to magic.[4] Saddam Hussein's threat and ties to Al Qaeda proved to be an embarrassing mirage as evidence leaked out that the administration had been looking for a pretext to attack Iraq from well before 9/11.[5] Iraq's governance, infrastructure, economy, and invaluable oil resources remained impaired; tens if not hundreds of thousands of civilians died in the crossfire; others fled the country.[6] The new dominance of Iraq's Shiites benefited their "axis of evil" neighbor, Shiite Iran. The suffering created a more representative but also brutal regime. Beyond the torment and death of American casualties, the war has been estimated to cost 3 trillion dollars over time, contributing to a budget crisis that rationalized subsequent attacks on social programs at home.[7]

But as in the Vietnam War, the planners badly misjudged. They proved to be out of touch with the inner lives of their soldiers, their enemies, and the Iraqi population. Almost from the start the occupation went awry. Looting and economic breakdown wracked Iraqi communities. Insurgents mimicked the invaders' lean-and-mean, shock-and-awe propaganda with spectacular bombings and torture. The military retaliated with escalating "collateral damage," annihilation of the town of Fallujah, and notorious torture. The official story of liberation and justice began to show the seething vengefulness characteristic of rampage killing.

In theory soldiers choose to risk death to defend the life they believe in. When home and command are incoherent, conflicted, or devious, soldiers are likely to falter or run amok. Global protests declared the rationale for the Iraq War to be faulty or cynical. From its inception the "war on terror" modeled unchecked and impulsive force. The "Bush doctrine" of preemptive war, "shock and awe" intimidation, torture, and illegal domestic surveillance resonated with the combat berserker's impulsivity, hypervigilance, and indiscriminate violence against civilians.

The analogies are more than clever abstractions. When the illicit surveillance program came to light, the editors of the *New York Times* asked "So why break the law, again and again? Two things seem disturbingly clear. First, President Bush and his top aides panicked after the Sept. 11 attacks. And second, Mr. Cheney and his ideologues, who had long chafed at any legal constraints on executive power, preyed on that panic to advance their agenda."[8] This is the familiar berserk dynamic: panic unleashes aggressive overconfidence that defies "legal constraints." Politicized corporate media amplified the ideological violence, treating forbearance and patient problem-solving as unthinkable folly.

The predisposition to panic was there from the beginning. Washington insisted that the nation faced enemies so berserk that only overwhelming preemptive force could stop them, echoing colonial attitudes toward crazed rebellious natives. Political scientist Ken Jowitt labeled them "movements of rage," and forecast "the likely proliferation of horrendous 'wildcat violence.'"[9]

These policies presented totalizing abstractions. In reality the "war on terror" and the "axis of evil" were episodes in a global struggle over energy resources and financial hegemony. With new challengers to its postwar economic preeminence and limited world oil reserves increasingly nationalized, the U.S. has good reason to fear a declining standard of living and the end of empire. The invasion of Iraq gave Washington an ideal opportunity to demonstrate the "global policeman's" military and economic power to the world—and to OPEC as well.

A nation that has sunk much of its wealth into history's most sophisticated and expensive corporate military will be tempted to use it. Since World War II, U.S. military spending has outstripped all competitors by a wide margin and now absorbs about 57 percent of the budget, though many expenses are secret and therefore incalculable. A Congressional study reported in September 2009 that "Despite a recession that knocked down global arms sales last year, the United States expanded its role as the world's leading weapons supplier, increasing its share to more than two-thirds of all foreign armaments deals."[10] An arsenal of remote-controlled cybernetic weapons and an all-volunteer force encouraged leaders to overreach without fear of public protest. Peacetime interventions—demonstration wars—energize military careers just as they enrich corporate military suppliers and boost national self-esteem.

The shock and awe campaign sought to minimize carnage. But threat display is a dangerous weapon. Once adversaries see through the bluff of "controlled" abandon, they may raise the stakes. In Iraq the insurgents quickly developed their own shock and awe campaign of torturing and beheading victims. One result was the unforeseen chaos that frightened and humiliated the nominal victors. The policy makers escalated the threat display—an overreaction epitomized by the annihilation of the town of Fallujah and the massacre of families in Haditha. Many soldiers were radically conflicted: asked to die for a mission they believed in only superficially. Many felt betrayed by leaders who failed to supply armor to survive roadside bombs (IEDs) and cruelly extended their tours of duty to compensate for bad planning. And the betrayal of course centered on the Iraqis. At any moment the people the troops were supposedly rescuing could suddenly try to kill them.

At the same time, as in Vietnam, many troops believed—or claimed to believe—that they were winkingly authorized and forced by necessity to skirt the rules of engagement. Although there is no delicate way to put it, "shock and awe" is, after all, the core principle of terrorism and a crucial theme in rampage killing. In practice a policy of deliberately trying to exploit boundary behaviors is bound to feel two-faced when it bridles at the obscene excesses bound to turn up from time to time.

To be sure, American soldiers were not the only source of violence. As confirmed in the military logs released by Wikileaks (October 22, 2009), Iraqi military and police also committed atrocities. "Trigger-happy," nervous private security contractors killed numerous civilians as well.[11] Like their counterparts in the Vietnam War, some veterans began to recognize the dangers of traumatic stress and vicious motives. Among the moving accounts of Iraq veterans, the "winter soldier" hearings (March 13-16, 2008) stand out as a brave effort to bear witness to atrocities and to restore moral clarity and calm.[12]

A MODEL MASSACRE

U.S. atrocities in Iraq fit the historical pattern. Under stress, predictably, some soldiers kill innocents, and nations rarely punish them. At My Lai in Vietnam (1968), U.S. soldiers gunned down whole families, gang raped women, and mutilated victims, leaving about five hundred dead. A participant in Operation Speedy Express in the Mekong Delta estimated that his division's atrocities "amounted to a My Lai each month for over a year."[13] By comparison, the scale of U.S. massacres in Iraq has been small. But the killing has been chronic and distributed. Pilots bombed houses by mistake; gunfire riddled "suspicious" cars on the highway and at checkpoints; troops and CIA personnel killed prisoners. In addition, legally unaccountable private security forces cut down civilians, and preliminary evidence signals that the environmental toxicity of depleted uranium munitions may eventually prove lethal as Agent Orange did in Vietnam.

When insurgency made a mockery of the "Mission Accomplished" story, panic and revenge sent death tolls sharply higher. The Iraqi prime minister al-Maliki protested that "violence against civilians had become a 'daily phenomenon' by many troops in the American-led coalition who 'do not respect the Iraqi people.'"[14] One Iraqi Health Ministry survey estimated 151,000 violent deaths out of 400,000 war-related deaths. But these figures are speculative, and since the Pentagon declines to release civilian casualties, we cannot be sure how many of those deaths American forces caused.

We cannot do justice to the inner life of a particular soldier who has run amok. Conventional accounts of combat massacres focus on stress-induced personal "breakdown" and loss of control. Here is a psychiatrist's list of characteristics associated with berserk frenzy (Shay 82):

Beastlike	Godlike
Socially disconnected	Crazy, mad, insane
Enraged	Reckless, feeling invulnerable
Insatiable	Devoid of fear
Indiscriminate	Inattentive to [one's] own safety
Cold, indifferent	Exalted, intoxicated, frenzied
Cruel, without restraint or discrimination	

The list emphasizes pathology. The berserk state reflects explosive disorder in the limbic system as stress chemicals disrupt the body's regulatory systems. Numbed to pain and fear, plunging forward on a surge of strength, the berserker is apt to experience "godlike" or "beastlike" alienation akin to the cold, depersonalized aggression of science fiction cyborgs such as the Arnold Schwarzenegger Terminator (1984).

But neurophysiology is not the whole story. Soldiers operate in a halo of motives. How individuals react to stress depends on how they are wrapped. Creaturely motives, character, and cultural themes condition strategic behavior. The men of Charlie Company who exterminated farm families at My Lai were said to be suffering traumatic stress, exhausted, fearful and vengeful, grieving for lost comrades, with no practical relief in sight. Ordered to destroy the villages, they later claimed, they spared no one. They were already adrenalized, and once inhibitions failed, violence escalated. The first assaults showed predictable creaturely motives. Rape and murder of a rival's women kills his posterity, steals his immortality, and demonstrates the victor's potency. As in branding a slave or marking a carcass in a hunt, carving initials into an enemy's flesh signifies mastery. It magically undoes the soldier's actual condition of enslavement to command. In effect, berserkers substantiate the imperiled self by "making their mark."

As the rampage at My Lai flashed into chaos, survival greed regressed to a tantrum: a wild bodily determination to annihilate everything feared and hated. While the victims cried out and floundered among the corpses in a ditch, Lt. Calley, the officer in charge, reloaded his weapon at least ten times. At such close range bodies disintegrated, yet the killers perseverated with robotic fixation. It took the intervention of a helicopter pilot and his crew to halt the frenzy at gunpoint.

Even when individuals are indisputably out of control ("crazy, mad, insane"), the boundary transition has to entail some interpretation. Stress may bring out fatalism or suicidal despair as well as rage. Not every soldier runs amok or does it in the same way. Individuals may kill for "what's right," but what's right is bound to be subjective. In a contrived war, soldiers are trapped in a fantasy system. In Iraq, for example, troops widely believed the lie that the Iraqis were behind the September 11th terrorism. Like Iraqis, the Vietnamese were a mistrusted, alien underclass, often despised, and correspondingly resentful. The air bristled with dehumanizing epithets such as "slopes," "gooks," and "dinks." Officially troops were rescuing innocent victims of Communism, and in theory risking their lives for them. Not only could soldiers not tell friend from foe—as in Iraq—but the Vietnamese friends were strangers, and inherently tainted by death.

Since berserk mentality appears to concentrate experience into a singular fury, it is easy to simplify the motivation, including the strong element of magical thinking. "Payback," say, may feed a demand for revenge, but it may also promise to compensate for, or magically restore, a life lost. "At some deep cultural and psychological level," says Dr. Shay, "spilling enemy blood is an effort to bring the dead back to life" (89).[15] After every killing, one veteran chanted to himself, speaking to his dead comrade: "Every fucking one that died, I say, '____, here's one for you, baby. I'll take this motherfucker out and I'm going to cut his fucking heart out for you.'" He spoke to the dead friend "as if he were alive and present, psychologically bringing him back to life" (89). The hallucinatory quality of the ritual chant and the underlying psychic economy—cutting out an enemy's heart to appease and restore life— resonates with many ancient rituals such as Mesoamerican blood offerings. Sacrificial killing renews life not only for the dead, but also for the killer. The effect is similar to the gain from scapegoat murders such as lynching.

The Army archive compiled by Col. Henry Tufts makes clear that atrocities in Vietnam were far more common than generally believed, and that investigations proceeded with the surreptitious aim of distracting public opinion.[16] American leaders could entertain fantasies of annihilation without censure once they were sufficiently sanitized as berserk style. Witness LBJ's quip to bring home the coonskin and hang it on the wall, as if the war were a folksy hunt with an obliging raccoon. Attacking critics of the war in 1965, implicitly countenancing extermination, Ronald Reagan scoffed that "[i]t's silly talking about how many years we will have to spend in the jungles of Vietnam when we could pave the whole country and put parking stripes on it and still be home by Christmas."[17]

Suffering reverses in Vietnam and in Iraq, American leaders called for more force. Between one and two million Vietnamese died in the conflict. An industrial war machine incinerated with napalm and poisoned with Agent Orange a basically agrarian world. By the time Saigon fell, the U.S. had dropped more bomb tonnage on a nation of farmers than it had in World War II. Embracing what military historian Michael S. Sherry calls the "technological fanaticism" of American air power, General Curtis LeMay urged bombing Vietnam "back to the stone age" (1968). This was a mindset established in his firebombing of Japan during World War II, when the American cremation of entire cities in firestorms "caused many more casualties among Japanese civilians than their armed forces suffered throughout the war."[18] Projecting the mythic awe of the atomic bombing of Hiroshima into Vietnam, berserk style made thinkable both exterminatory ideation and the conviction of godlike power that the psychiatrist counts as a symptom.[19]

One influence on the berserk mentality was the reorganization of the U.S. military along corporate lines. Under Secretary of Defense McNamara, a former Ford Motor president who had worked with General LeMay on the bombing of Japan, the Army had instituted industrial models of efficiency and control. The premise was that the military is a machine that operates rationally at the push of a button, subject to corporate cost-benefit analysis and economic logic. To maintain career momentum, officers were speeded through tours of duty in Vietnam and therefore less in touch with men at the level of Charlie Company. Trying to quantify—and advertise—progress, headquarters demanded "body counts" from troops in the field. The inflated numbers sent in quickly became suspect among journalists and a marker for industrial callousness. [20] This is the mentality that outraged the veteran quoted earlier, who protested that he had become "a fucking animal" because "I didn't give a fuck anymore. Y'know, I wanted—They wanted a fucking hero, so I gave it to them. They wanted fucking body count, so I gave them body count" (83). He seems to be saying, "I wanted heroism, a value to make the struggle meaningful, but finally I could believe in nothing anymore."

As stress intensified and rage became less unthinkable, the sense of betrayal spurred an epidemic of fragging: assassination of officers by fragmentation grenades. The attacks were akin to a workplace rampage by disenchanted employees, and like workplace rampages, as dramatized by Tim O'Brien's novel *Going after Cacciato* (1979), they escalated as anger and opposition became the norm.

THE ALLURE OF LEVERAGE

In economics, leverage is the use of borrowed money as a tool to increase financial power. But the term can also describe the use of technology as a lever to create force-multiplying effects. In warfare, tools such as the sling, the club, and the nuclear warhead leverage up the force of the fist, magnifying firepower and "kill-ratios." The term is useful for this book because it calls attention to the corporate-military's use of technology to magnify the soldier's destructive force, in theory reducing casualties and even the number of soldiers needed. In World War II military-industrial leverage revived the Depression economy. For a giddy moment the atomic bomb seemed to be the ultimate leverage, promising a monopoly of force so massive that it would preclude all war.

Leverage is inherent in the warrior's role. Soldiers live in a state of threat display, needing to pump up the self to face danger the way our primate cousins use threat displays to look large and fearsome. Pylo-erection, rearing up, baring teeth, thumping the chest, and screaming are all signals that warn off or overawe enemies. Military culture vividly illustrates the way physiology and ideation reinforce each other, inducing central nervous system flooding and an aggressive mindset. The paraphernalia of martial threat-display has included animal skins, war paint, armor, horses, drums, and bagpipes, not to mention tanks, cannon, and other prosthetic enhancements.

The drawback with leverage of any kind is that it increases risk as well as power and rewards. Leveraged force can go out of control so fast that panic overrides strategy. Especially when leverage is exponential, its rewards and failures are likely to seem utopian or death-tainted. To be sure, all tools magnify our capabilities: we have always been leveraged animals. But the scale of leverage has changed in recent centuries, enriching our behavior and potential for self-control while also exposing us to spectacular abandon.

In the invasion of Iraq the hawks promoted "smart" weapons and computer-assisted communications that easily overestimate executive control of the battlefield. Retired Army Col. Andrew Bacevich warned of "the OSD's [Office of Secretary of Defense] contempt for the accumulated wisdom of the military profession" and infatuation with technology, calling it "really the height of recklessness."[21] The "surgical strike" promised to pacify antiwar critics and make killing a life-saving "procedure."[22] But "smart" weapons have human operators, and they have massacred wedding parties and sleeping families.

Propaganda is a crucial form of leverage. Like the veiled interest in Iraqi oil reserves, the effort to manipulate public support kept unraveling. Dead soldiers were sent home in secrecy. Scandals broke out at Abu Ghraib and in the privatized, fabulously profitable support industry. Security mercenaries drew salaries that mocked soldiers' pay. Military recruitment dried up; reports of post-traumatic stress and atrocities multiplied. As in Vietnam, hawks blamed the problem on morale management. "We lost the war—not because we were out-fought, but because we were out Psyoped," wrote Paul E. Vallely, a retired general and specialist in psychological warfare. As a Fox News "analyst" from 2001 to 2007, Vallely foregrounded his "psyops" craft: public relations, advertising, and propaganda. He "co-authored a paper in 1980 that accused American news organizations of failing to defend the nation from 'enemy' propaganda during Vietnam [and] urged a radically new approach to psychological operations in future wars—taking aim at not just foreign adversaries but domestic audiences, too." He called his approach "MindWar"—the use of network TV and radio to "strengthen our national will to victory."[23] In theory, as Deputy Secretary of Defense Paul Wolfowitz argued, the war would pay for itself through access to Iraqi oil.[24] Such sinister aims had to be dignified for the public and the troops by an apocalyptic melodrama of "WMDs," an "Axis of Evil," and "movements of rage."[25]

The emphasis on leveraged force obscured the conflicted content. Rather than examining motives on a field in motion, the hawks construed behavior as ballistic forces, impersonal as trajectories in billiards, and controlled by executives at the center of cybernetic communications webs. Many of the core ideas derived from Reagan-era managerial models. On paper, lean and mean troop detachments would fly to a global "trouble spot" and impose order. In reality, as in Iraq, the corporate military installed bases that were "full-scale 'American towns,' well guarded, 15-20 miles around, with multiple PXes, fitness clubs, brand fast-food outlets, traffic lights, the works." "Bumper to bumper, the tens of thousands of trucks, tanks, and humvees would stretch, from New York City to Denver."[26] Like the belated realization that lightning intervention would require forced redeployments of exhausted troops, the contradiction between bases dubbed "Camp Cupcake" and Humvees blown apart by crude roadside bombs exemplifies the conceptual conflicts that led to atrocities and abandon.

When insurgent atrocities wracked Iraq, the American reaction was sometimes brutal precisely because it had taken so little account of motives. American planners downplayed or screened out the reality of other selves. This is not a sentimental criticism. As in Vietnam, to maximize leverage the hawks paid little attention to the inner lives, history, and contingencies of those to be rescued or their enemies.

LEVERAGE AT WAR

Leveraged firepower did not work as planned. Evan Wright recounts the approach to Baghdad on April 6, 2003, when the Marines confronted "a horrorscape of human corpses and of dead cows.... Sergeant Espera's vehicle swerves to avoid running over a human head lying in the road. When the vehicle turns, he looks up to see a dog eating a corpse. 'Can it get any sicker than this?' he asks. Reflecting back on the battalion's performance to this point, he says, 'Do you realize the shit we've done here, the people we've killed? Back home in the civilian world, if we did this, we would go to prison.'"[27]

"Do you realize—?" Killing from behind a shield of massive firepower has the quality of half-knowledge and denial. In its way the "horrorscape" was one outcome of the furious doublethink that gripped American culture after the September 11th attacks. In the

National Review Online (Sept. 13, 2001), pundit Ann Coulter blustered that "We should invade [the terrorists' Islamic] countries, kill their leaders and convert them to Christianity." With blithe, sadistic illogic she switched from Christianity to genocide: "We weren't punctilious about locating and punishing only Hitler and his top officers. We carpet-bombed German cities; we killed civilians. That's war. And this is war."[28]

The sergeant's anxiety about punishment ("we would go to prison") anticipated what would turn out to be insurgent mania for revenge. Exemplary violence—teaching "a lesson"—always risks inciting retaliation.[29] "At least some of the initial impetus for Iraq's insurgency came in the spring of 2003, when American troops in Fallujah shot and killed seventeen demonstrators, and kinsmen of the dead sought revenge by killing Americans."[30] Unlike many animals hard-wired to signal submission and halt a conflict, human cycles of revenge have no natural upper limit.

Economic leverage also backfired in the occupation. Staggering infusions of taxpayer money went to privatized military support and to outside contractors rehabilitating Iraqi infrastructure. But the work was plagued by ineptitude and waste. When L. Paul Bremer's Coalition Provisional Authority (the CPA) disbanded the Iraqi army to purge all Baathists, the decree spawned mass unemployment, hardship, and fears of social death. In an absurd failure of imagination the CPA never disarmed the soldiers. Like terminated employees, many joined the insurgency, with suicidal attacks akin to workplace rampages.[31]

The immediate response to the "liberation" of Iraq was the looting rampage that plundered government offices, utilities, and national treasures, crippling Baghdad. Many accounts blamed the disorder on troop shortages—the Pentagon's "lean and mean" reliance on technological leverage. "Stuff happens," Defense Sec. Rumsfeld quipped, playing on a bumper sticker associated with pickup trucks, rednecks, and cool toughness. As berserk style, however, his joke euphemizes an assumption that social disintegration would make Iraqis more compliant. His disarming nonchalance similarly masked berserk style when film-maker Errol Morris asked "How do you know when you're going too far?" and Sec. Rumsfeld replied, "You can't know with certainty."

Critics contrasted the Pentagon's tolerance of the urban looting to the forceful occupation of Iraq's oilfields. Klein argues that neglect of the looting was a deliberate application of shock doctrine, since it weakened the Iraqis' powers of self-governance and strengthened the hand of the occupiers.[32] Yet the rampage turned out to be an early sign of an insurgency that a decade later was still wreaking havoc. By 2014, calling themselves "ISIS" or the Islamic State, Sunni insurgents controlled parts of Syria and Iraq, earning UN condemnation of their brutality—another instance of the blowback that has plagued American foreign policy since the Cold War.[33] In 2006, retired Maj. Gen. John Batiste, an Iraq War veteran, openly accused Sec. Rumsfeld of causing "uncontrollable chaos" in Iraq.[34] Six months later (November 6), proposing "an accelerated drawdown of U.S. bases," Rumsfeld resigned.

After the dust settled, financial leverage was supposed to generate model prosperity through free markets and multinational corporations.[35] "Getting the rights to distribute Procter & Gamble products would be a gold mine," one corporate warrior vowed. "One well-stocked 7-Eleven could knock out 30 Iraqi stores; a Wal-Mart could take over the country."[36] Free market breakup of state-owned enterprises exacerbated unemployment; unsupervised American contractors repeatedly proved incompetent and corrupt. In the event, insurgents kept the country unstable, and corporate money fled.

In its freewheeling efforts to jumpstart the Iraqi economy, Washington dispatched shrink-wrapped bundles of dollars—some of it Iraqi oil money—to Baghdad from U.S. repositories, billions of which vanished.[37] Some of the money kept Iraqi ministries afloat, some apparently bought off warring groups. In the scramble to transform Iraq, hasty contracts sent unaccountable sums of U.S. taxpayers' money to "privatized" contractors for dubious performance. No-bid profits poured into corporations such as Halliburton that were closely connected to Vice-President Cheney and his circle. During the Vietnam War the construction company Brown and Root—a Halliburton subsidiary, now KBR—had been known as "Burn and Loot."[38] Privatization encouraged short-term thinking and sky's the limit pricing. Since contractors' compensation vastly exceeded soldier's pay, free market strategy proved demoralizing. An exasperated Rep. Henry Waxman protested that the privatized contracts "may well turn out to be the largest war profiteering in history."[39]

Berserk style was both a cause and an effect of the chaotic occupation. Regional tribes and religious sects were embroiled, as well as some foreign jihadis and opportunists such as Abu Musab al-Zarqawi, not to mention predatory militias and police death squads as well as criminal gangs. Disoriented American troops and their leaders were unable even to name all the shadowy actors or their motives.

As casualties rose and control failed, commanders retaliated as they had in Vietnam with ferocious force. When a mob in Sunni Fallujah killed four Blackwater mercenaries in March 2004, media branded the town a "hotbed of hatred" and the mob criminals to be "hunted down" with a "precise," "deliberate." and "overwhelming" response.[40] The military obliterated the city. "U.S. soldiers opened fire on houses, and U.S. helicopters fired on and killed women, old men and young children, according to Associated Press photographer Bilal Hussein."[41] The Italian documentary "Fallujah: The Hidden Massacre" includes interviews with witnesses who report that the military used the banned chemical white phosphorus. "'Phosphorus burns bodies, melting the flesh right down to the bone,' says one former U.S. soldier, interviewed by the documentary's director, Sigfrido Ranucci."[42] After a year of denials the Army acknowledged use of the banned munitions, but only against enemy combatants—a claim disputed by eyewitnesses.[43]

In Fallujah as in Vietnam, the determination to crush all resistance led to a "free fire zone" policy. By 2005, "faced with intractable and growing armed resistance in Iraq, the Pentagon has drafted plans for the organization of death squads to assassinate political opponents of the U.S. military occupation and terrorize the civilian population. The plan...has been dubbed by Pentagon planners as 'the Salvador option.' It was a measure of the leadership's growing desperation over the deteriorating situation in Iraq. 'We have to find a way to take the offensive against the insurgents,' a senior U.S. military officer told *Newsweek*. 'Right now, we are playing defense and we are losing.'"[44]

LEVERAGE AMOK

Beginning in the Vietnam War, American soldiers carried more ammunition and were trained to achieve a strikingly higher "kill ratio" than in previous wars. The success in overcoming inhibitions registers tragically when soldiers commit murder on or off the battlefield without compunction, as in the premeditated "kill team" slaying of civilians "out of pure bloodlust" in Afghanistan.[45] For a military culture striving to maximize its lethality, particular individuals with a heightened potential for violence are attractive but risky prospects.

From the start American troops in Iraq showed confusion about their motives. A February 28, 2006 poll showed that "58% of those serving in country say the U.S. mission in Iraq is clear in their minds, while 42% said it is either somewhat or very unclear to them, that they have no understanding of it at all, or are unsure. While 85% said the U.S. mission is mainly 'to retaliate for Saddam's role in the 9-11 attacks,' 77% said they also believe the main or a major reason for the war was "to stop Saddam from protecting al Qaeda in Iraq." [46] While the poll says that most troops didn't "blame [the] Iraqi public for insurgent attacks," they were operating on discredited, unrealistic beliefs that would polarize their feelings about the Iraqis. It is logical that vulnerable soldiers in morally queasy operations needed to believe the MindWar canard that Saddam Hussein was behind the terrorism.

In a combat emergency, experience sharpens beliefs. "They're all guilty," former Pvt. Kenneth Eastridge told an interviewer, "all hadjis. They're not human like us."[47] In places such as Ramadi soldiers felt hated and futile. When terror flared into panic and rage, their killing became indiscriminate and, as in the Bush doctrine, preemptive. Ramadi, said Marcus Mifflin, "was just a free-for-all," [48] a term reminiscent of "free-fire zones" such as My Lai. And berserk style conditions such deluded explanations.

One of the first massacres to come to light took place in Haditha after a roadside bomb killed a Marine on November 19, 2005. Lance Cpl. Roel Briones reported that "A lot of people were mad. Everyone had just a [terrible] feeling about what had happened to TJ," their dead friend.[49] It was a classic scenario: shocked, terrified, grieving men, and a highly aggressive sergeant leading the way to further killing by allegedly shooting dead a taxi driver and his four student passengers. They felt hate and hated; they wanted revenge. The ensuing slaughter left nineteen people in two families dead in adjacent houses, including mothers and children and a wheelchair-bound grandfather.

The official reaction medicalized the rampage as a symptom of traumatic stress. "'Many of our Marines have been involved in life or death combat or have witnessed the loss of their fellow Marines, and the effects of these events can be numbing,' said General Hagee. 'There is the risk of becoming indifferent to the loss of a human life, as well as bringing dishonour upon ourselves.'"[50] Trying for balance, the general warned about "indifference to the loss of human life" and "dishonor." Despite humane intentions, these euphemisms distort the reality of atrocity. After all, the problem at Haditha was not an isolated slip; not indifference but rage and chaos; not "loss of human life" but the murder of innocent families; not just dishonor but the risk of war crimes prosecution and disgrace to a nation waging an unprovoked war.

The core dilemma is that trauma is an injury that entails interpretation of the injury. Shock and exhaustion may seriously disturb body and mind; but much depends on the way you understand the experience. How you—and those around you—are wrapped determines how you will respond to traumatic stress. In turn, how you interpret is part of how you are wrapped. U.S. Army Field Manual 22-51 acknowledges in bureaucratic jargon that "misconduct combat stress behavior" is likely in guerrilla warfare. The manual notes that, "even though we may pity the overstressed soldier as well as the victims," such cases "must be punished." What the manual cannot acknowledge is that the rules themselves exist in a cultural environment that may be profoundly compromised by conflict and denial. In actual combat soldiers develop styles of thinking and acting that try to match rules of engagement to real world exigencies. Style mediates between an idealized blueprint and the "fog" of war. Berserk style, whether in General Hagee's euphemisms or in the decision to kill "suspect" Iraqis, preserves possibilities of empowering violence that otherwise might be ruled out. And in the end, as the Marines in Haditha knew, the murder of civilians is rarely punished.

To be sure, war attracts aggressive personalities. And an Army short of manpower has been known to wink at recruits with criminal records.[51] Yet even antisocial personalities will be affected by living in a fractured environment that fears, condemns, but also surreptitiously praises berserk behavior. Occupation soldiers experienced a fractured reality every time they left familiar American bases to patrol a world in which strangers could be suicide bombers. The reality of the streets, that is, was always potentially berserk. At once the selves in view were "just like you and me" and yet also specters of death. They were familiar parents and children, but also predatory animals, invisible demons, and contemptible losers.

At home reality was fractured as well. The American public was torn between yellow ribbons and antiwar banners, sympathy for Iraqis and masked rage. These Marines "suffered a total breakdown in morality and leadership, with tragic results," an unnamed "U.S. official" told the *Los Angeles Times* (Cohn), as if the atrocities could be an isolated anomaly. Right-wing media, by contrast, vociferously defended the Marines, and shock jock Michael Savage ranted that the Marines arrested for the massacre in Haditha were being treated even more harshly than the Afghan War prisoners that the U.S. was holding—over a hundred of whom had died in American custody by 2008.

None of the Marines in the Haditha massacre were charged with murder. Charges of manslaughter were dropped. Staff Sgt. Frank D. Wuterich, who ordered the killings, faced nine counts of voluntary manslaughter (maximum penalty three months), but eventually went free on a plea agreement (1/25/12). In accounts of the incident, "complexity" and bureaucratic terminology sanitized the killings: "Initially called a massacre by Iraqi residents of Haditha and later characterized as coldblooded murder by a U.S. congressman, the case has turned not on an alleged rampage but on a far more complex analysis of how U.S. troops fight an insurgency in the midst of a population they seek to protect."[52]

LOSS OF SELF

When boundaries are violated, it can feel like ecstatic freedom or insane chaos. Empowered to kill with impunity, soldiers can feel god-like. But the experience is treacherously unstable. The excitement is, literally, like nothing else in life. Without boundaries the self threatens to come apart. In the wisdom of slang, you "lose it." After the Haditha massacre, Lance Corporal Briones felt himself eaten alive. In Marjorie Cohn's account "he was ordered to take photographs of the victims and help carry their bodies out of their homes. He is still haunted by what he had to do that day. Briones picked up a young girl who was shot in the head. 'I held her out like this,' he said, extending his arms, 'but her head was bobbing up and down and the insides fell on my legs. I used to be one of those Marines who said that post-traumatic stress is a bunch of bull,' said Briones, who has gotten into serious trouble since he returned home. 'But all this stuff that keeps going through my head is eating me up. I need immediate help.'"

His metaphor says he feels that a predator is consuming his identity, as if he has fallen victim to cannibals or to the hunter he was. But the predators, unthinkably, are his own country and his buddies who have destroyed a child and exposed him to guilt, grief, disgust, terror, and alienation. Behind them is the most terrifying predator, death, which reveals life as nothingness: a smear of brains on a pant leg.

Psychic defenses usually keep the ephemeral nature—the nothing-ness—of the self hidden from us. To "lose it" is to lose self-control and in turn, self. Even in the face of actual death, that terrifying abyss is likely to remain disguised or denied. Consider the way berserkers may mutilate enemies. John Needham, who tried to commit suicide in Iraq, reported that Iraqis were shot for invented reasons, then mu-tilated. "The sergeants particularly liked removing victims' brains, Needham said, and had photographs to prove it."[53] Whatever they thought they were doing, the sergeants were unwittingly emulating American culture's focus on the evil "mastermind" Saddam Hus-sein (or Osama bin Laden). After all, the war opened with a missile bombardment specifically targeting Saddam's palaces, hoping to "be-head" the enemy.

But the behavior has a deeper dimension too. By carving out an enemy's brain you take apart his personality as if to discover a core self, even as you annihilate him. In this way the sergeants were doing to enemies what the war—the enemy—was doing to the Americans' inner lives. They were acting out their distress. John Needham's fa-ther, a retired Army officer, recognized the fragmentation when his son was on trial for murdering a girlfriend after his discharge: "He was a good soldier, and his group was doing things he knew was wrong. And he was in this prolonged combat situation where they have all this armor and lifesaving technology to keep them alive, but mentally, they are in pieces." On his MySpace page the young soldier had written: "I'm falling apart by the seams it seems the days here bleed into each other I have to find the will to live man I miss my brothers. These walls are caving in my despair wraps me in its web, I feel I'm sinking in, throw me a lifesaver throw me a life worth liv-ing. I'm a part of death I am death this is hard to admit but this shits getting old."

To feel yourself "a part of death" is to experience the annihilation of meaning, which is the nothingness of the self. As Ernest Becker says, we depend on heroic purpose—a sense that our lives have some sort of enduring significance—to manage the terror of death that is built into us.

In this context atrocious aggression acts out a struggle not sim-ply to avoid death but to substantiate the self. This helps to explain the otherwise pointlessly cruel hazing Marines inflicted on "weaker" comrades.

Domination of a "bitch" creates a conviction of alpha mastery as slavery does. In crushing the will of the victim, the master not only appropriates it to building himself up, but does so with a special surge of righteousness—"I'm doing this for your own good." When soldiers committed suicide, turning aggression against the tormented self, their suicide notes "almost always cited hazing." [54]

As a ferocious and fearless gunner, Kenneth Eastridge was decorated and praised. He was important to others. He was somebody. His tattoos boasted of his power as a killer. Yet one tattoo, an SS insignia, revealed an awareness of evil: a devil's pact. And as combat stress wore him down, Eastridge began to "lose it." Once while his platoon searched a house in Ramadi and he covered the street, Eastridge began firing as Lt. Calley did at My Lai. "Families were out playing soccer and barbecuing," and fled when the gunfire erupted. "Orders came over the radio to cease fire, he said, but he kept yelling, 'Negative! Negative!' Eastridge said he shot more than 1,700 rounds. When asked how many people he killed, he said, 'Not that many. Maybe a dozen.' "

Eventually Eastridge was court-martialed for "sex and drugs," but not for "Things that can never be told, but that everybody knew about and approved of—basically war crimes." On his return home Eastridge was convicted in the murder of another soldier and sentenced to prison. "I had no job training," he explained. "All I know how to do is kill people." [55] On the brink of nothingness, emergency physiology and the illusion of godlike power can be self-intoxicating even as it overrides the governing limits that define personality and puts you—as slang has it—"out of it."

Looking back, combat berserkers and rampage killers may describe a feeling of blackout or dissociation. "Did I do that? Was that me?" At the court-martial of a sniper accused of murder, another sniper, Sgt. Evan Vela, "all but broke down as he described firing two bullets into an unarmed Iraqi man [that] his unit arrested last May." After his squad leader, Sergeant Hensley, cut off the prisoner's handcuffs, "I heard the word 'Shoot,'" Sergeant Vela recalled. "I don't remember pulling the trigger," he said. "I just came through and the guy was dead, and it just took me a second to realize the shot had come from the pistol." As the suspected insurgent convulsed on the ground, "Sergeant Hensley kicked him in the throat and told Sergeant Vela to shoot him again. Sergeant Vela, who is not on trial but faces murder charges in connection with the killing, said he fired a second time." [56]

In Iraq troops were often exhausted because of extended tours, insomnia, and unrelieved nervous system arousal. In addition, they personally or officially treated exhaustion and post-traumatic stress

(PTSD) with drugs and alcohol that affected judgment. Mentally they lived out impossible conflicts of right and wrong, sympathy and hate, trigger-finger omnipotence and relentless terror. Not least of all, they struggled with conflicts over nervous system fight or flight. Escape into drugs, distraction, or depression can try to leave the troubled self behind. But flight may explode into fight, and fight may plunge into depression.

Military culture and militarized American culture are complicit in the problem. Military obsession with obedience and threat constricts awareness and intensifies the explosive potential of stress. Armies have routinely used berserk style to harden recruits. The Japanese military in the 1930s engrained in recruits the Three Alls Policy: kill all, burn all, and loot all. The temptation to reduce the soldier to an insensate weapon is strong. The power of technological leverage promises to bypass or overcome the psychic conflicts that can torment soldiers, but it can also make them expendable and literalize their enslavement to command. The frightening possibilities register in popular fantasies such as James Cameron's *Terminator* (1984). Michael Belfiore describes military research in which machines co-opt the human bodies with which they merge, given so much autonomy that they run amok when subject to hacking or malfunction.[57] Americans are horrified by terrorist fanatics, yet such fanatics are a version of "smart" weapons and proof that people can be trained to self-destruct.

This is no academic cavil. Perhaps the cruelest use of leverage by the corporate military is its new reliance on psychiatric drugs to get more fight out of soldiers who are coming undone from combat stress. The soldiers quoted above showed severe symptoms of PTSD. Yet in case after case they were treated as high-tech machines to be lubricated with prescription drugs and returned to battle. Worn out and badly shaken, they kept going with antidepressants such as Celexa and the mitrazapines, Valium, Ambien for insomnia, antipsychotics, plus alcohol, marijuana, and other drugs. Often they combined official prescriptions and self-medication, with perilous side effects. Coming home they faced withdrawal and an appalling void. In Eastridge's words, "All I know how to do is kill people."

Doublethink haunts the problem of combat stress. Since berserk frenzy can make soldiers exceptional fighters if it doesn't destroy them, it is tempting to tolerate or even wink at the role of trauma. In *Shock and Awe* (1996), Harlan K. Ullman and James P. Wade enthused about the use of trauma as a weapon against enemies without acknowledging its paradoxical effects. They adduced "the comatose and glazed expressions of survivors of the great bombardments of World War I" as proof of the power of shock to immobilize enemies. Ullman defended the "life-saving" annihilation of Hiroshima as a model. Yet despite "great bombardments," Germans and Vietnamese fought on for years.

While everyone deplores traumatic injury in soldiers, military thinking also allows for, or even sustains, traumatic stress when it leverages up ferocity and daring in combat, or unless it cripples operations. The ambiguities of the syndrome make it possible to rationalize injury.[58] Military psychiatry treats PTSD with a mix of talk therapy and drugs, but help is not always available. A Rand study estimated that nearly one in five veterans of the Afghanistan and Iraq wars suffered symptoms of PTSD or depression, although many avoid seeking help for fear that the stigma of weakness will hurt their military careers.[59] Researchers are currently testing drugs that may block overreaction to traumatic memories rather as ice applied after a burn prevents the body's emergency response from causing more serious harm.[60] One concern would be that efficient relief of symptoms could support the dream of cyber soldiers who could be more deliberately driven to frenzied aggression and then pharmaceutically disarmed and restored to civilian life—a version of the *Terminator* scenario.

AT WAR WITH STYLE

As havoc overtook the occupation, the berserk trope began to surface in accounts such as Pepe Escobar's "Counterinsurgency run amok" (*Asia Times*, Nov 18, 2004). The Internet and even embedded journalists began to recognize berserk style at work. The psychiatrist's category "beastlike" found euphemistic expression in a few instances such as Oliver Poole's description of "feral" Marines on their third tour of duty in Iraq who had been involved in the mayhem at Fallujah and Haditha.

At Kilo Company's encampment at a dam on the outskirts of Haditha, Poole observed that "institutional discipline had frayed and was even approaching breakdown." As a rule, "American camps in Iraq are almost suburban, with their coffee shops and polite soldiers who idle away their rest hours playing computer games and discussing girls back home." By contrast, these Marines had set up a separate camp that was "a feral place [and] resembled something from *Lord of the Flies*...and on the "day before my arrival one soldier had shot himself in the head with his M16. No one would discuss why.[61]

The group had withdrawn to an emergency culture signposted with death's heads to warn off strangers. Their fears showed in the stereotyped bravado of their skull-and-crossbones threat displays. They were encamped at a massive dam that was a constant reminder of their precarious situation. With its chronic alarms and broken machinery, the dam was under terrific strain, holding back a flood as the troops were tenuously holding in check a lethal insurgency, every Marine casualty another crack in the structure.

The "feral" metaphor evokes the berserk style fantasy that by shedding civilized restraints we can access extraordinary instinctual resources. It also picks up on the idea of war as predation. An article in the *Marine Corps Times* quotes Col. Clarke Lethin: commanders "believe that if we create a mentality in our Marines that they are hunters and they take on some of those skills, then we'll be able to increase our combat effectiveness." He adds: "The Corps hopes to tap into skills certain Marines may already have learned growing up in rural hunting areas and in urban areas, such as inner cities." Nick Turse points out that the colonel's language implicitly compared "enemies in urban warfare, today largely Iraqis and Afghans, to animals that are hunted and killed as quarry. As Lethin had unabashedly noted, 'We identified a need to ensure our Marines were being the hunters. Hunting is more than just the shooting. It's finding your game.'"[62] Just this idea turned up in the prosecution of snipers allegedly authorized to operate as "death squads," using "bait" such as fake explosives and spools of wire to lure Iraqis into shooting range.

As a style of organizing aggression, the trope of the hunt reaches from firefights in Iraq through U.S. inner cities to the leaders dictating policy. President Bush outdid LBJ in faux-heroic references to "hunting" the enemy. Of Al Qaeda terrorists he liked to say, "We're hunting them down, one at a time," or as he put it in November 2001, "we're smoking them out." The president "talked incessantly of hunting humans—in speeches to American troops, at photo ops with foreign leaders, at family fundraisers, even in the midst of remarks about homeownership."[63]

To recognize what Robert J. Lifton calls "atrocity-producing situations," we need to see more clearly the deep tropes such as hunting and predation that shape them, even when they are transparently packaged. A style preconditions a behavior so that it can be put on like a costume off the cultural rack. What begins as style can trigger actions, but the reverse is also true. For example, in the Iraq War ubiquitous digital cameras have filmed actual killing. On the Internet the photos are equivocal: they can be taken as trophies that prove heroism, but they could also enhance legal and moral oversight, as did a video clip released by the whistleblower website Wikileaks of two U.S. helicopters mistakenly or wantonly slaughtering two journalists and six other people on a street corner in New Baghdad on July 12, 2007. Killings may arouse abhorrence but also become war porn.

In style, tropes may insidiously combine. The camera can also be a weapon, seeming to tame the killing it witnesses or even enables. Sniping and photographing from cover are kinds of ambush, a predatory strategy. The implicit breakdown of cultural categories and rules that protect our sense of human rightness is evident in the prominent symptoms of godlike (spying on quarry from an invisible, commanding blind) and beastlike behavior. A Marine blog called Slaglerock Slaughterhouse[64] posted a photo of a large-caliber automatic weapon behind an armored housing with the hand-painted sign:

Iraqi photo's [sic]
Look here
Smile
Wait for
Flash

The macabre joke is a threat display to intimidate Iraqis and to advertise alpha male confidence to other Marines and, on the web, to the world. The intuitive nature of the wit is striking, since the joke parodies a photo studio but turns the portrait's substantiation of identity into a threat of annihilation in a "flash" of gunfire. Further, the joke associates military conquest with the photo studio "business," the more disturbingly conflicted since the business of rescuing and rebuilding Iraqi identity in reality means the "flash" of death. The blog's title, "Slaglerock Slaughterhouse," implies rampage killing while the joke daydreams about total Iraqi compliance. The instructions—"Look here and smile"—evoke a carnival shooting gallery with passive targets, even as it commands the victim's smiling assent to murder.

This cluster of tropes can be seen extending to wartime rape. Like killing at will, rape promises godlike mastery over life and death. The rapist acts out mind and body's appetite for more life: but evil in its destruction of the love that nurtures new life. Like war, it is a fantasy of putting in seed to overcome death. In his rape of Europa and Leda, Zeus acts out the clinical qualities of the berserk state, at once god and beast, forcing life into being. In wartime rape victims take on the soldier's enslavement to command, his terror, his threatened loss of self. Their suffering and abjection confirms his being.

Rape, then, merges the physiology and ideation of taking and giving life: of killing and fucking as a means to survival ecstasy. Shay points out that some people experience the "adrenaline rush" of the berserk state "as immensely pleasurable and willingly refer to [it] as exaltation or intoxication. Some combat veterans speak of it as 'better than sex'" (92).

This is the psychic economy underlying one of the war's most appalling atrocities: the gang rape and murder of fourteen-year-old Abeer Qassim Hamza al-Janabi following the slaughter of her parents and five-year-old sister.[65] Berserk style influenced the crime from the moment the girl caught the attention of four soldiers from Bravo Company in a town southwest of Baghdad at a time when insurgents had killed seventeen from their battalion in four months. The four men stalked the girl and searched her family's isolated farmhouse as a pretext to make advances toward her. The alarmed family allowed the girl to sleep at a neighbor's house for safety, but on the afternoon of March 12, 2006, after drinking and hatching plans, the soldiers acted.[66] Subsequently insurgents abducted and beheaded two of their fellow soldiers in revenge.

All of the accused invoked traumatic stress in their defense. Before the rampage came to light, Pfc. Stephen D. Green was discharged for a personality disorder that according to an Army spokesman, "does not necessarily indicate a mental disorder. Such a notation can be used to document willful disobedience or a personality that does not mesh well with military life."[67] Yet Green had been welcomed into the army despite a criminal background, and had boasted to a neighbor that he was "gonna go over there and kill 'em all." In effect, he was already planning a rampage.

To appreciate the role of style in the "atrocity-producing situation," recall the joke about photographing Iraqis to death. As Brian Nicol observes about paparazzi who stalk celebrities using the language of hunting and prey, "The camera 'shoots', it *takes* (i.e. steals) pictures." In the soldiers' photo the gun "shoots" people and "takes" their lives. Nicol cautions that "It would be a mistake to overstate the links between photography and serial murder, but there is a similar logic at work in both, which revolves around the 'capturing' of a targeted individual (often for the image they represent) and involves a similar dynamic of power and control."[68] The ambivalence implicit in the relationship of stalker and prey also resonates with the soldiers' role as would-be liberators of Iraqis. Instead of being greeted with kisses and adulation, the invaders meet ambush and death and feel enraged at what seems to be a betrayal.

The stalking soldiers pumped up sexual excitement and rage, as in sadistic pornography, and echoing the "war porn" photos of Iraqi deaths on the Internet. A sublimated echo of these themes captured media attention in mid-2006 and resonates with the rape and murder of Abeer.[69] At his base Corporal Joshua Belile performed an original folksong called "Hadji Girl" for an audience of laughing, applauding fellow Marines. The song is about erotic attraction to an Iraqi girl that leads to a Marine's slaughter of her family. Videotaped, the song appeared on the Internet, where it was officially censured. The performer apologized that it was only a joke, and some soldiers vehemently justified it. In the lyrics the speaker is under fire in Iraq. Facing death, he "looked up and I saw her eyes / And I knew it was love at first sight."

And she said...
"Dirka Dirka Mohammed Jihad
Sherpa Sherpa Bak Allah."
Hadji girl, I can't understand what you're saying.
Invited "to meet her family," unable to "figure out how to say no. / Cause I don't speak Arabic," the soldier goes home with her to a "side shanty." There,
Her brother and her father shouted...
"Dirka Dirka Mohammed Jihad
Sherpa Sherpa Bak Allah."

They pulled out their AKs so I could see ....
So I grabbed her little sister and pulled her in front of me.

As the bullets began to fly
The blood sprayed from between her eyes
And then I laughed maniacally

Then I hid behind the TV
And I locked and loaded my M-16
And I blew those little fuckers to eternity.

And I said...
"Dirka Dirka Mohammed Jihad
Sherpa Sherpa Bak Allah."

They should have known they were fucking with a Marine.

A theatrical occasion can accommodate scathing satire, and in its origins satire is a form of cursing,[70] so the murder of the "little sister" could be taken as gruesome gallows humor about insurgent treachery. But the same text is also projecting aggression onto the Iraqi father and brother in order to enable the Marines onstage and in the audience to fantasize about romance, sex, fertility, and an orgasmic rampage that could discharge tremendous internal stress and reinforce a conviction of godlike inviolability. The enemy males are rivals for the "Hadji girl," and the song substitutes the "Hadji girl's" alter ego, the little sister, in order to kill the rivals and take the girl.

Style conditions the psychic *stage* on which life stories play out. Just as the gunner in the photo imagines manning a machine gun and a camera, using witty condescension to manage his own psychic turmoil, so the song acts out an inner storm of conflicts in a "safe" play space. In the videotaped performance at his base in the war zone, Corporal Belile is actually on a stage with a microphone and his guitar before an audience of buddies, behind him a set of drums, and trained on him a "TV" camera. His "act" emulates American industrial entertainment: talent shows, American Idol, pop protest music, and the television cartoon satire "South Park," from which he took the mock-Arabic phrases in his lyrics. At the same time his audience applauded the sadistic fantasy they shared, either blowing off steam— or tragically reinforcing—the group's urge to "blow those little fuckers to eternity."

In the song the soldier hides behind the TV set. As a style, television provides a shield. It stands for home: it literally contains familiar icons and values that can make a soldier's sacrifices meaningful. To the extent that television style shapes the warrior's actions, it is formative. For the self under stress, TV-as-style provides a platform like the machine gun "camera" from which to kill the hostile, alien Iraqi family. In the pervasive idea of performance the unthinkable becomes thinkable, and an "act" may also be an action, ambiguously scripted and visceral. Stylized, violence masters death by dispatching enemies who represent death, even as its element of play and controlled unreality tames—or promises to tame—death's terror.

THE ECONOMY OF TORTURE

Though torture inflicts pain, it is at bottom, like war, an economy of creaturely motives. The ultimate leverage in torture is the threat of death, just as the ultimate prize is supposed to be life-saving information. The torturer seeks to break the will of the victim. The term "brainwashing" points to the underlying idea of a conversion experience in which the prisoner's will is "washed" away and replaced by the will of the torturer. The torturer consumes the victim's will and life-giving secrets. Bureaucracy may disguise it, but torture acts out the creaturely drive to consume the vitality of others evident in slavery, vampire fantasies, and in the cannibalistic obsessions of a Jeffrey Dahmer or the berserk sergeant's scooping out of an enemy's brain. At Abu Ghraib the motive crystallized in the bared fangs of guard dogs attacking prisoners.

In these terms torture is a form of virtual killing. Carried to its conclusion, as in lynching, it shares the dynamics of human sacrifice, epitomized in the interrogation and ritual burning of witches. In witchcraft prosecutions and show trials, for example, a vicious feedback loop of pain, paranoia, and panic reliably extorted confessions that rationalized judicial murder. Torture by the Argentine and Chilean juntas in the 1970s regularly led to murder.

In the "war on terror" an unknown number of prisoners have died in American custody.[71] At Abu Ghraib, a badly beaten prisoner kept shackled in a "stress position" suffocated as in crucifixion. His CIA interrogator allegedly expressed surprise at the outcome. By contrast, berserk rage is unequivocal when guards have literally beaten a prisoner to a pulp, as in the death of an Afghan civilian recounted in Alex Gibney's documentary *Taxi to the Dark Side* (2007).

Viewed in terms of berserk style, torture grades by degrees toward atrocity. In the Bush administration's justifications of "harsh interrogation," jargon sanitized the cold rage. The practice of "waterboarding," which fascinated the media, is not "simulated" drowning regulated by legalistic adjectives, but actual drowning carried to the brink of death. The suffering comes not merely from pain but from the terror of knowing that someone is killing you.

Torture is always latently berserk because it is a self-fulfilling and self-intoxicating system. Operating to revenge or prevent injury, it is incipiently paranoid, driven by suspicion and anxiety. As in witchcraft interrogations, innocence is virtually impossible to prove. If a victim has some information, it raises the possibility that pain will force out more. Likewise, the proximity to pain and death may excite in the perpetrator fear, guilt, frustration, and survival rage that only the victim's guilt can relieve, so the process feeds on itself. The victim's helplessness invites the sadistic total control that Erich Fromm linked to authoritarian fantasies of invulnerability and immortality.

The Geneva Conventions and habeas corpus in American jurisprudence developed for good reason. The Senate Armed Services Committee report on torture (2008-09) shows that when President Bush stripped suspects of those protections (February 7, 2002), his inner circle sprang into action. The principals were "obeying orders" but also licensing aggression.[72] The administration's hair-splitting embrace of torture cost the nation so much prestige and moral authority that its motives remain puzzling. Since evidence shows that torture produces unreliable information, it is unclear how fully Vice President Cheney, his legal advisors, and the C.I.A. believed in its efficacy. One answer is that conspicuous torture is berserk-style threat display, exaggerating the "tough cop" face of the global policeman in hopes of intimidating adversaries. In addition, since the administration was defying international law, possible prosecution for war crimes, as in the belated arrest of Chile's Gen. Pinochet in 2000, gave policy makers reason to defend their decisions aggressively.

The improvised and incoherent policies at the top played out in the Abu Ghraib scandal. The Army's initial investigation recorded that "Numerous incidents of sadistic, blatant, and wanton criminal abuses were inflicted on several detainees...systemic and illegal abuse."[73] A former intelligence official told Seymour Hersh that the photos of torture "turned out to be the result of the [approved 'special-access'] program run amok."[74] Conditions at Abu Ghraib were chaotic. "As mortar attacks rained down on the overcrowded prison—at one point there were only 450 guards for 7,000 prisoners—its command structure broke down. At the same time, the pressure from the Pentagon and the White House for "actionable intelligence" was intense.... Intelligence agencies such as the CIA were apparently given the green light to operate by their own set of secret rules."[75] With the arrival of Major Gen. Geoffrey Miller, the former Guantánamo interrogation commander who allegedly brought tougher intelligence tactics to Abu Ghraib, the confusing and sometimes disingenuous orders to "soften up" prisoners intensified pressure on the blundering young military police staff in the prison.

On March 15, 2006, Salon.com published extensive official documentation of the abuse. In a report written by Special Agent Seigmund for CID (June 6, 2004), "A review of all the computer media submitted to this office revealed a total of 1,325 images of suspected detainee abuse, 93 video files of suspected detainee abuse, 660 images of adult pornography, 546 images of suspected dead Iraqi detainees, 29 images of soldiers in simulated sexual acts, 20 images of a soldier with a Swastika drawn between his eyes, 37 images of Military working dogs being used in abuse of detainees and 125 images of questionable acts."

Sensationalized in global media, torture in the prison was a sinister, squalid carnival. In much of the low-level abuse the low-ranking young soldiers attempted to humiliate Iraqi men with infantile sexual aggression and violated cultural taboos. Abuses included urinating on detainees, sodomizing with a baton or possibly a broomstick, smearing them with excrement, putting women's underwear on them, forcing them to masturbate, riding naked prisoners like donkeys, and "Tying ropes to the detainees' legs or penises and dragging them across the floor."[76]

The obtuse rationale for such practices—that they would distress macho Iraqi men, for instance—says much more about the psychology of their tormenters than about the detainees. The aggression shows immature young people under stress and taking shelter in fantasies of humiliation and mastery. By posing for photos gleefully showing off their socially dead "trophies" for the camera, soldiers could play heroic warrior to support shaken self-esteem. At the same time the infantile sexual themes expressed childish rebellion against the authority that, after all, had the soldiers imprisoned along with the Iraqis.

Two of the young women soldiers were drawn into charged sexual relationships with Cpl. Charles A. Graner, Jr., who also directed most of their abuse of prisoners.[77] Given the atmosphere of death-anxiety and caged rage, it is not difficult to understand the fantasies of intimacy and fertility that seduced the trio. For the alpha male Graner and his small harem, the social and sexual humiliation of Iraqi prisoners on display in the famous photographs confirmed the soldiers' superior status. Dominating frightened and angry Iraqi men, Graner could act the protector to the younger women.

In "Iraq for Sale" Michael Greenwald shows CACI personnel, deployed as "expert" interrogators, tying men together with cords looped around their penises and then pushing them over, symbolically castrating them. Castration of rival males is a feature of ancient warfare. Likewise, anal rape is a marker for male dominance, just as confining prisoners in their excrement literalizes the verbal assault in slang insults such as "asshole" and "shit." The taboo is especially sensitive in the military, where soldiers are nominally heroes yet enslaved by command, and in recent years homophobia has protested attempts to legitimize gay enlistment. When Gen. Taguba reported to Sec. Rumsfeld about the Abu Ghraib scandal, someone asked, "Is it abuse or torture?" As Taguba recalled, "I described a naked detainee lying on the wet floor, handcuffed, with an interrogator shoving things up his rectum, and said, 'That's not abuse. That's torture.' There was quiet."[78]

When berserk style goes amok, humiliation and social death turn into real death. In the military, brutality against prisoners is common enough to have its own slang term, "to fuck up PUCs" (= Persons Under Control). At Abu Ghraib, where outnumbered guards were always potentially in danger, some beatings expressed retaliatory rage. More difficult to sort out is the influence of the secret CIA task-force teams on the young military subordinates. A CIA source told Seymour Hersh that "the task-force teams "'had full authority to whack—to go in and conduct 'executive action' "—meaning assassination. "'It was surrealistic what these guys were doing,' the retired operative added. 'They were running around the world without clearing their operations with the ambassador or the chief of station.'" Cpl. Graner confirmed that CIA interrogators operated outside the law. "You know these guys can kill people," Graner said in an April 2005 statement to the Army Criminal Investigation Command (CID). "The OGA guys do whatever they want. They don't exist."[79]

Like secret police the world over, clandestine OGA or "other government agency" operatives were unaccountable. By cooperating with vicious regimes, the CIA maintains a screen of deniability for policy makers. When the mayhem at Abu Ghraib became public, sophistry and denial echoed up the chain of command. The president and vice-president confronted allegations with a campaign to sanitize torture as "enhanced interrogation"—a term echoing the Gestapo's "Verschaerfte Vernehmung," going on the offensive to justify their involvement.[80]

This boldness about torture is the more puzzling because the risks of injustice and inefficacy could scarcely be more obvious. Without access to courts, prisoners were subject to suspicions that could be neither proved nor disproved. In her memoir Brig. Gen. (now Col.) Janis Karpinski, the prison commander, estimates that 90 percent of detainees in the prison were innocent. However, when military intelligence ordered the release of all but a few detainees, Gen. Wodjakowski summarily overrode the decision. In one exchange he vowed, "I don't care if we're holding 15,000 innocent Iraqis, we're winning the war." And I [Karpinski] said to him, "No, sir, not inside the wire you're not, because every one of those detainees becomes our enemy when they're released, and they will be released one day."[81]

Gen. Wodjakowski's tough-guy reflex trivializes the suffering and deaths at Abu Ghraib as mere detention ('holding'). Yet his response dimly recognizes that cruelty is supporting or feeding his triumphant conviction. The acute excitement of a contest ("we're winning"), the impatience with systematic interrogation, and the self-defeating creation of more enemies suggest the berserker's godlike indifference to risk and pain. The problem is not simply that the general ignored justice and truth, but that style overwrote the motives he needed to manage. The core conflict is the old colonial conundrum, the need to dominate yet win the cooperation of a subjugated people.

Trying to manage with incoherent policies, the Guantánamo lawyers charged with devising interrogation techniques found inspiration in the television series "24."[82] As Jane Mayer has reported, the show's producer, Joel Surnow, systematically uses the unspoken premise that the show's anti-terrorism agents, especially their leader Jack Bauer, are actually in emergency-panic mode.[83] During the Iraq War a delegation from the military academies complained to Surnow that the show's sensational treatment of torture was encouraging young officers to disregard legal codes and the inefficacy of torture. In reply, echoing debates over violence in children's programming, Surnow scoffed that the show was "only fantasy."

Surnow systematically uses Orwellian doublethink to rationalize Jack Bauer's viciousness. In Jane Mayer's account he claims the show is "all just fantasy." Letting down the mask of facetious dismissiveness, however, he can comment "in a more sober tone" that

> "We've had all of these torture experts come by recently, and they say, 'You don't realize how many people are affected by this. Be careful.' They say torture doesn't work. But I don't believe that. I don't think it's honest to say that if someone you love was being held, and you had five minutes to save them, you wouldn't do it. Tell me, what would you do? If someone had one of my children, or my wife, I would hope I'd do it. There is nothing—nothing—I wouldn't do." He went on, "Young interrogators don't need our show. What the human mind can imagine is so much greater than what we show on TV. No one needs us to tell them what to do.

It's not like somebody goes, 'Oh, look what they're doing, I'll do that.' Is it?"

This argument turns on non sequiturs. But its core is pure berserk style in the service of self-abandon: "There is nothing—nothing—I wouldn't do."

Surnow's fantasy of abandon is psychologically blind or dishonest. He gives no hint that authority might take out its rage and fear on an innocent victim. His language is deviously indirect: if someone you love "was being held" [by whom?]; "if someone [who?] had one of my children." Thinking himself a self-made Hollywood success, he imagines that all behavior comes from within: "No one needs us to tell them what to do."

Ironically, Surnow's prosperous connections to the rightwing media establishment and to the White House dramatize precisely the sort of social influence on individual thinking that he denies, since they are rewarding him for his show. "'It's been very heady,' [lead writer Howard] Gordon said of Washington's enthusiasm for the show. Roger Director, Surnow's friend, joked that the conservative writers at '24' have become 'like a Hollywood television annex to the White House. It's like an auxiliary wing'" (Mayer). The fantasy explicitly makes broadcast fantasy a function of government.

Style mediates creaturely motives but cannot entirely dispel them. Laura Ingraham, the talk-radio host, has cited the popularity of "24" as proof that Americans favor brutality. "'They love Jack Bauer,' she noted on Fox News. 'In my mind, that's as close to a national referendum that it's O.K. to use tough tactics against high-level Al Qaeda operatives as we're going to get.'" So far Ingraham's plug for the series is merely intellectually dishonest: euphemistic ("tough tactics" not torture) and demonizing ("high level Al Qaeda" instead of possibly innocent suspects). But then come some unwitting revelations: "Surnow once appeared as a guest on Ingraham's show; she told him that, while she was undergoing chemotherapy for breast cancer, 'it was soothing to see Jack Bauer torture these terrorists, and I felt better.' Surnow joked, 'We love to torture terrorists—it's good for you!'" (Mayer). Vicariously inflicting pain and death on an "enemy," the cancer sufferer relieves her death-anxiety and enjoys a boost to morale.

Throughout history the sacrifice of enemies and scapegoats has been a common practice to generate exaltation. Style can help to dissolve taboos and makes the psychic economy of killing available for vicarious mass consumption. Laura Ingraham is "fighting" her illness, but in her radio broadcast she is also propagating berserk style, modeling aggression, for a mass audience. The style may be ceremonial, even festive, as in the Roman amphitheater's choreographed torture and death, which took place in a holiday atmosphere, with the crowd excitedly participating in the coup de grace, and prostitutes at the exits to fulfill the creaturely drives excited by the show. The Aztecs invited foreign dignitaries to be impressed by their periodic ritual slaughter of captives. Photographs of American lynch mobs commonly capture signs of expansiveness and glee. When the sadistic exhilaration includes a conviction of heroism and righteousness, it can be irresistible.

The abuse of captives in modern warfare perpetuates a kind of ecstasy common in history. The Iraq war began with the usual sanitized belief in "surgical"—that is, healing—intervention. In practice it is nearly impossible to determine exactly the extent and nature of the self-deception: the *quality* of the belief. In *Fiasco,* Thomas Ricks describes U.S. troops taking turns assaulting prisoners, as in one unit where a cook took part, breaking a captive's legs with a Louisville slugger. [84] The baseball bat evokes fantasies of sports heroism, but also the war club and its euphemistic offspring, the royal scepter. As a prop of berserk style, the bat stands for play, the pieties of home and childhood that armies fight for, and the thrilling exertions of the playing field. Like the machine gun jokingly analogized to a camera, the baseball bat dispels guilt and horror.

The contrast between the unreported testimony of experts opposed to torture and the "speculative defense of waterboarding offered by semiofficial advocates," says David Bromwich," has been among the most disquieting revelations of these years. A group of men who think what they want to think and pay little attention to evidence have been running things, and they are guided not by experience but by words that were constructed for the purpose of deception."[85]

Ironically, when Laura Ingraham fantasized on the air about torture as therapy, her guest Joel Surnow applauded with a chuckle, sounding like an infomercial for a health product: "'We love to torture terrorists—it's good for you!"[86] His smart-aleck quip reflected not only his position as a businessman in Hollywood making a profit from representations of torture, but also another facet of the privatization of torture, removed from and yet not unrelated to the private security agents hired to conduct torture at Abu Ghraib.

The businessman's sinister quip points investigation toward the following chapter, which examines berserk style in American economic life.

THE PEAK OF THE PEAK

American culture in the new century moved through a series of peaks, nominally—but only nominally—beginning with the September 11 terrorism. Thereafter the nation undertook confrontations with one enemy after another. As Iraq became calmer in 2007, sirens were already whining for a renewal of hostilities in Afghanistan and a battle with Iran. An October 21, 2007 editorial the *Los Angeles Times* captured the operation of berserk style in U.S. policy:

The war of words against Iran grew scorching this week when President Bush declared that "avoiding World War III" requires preventing that country from developing nuclear weapons....[T]he escalation of American threats against Iran is unwise. It is grossly premature. It is dangerous, as it greatly increases the likelihood of accidental escalation into a preventable war. It is alarmingly ill-timed, as an isolated United States wages simultaneous ground wars in Iraq and Afghanistan, and both conflicts are going badly....

So why rattle the sabers now, at a moment of U.S. military weakness? In 1969, with the Vietnam War going badly, President Nixon devised a plan to spook the Soviets and the North Vietnamese into making concessions by making them think that he was just crazy enough to use nuclear weapons. Nixon called it the "madman theory." There is speculation that the Bush administration could be trying out its version of the madman gambit."

What makes the "madman gambit" so trenchant is that its use against Iran coincided with the first rumblings of collapse on Wall Street. President Bush, the secretary of the treasury, and the Federal Reserve head warned that the American-led global financial system was about to implode. Financier Warren Buffet had dubbed the Wall Street derivatives "weapons of mass destruction." Naomi Klein has summed up the intersection of the Pentagon, Wall Street, and the federal government as a central feature of the "Disaster Capitalism Complex."[87]

With the all-in costs of the post-9/11 wars projected to be in the trillions, the nation's financial health required reining in military spending. The Defense Business Board, which includes corporate executives, concluded that the spending binge was no longer tenable.

The berserk dynamics surface in the analysis of Winslow Wheeler, director of the Straus Military Reform Project at the Center for Defense Information in Washington, who presents congressional efforts to confront the corporate military as a suicidal assault: "The forces arrayed against terminating defense programs are today so powerful that if you try to do that it will be like the British Army at the Somme in World War I.... You will just get mowed down by the defense industry and military services' machine guns."[88] The corporate military economy, that is, fights Americans at the cash register as well as distant enemies.

By 2014, multi-party civil war was raging in Syria, Iran had relaxed into the background, and U.S. public opinion was weary of U.S. war in the region. As President Obama was systematically withdrawing troops, radical jihadis fighting in Syria recruited disaffected Iraqi Sunnis and reignited the insurgency that had disrupted the U.S. pacification of Iraq a decade earlier. The Islamic State (ISIS) rapidly took over traditional Sunni territories and threatened the rest. Within weeks U.S. bombs were once again trying to remake the map, and in classic berserk style, former national security advisor Henry Kissinger was warning that "The concept of order that has underpinned the modern era is in crisis."[89]

CHAPTER 4

MAKING A KILLING

The massive global pool of speculative finance has run amuck.
Doug Noland, *"Riddle of the Burst Bubble"*

*The banks were allowed to run wild by those
charged with regulating them.*
Roger Alcaly, *"The Right Way to Control the Banks"*

In the wake of the financial crisis of 2007-08, a Google search for "economy amok" turned up 595,000 hits, one sign of the role berserk style played in the mayhem. As early as November 2009, Federal Reserve chair Ben Bernanke was calling the 2008 crisis "the worst financial crisis in global history, including the Great Depression."[1] Most commentators blamed excessive debt and lax government regulations. Joseph Stigitz deplored not only the crisis but the collateral damage, the foreclosed houses and lost jobs that open the abyss of social death underfoot: "No democratic government...has ever wasted resources outside of war on the scale which our private sector misallocated capital...a massive, massive failure [sic]. But after the crisis the consequences are even larger, the gap between full employment, potential output and actual output, is trillions of dollars and mounting."[2]

Comparisons abounded to the 1929 crash, to the recurring bank panics of the nineteenth century: to the Mississippi Bubble, the Dutch tulip mania, and the 1720 British South Sea bubble, which climaxed in daily suicides, expulsion of the Chancellor of the Exchequer, mob demands for vengeance, and reading of the Riot Act—that is, in rampage. Critics routinely described the speculative bubbles and the "meltdown" as berserk: meaning out of control. But speculative mania is a familiar liability of capitalism. No less interesting is the berserk style that rationalizes that mayhem.

In the 2008 crash, banks and mortgage lenders financed—and finagled—a housing bubble that imploded. Investigators found perilously ingenious financial engineering and operators amok. In the aftermath conventional wisdom wondered aloud why taxpayers had rescued Wall Street investors but not taxpayers put out on the kerb by mortgage fraud. And why were no bankers punished?

The idiom "making a killing" preserves the ancestral relationship of prosperity to hunting and warfare. Bull and bear markets take the names of awe-inspiring totem animals that humans have hunted, fought, and tamed. In a *New Yorker* cartoon a businessman queasily notices that the Wall Street statue of a bull, the mighty inseminator, has been marked out in choice cuts for butchering.[3] Finance is food: more life. At the same time it is butchery: fighting and killing. In business slang, competition is "cutthroat." Buying a stock you "pull the trigger." A small, quick profit is "scalping." When markets fall, there is "blood in the streets" and "carnage"; equities may be "slaughtered" or rally in a "dead cat bounce."

Where tribal societies valued equilibrium, capitalism stresses dynamism: insemination and more life. In the *Grundrisse*, Marx held that the circulation and accumulation of capital cannot abide limits. Capital creates barriers and strives to overcome them. Cartoonists satirize obsessive concerns for growth and profit by associating business life with charts whose trends point up toward prosperous abandon ("off the charts") or downward, toward doom (an "abyss"). Fear and greed drive markets. A "bull" market gives off potency: a "bear" will devour you. investors develop or lose an "appetite for risk." The feeding frenzy of "dog-eat-dog" competition is implicitly cannibalistic. Matt Taibbi named the taboo, oft talked about yet ever struggling to be heard, when he described Goldman Sachs as a "great vampire squid wrapped around the face of humanity, relentlessly jamming its blood funnel into anything that smells like money."[4] The trope struck a nerve, and in no time vampire squid were swarming in financial journalism.

The aggression and death-anxiety in this market glossary help to explain why berserk style figures so strikingly in economic relationships, and why societies have always had to regulate market behavior. Charles Mackay's *Extraordinary Delusions and the Madness of Crowds* (1841) and Keynes's "animal spirits," for example, recognized creaturely motives as an economic force, and today the term has entered into mainstream economic thinking. "Irrational exuberance" inflates bubbles; survival panic—hoarding, paralysis, paranoia—drives a depression.[5] Setbacks have an apocalyptic quality when described as an economic "blow off," "tsunami," or a "meltdown."

We are social animals. Traders have to be able to see that there are at least two sides to every transaction, and that all the parties have to satisfy their needs. Business requires imaginative sympathy in order to understand what others want and to determine the value of things. Traders need psychological and diplomatic skills. The problem is that these qualities are richly ambivalent, since the trader's imaginative sympathy can foster mutuality, but it can also be the weapon of a sociopath seeking advantage. And in the real world, although the balance scale symbolizes objectivity, economic behavior is almost always conditioned by scheming and social relationships, including the enduring childhood urge to grab what we want.

Since people are often irrational, unaware, or mistaken, economic thinkers usually schematize or exclude unruly motives. Modern economies have invented the corporation to juggle this problem. With double vision the law treats corporations as persons, with the right to free speech, even the right to influence elections. Yet by design, corporations exist to shield their owners from liability. In simple markets owners are responsible for the debts and liabilities of their business. But by permitting so much risk, a simple market limits economic activity. By allowing corporations to declare bankruptcy and reorganize, diluting the risk, the political system shields the owners, and business can survive.

As corporations become "too big to fail" and monopolistic, even the prospect of bankruptcy is too destabilizing to tolerate, and so a culture of impunity and survival dread develops. When corporations run amok, who or what is making—or doing—the killing? Officers? investors? Company policy? "Corporate culture?" If taxpayers are silently guaranteeing corporate risk-taking, socializing risk and privatizing reward, whose motives are in play? Do the public's unwilling and often invisible subsidies make corporations kleptocracies? The question makes the idea of the corporation one of the most elegantly useful and pernicious forms of berserk style.

BUBBLE TROUBLE

Markets determine the value of things by discovering how much people will pay for them. In a bubble, too much available money distorts values. In 2008, for example, house prices rose so far, so fast, that as in an arms race, institutions and individuals borrowed more and more in hopes of preempting a coming price increase, or in hopes of flipping a property for a profit that seems as certain as it is outsized. The analogy to war is not frivolous. War also discovers valuations by determining how much life people will give to capture a goal. As the previous chapter noted, the treasure that victory brings is at bottom associated with creaturely motives: namely more life. In a war, the contenders will pay with lives—the ultimate price—so wars readily distort values as bubbles do. As President Eisenhower famously warned in 1961, postwar Washington and the corporate military were striving to keep the stimulation and heroic self-esteem of World War II pumped up. Nevertheless, in his inaugural address of 1961, President Kennedy vowed that for "the survival and success of liberty," we "would pay any price." In short order, the Vietnam War would demonstrate that as berserk style, the idea of a bubble is deeply embedded in American habits of thought.

As the world rebalanced after World War II, the U.S. maintained its dominance by unprecedented investment in military power. But global competition exposed the bubble. "Since the 1970s...the U.S economy has grown more slowly than in the thirty-year period after the end of World War II, but also very likely more slowly than in any other period in the nation's history."[6] "America's actual share of global wealth has been in almost continuous decline since the end of World War II. By 2012, the United States controlled roughly 25% of the world's wealth, compared with roughly 50% in 1948."[7] In these years the "heartland" became a "rustbelt," and as factories closed, a lower-paying service economy emerged. Business philosophy shifted from long-term investment to entrepreneurial risk.

In a momentous shift from labor to capital, finance doubled its share of the economy, and with the aid of free market policies and tax reductions for upper brackets, income inequality dramatically reversed. During 1949-1953, 80% of average income growth went to the bottom 90% and 20% to the top 10%, but the trend favored the top. After the Vietnam War, distribution shifted dramatically. By 1982-1990, the top 10% claimed 80% of income growth, while for the bottom, 90% growth had collapsed to 20%. In 2008 real wages for most were lower than in 1972.[8] By 2009-2012, the top 10% had captured about 117% of income growth, while the bottom 90% were now about 17% below the baseline of 1949.[9] By 2009, the 74 wealthiest people in the nation "made as much as the 19 million lowest-paid people in America, who constitute one in every eight workers."[10]

This distortion in income recalls 1928, the trigger point of the Great Depression. It has been momentous in part because the nation maintained the illusion of prosperity through bubble psychology and sloshing debt. In different ways those at the top and those below were both susceptible to fantasies of abandon. In the 1980s, as "free market" ideology became dominant, business culture fought to eliminate regulatory oversight. Global competition excited a "decade-long "golden age of junk financing [that] built to a virtual frenzy." Even some partisans of creative finance acknowledge the berserk dynamics that in 1989 and 1990 resulted "in an unprecedented number of defaults by junk bond issuers and the bankruptcy of Drexel Burnham."[11] The new leverage provided much-needed capital and flexibility, but with dubious transparency, creating corporate agglomerations on a scale that recalled the trusts of the pre-Depression era, and the speculative overreach evident in the Black Monday (1987) stock market swoon.[12]

Junk finance aroused familiar ambivalence. When abandon worked magic, the magicians were celebrities; when it failed, they faced prosecution. In Oliver Stone's *Wall Street* (1987) the speculator Gordon Gecko (Michael Douglass) was partly modeled on Ivan Boesky, one of the few junk bond desperados jailed for trading violations. Gecko made famous the battle-cry of berserk finance: "Greed is good."

The decades to come stressed "conservative" responsibility but favored enterprising laissez faire and "creative destruction." President Reagan called for revolt against "big government" and yet overspent. In the new adventuresome atmosphere of the 1980s, over a thousand deregulated savings and loan institutions self-destructed in "the largest and costliest venture in public misfeasance, malfeasance and larceny of all time."[13]

Belief that "the sky's the limit" because "it's different this time" rationalized abandon and a massive capture of wealth and power in fewer and fewer hands. Critics harped on the dangers of inebriation and blamed the Federal Reserve's Alan Greenspan for refusing "to take away the punch bowl." Hedge funds, easy credit, and ungrounded valuations made for "casino" markets.[14] With the Glass-Steagal Act and other Depression era firewalls dismantled in the 1990s, banks joined the ranks of speculators at the gaming tables.

The atmosphere was self-intoxicating. Technology and dotcoms contributed to a cycle of increasing perturbations. In the 1980s, metaphors of piracy invaded board rooms: corporate "raiders" and "buccaneers" used overpowering leverage to "loot" companies.[15] The liquidation or monetization of productive assets for windfall gains marked a new era of stress in the workplace.[16] To be sure, some of the restructuring led to needed innovation and efficiencies, and the myths of the day celebrated the wholesome birth of Apple Computer on a shoestring in a California garage. But the bailouts of the 1990s revealed underlying instability and prefigured the 2008 bust.

When the tech bubble popped (1999-2001), the finance industry turned to mortgages. Wall Street fashioned ingenious derivative instruments that promised to expand leverage for bankers and the poorest homebuyers without limits or risk. Selling and reselling derivatives, giving chimerical guarantees to mortgages repackaged to mask risk, bankers collected outsized fees and paid themselves piratical bonuses. Since housing prices seemed destined to soar forever, the prosperous beyond lured many borrowers, lenders, and home-builders into risk-taking at a time when wages were stagnant, consumer credit already overextended, and savings rates negligible.[17]

By then, Wall Street banks were "too big to fail" and berserk style became more openly violent in its ideation. The emergency bailouts of 2008 spurred some in Congress to speak as if the banks were rampage killers holding the government hostage. Some critics saw it as a coup d'etat: "the finance industry has essentially captured our government."[18] The bailouts took place in an atmosphere of suppressed panic: "The Bush administration and Congress discussed the possibility of a breakdown in law and order and the logistics of feeding U.S. citizens if commerce and banking collapsed as a result of last autumn's financial panic.... [The] former Treasury secretary Hank Paulson said it was important at the time not to reveal the extent of officials' concerns, for fear it would "terrify the American people and lead to an even bigger problem."[19] With former Wall Street executives managing the epic bailouts as government officials, it was symptomatic of abandon that some critics saw talk of panic as self-serving.

In bubbles, frames of reference blur. Wall Street banks devised a shadow banking system to veil their innovative derivatives from regulatory challenges. In 1997, in *The Innovator's Dilemma* (1997), Clayton M. Christensen held that unforeseen and even unlikely products could revolutionize a market and blow up strong conventional businesses. The idea resonated from board rooms to the Pentagon, inflaming giddiness but also uneasiness about devastating innovations. Enron fell to ruin boasting that its innovation would outwit competition. As Jill Lepore sums up, "Disruptive innovation is a competitive strategy for an age seized by terror." Of the 2008 meltdown, she concludes, "When the finance-services industry disruptively innovated, it led to a global financial crisis. Like the bursting of the dot-com bubble, the meltdown didn't dim the fervor for disruption; instead, it fuelled it, because these products of disruption contributed to the panic on which the theory of disruption thrives."[20]

As frames of reference erode, risk analysis is impaired, and the effect goes beyond decimal points and dollar signs. Like nervous system flooding under stress, gambling feeds on itself and becomes addictive. Nick Paumgarten tuned in to the behavior when he described one of 28 million pens given away by New Jersey's failed, flashy Commerce Bank. "The pens were, in a way, a souvenir of the shadow banking system, a by-product of securitization. Finding one was a little like stumbling on an empty crack vial in the public park."[21] Some personalities were more susceptible than others, but addiction was also a cultural predilection, as if a force of nature was directing the participants: "The price of things came to be determined largely by how easily they could be financed. A long-term decline in interest rates, promoted and abetted by the Federal Reserve, helped create a perpetual motion machine that encouraged people to borrow, buy, and borrow some more" (48). Paumgarten quotes a business professor who regards securitization and its fabulous fees for banks as "a machine that said, 'Feed me.'" And so "debt was created to sate the machine" (49). The underlying notion is akin to an addiction. A "perpetual motion" machine represents addiction's promise of deathless intoxicating promise—the bliss of the beyond. Perpetual motion appears to be free, bountiful, unforced, like the early stages of a Ponzi scheme, when the transactions seem magically self-sustaining.

One addictive property of the securitization machine was the illusion that it guaranteed against risk. Hedge funds similarly relied on machines in computer programs whose arcane formulas promised to guarantee profits by detecting the subtlest market signals and responding faster than a live trader. The computer revolution promised new controls over price discovery and risk, even at giddy levels of abstraction. Algorithms (in Wall Street jargon "Algos") acquired the magical aura of alchemy.[22] Like military drones, the computer programs were designed to see over the horizon and make a killing while safeguarding the operators. And like other strategies, hedging—combining long and short positions to offset risk—is more reliable when markets are bubbling upward and nearly every investor is a genius. The relentless rise in house prices since World War Two convinced many in real estate that it was an unshakable formula. Hence the unrealistic mortgages, the purchase of houses "on spec" to "flip" them—as in judo's cunning leverage—at a higher price. And hence the loans subsequently drawn against home equity that could transform the house into a cash machine.

The atmosphere was feverish with possibility. More money. More prestige. More autonomy. More future. More life. According to critics such as Jonathan Walton, a professor of religious studies, the growth of the popular Christian "prosperity gospel"—that God wants everyone to be wealthy—"tracks fairly closely to the pattern of hotspots" for house foreclosures as mortgage lenders teamed up with pastors and blind faith overrode financial prudence.[23]

When the crisis finally broke, the distress rumbled across the globe. Analysis of the chaos tried to sort out villains, and the business press turned to the idea of abandon in reports such as "Berserker Funds in Commodities."[24] As political power shifted in the 2008 elections, images of civil insurrection and rage boiled up. Like an unemployed worker on a crime spree, "Wall Street put a gun to the head of the politicians and said, 'Give us the money [for a bailout]—right now—or take the blame for whatever follows.'"[25] On October 2, 2008, Rep. Brad Sherman reported that members of Congress faced threats of "martial law in America if we voted no."

The rage was not all just journalistic spice. Caught up in the derivatives fever, Richard Fuld, CEO of Lehman Brothers, had turned a deaf ear to warnings from his subordinates. On the afternoon he announced the firm's bankruptcy to shocked employees, Fuld—once known as "the Gorilla"—was on a treadmill in the company gym wearing a heart monitor when someone "pumping iron...walked over and...knocked him out cold."[26]

LIFE AS LEVERAGE

A club, a slingshot, a cannon, and a nuclear missile all magnify the impact of a fist. Similarly financial instruments such as bonds, options, derivatives, margin, and other instruments magnify the impact of capital. They are all force-multipliers.

Berserk style expresses the creaturely motives that link financial leverage to other forms. In the military, leverage is technological firepower. But in wartime the military also "borrows" the autonomy and savings of citizens to maximize its force for the projected gains of victory. It hopes to pay back the "loan" through more life: survival, glory, loot, veterans' benefits, and other rewards. The factory borrows the autonomy of its "hands" to magnify productivity till payday pays it back with—in theory—the means to a better life. In the cosmic scheme of things all lives are on loan. As Hal says to Falstaff before battle in Shakespeare's *Henry IV*, "thou owest God a death."

Leverage opens toward the beyond. If borrowed money can be used as collateral to borrow more money, and the process is repeated, the gains are potentially infinite. As the scale of the lender's loans and the debtor's debt increases, however, so does contingency. When sums borrowed exceed collateral or bank reserves, the sum becomes hypercritical, since a failure can destroy both parties.

In the pre-2008 bubble, easy money, lax regulation, and the cult of innovation lubricated speculative excess. The tech boom and the postwar history of rising real estate prices seemed to justify maximum leverage for borrowers and lenders. Overextended parties kept parlaying gains from the prolonged economic bubble. With regulatory firewalls coming down, Wall Street banks began acting like brokers and hedge funds, devising and repackaging derivatives so complex that rating agencies—hired by the banks—later confessed to vetting them more or less on faith.

Frames of reference deteriorated globally. Nouriel Roubini described the effects on abandon: "The crisis was caused by the largest leveraged asset bubble and credit bubble in the history of humanity where excessive leveraging and bubbles were not limited to housing in the U.S. but also to housing in many other countries and excessive borrowing by financial institutions and some segments of the corporate sector and of the public sector in many and different economies: a housing bubble, a mortgage bubble, an equity bubble, a bond bubble, a credit bubble, a commodity bubble, a private equity bubble, a hedge funds bubble are all now bursting at once in the biggest real estate sector and financial sector deleveraging since the Great Depression."[27]

In 2006 it was still possible to marvel at the "Mind-boggling growth in derivatives."[28] Simple derivatives can be a practical commitment to a future act: say, to buy or sell a crop at an agreed price. The contract in effect uses leverage to "buy" time and stability. The new generation of "high-tech" derivatives used intricate mathematical formulas to justify greatly expanded leverage by creating networks of counter-parties that would insure the values in a given deal. This made it possible for banks and shadow banks to bundle and resell through tax-exempt conduits contracts of unaccountable soundness involving a multitude of participants. Collecting rich fees and bonuses at every step, the banks mixed dubious mortgage debt into sanitary packages for global resale. [29] So fatally opaque and feverish was the repackaging process that incompetent or dodgy records eventually put many failed mortgages in limbo. By 2010 the uncollectible debt precipitated yet another crisis, called "foreclosuregate."

The scale of the derivatives bubble defied ordinary analysis. As in a Ponzi scheme, the expanding pyramids of counterparties seemed to guarantee ever-enlarging hypothetical value in the rosy beyond. With only $1.2 billion in equity J.P. Morgan controlled $91 trillion in derivatives.[30] As in junk finance, the parties kept transactions private, creating their own clearing agent so that the products and their web of derivative formulas bypassed market corroboration. In 2008 the Bank for International Settlements [BIS] estimated that the global Over the Counter derivatives market had grown almost 65 percent from $414.8 trillion (December 2006) to $683.7 trillion (June of 2008).

The new instruments promised to magnify the safety as well as the velocity and impact of credit. Lenders could "securitize" risk by arranging for counter-parties to guarantee loans, then repackaging and reinsuring them, distributing risk over the horizon. "By appearing to provide an interlocking safety net, derivatives had the unintended effect of encouraging more risk-taking. Investors loaded up on the mortgage-based investments, then bought 'credit-default swaps' to protect themselves against losses rather than putting aside large cash reserves." When real estate valuations slumped, the guarantors were caught up in a dizzying web of obligations magnified by feedback loops. The result was a whirlwind of losses. "Instead of dispersing risk, derivatives had amplified it."[31] Nominal wealth vaporized overnight.

The prestige of computer technology and mathematical models conditioned risk-analysis. All such machinery depends on the quality of the data fed into it, and the questions being asked. Wall Street's ratings agencies proved treacherously inept not because risk-analysis was impossible—if it was, they had a fiduciary obligation to sound a warning—but because they were swept up in, or played along with, the Street's profitable delirium.

Mystification penetrated to the world's central banks. In 1998, the master of "masters of the universe," Federal Reserve Chair Alan Greenspan, "had assured an annual meeting of the U.S. Securities Industry Association that 'Dramatic advances in computer and tele-communications technologies in recent years have enabled a broad unbundling of risks through innovative financial engineering. The financial instruments of a bygone era, common stocks and debt obligations, have been augmented by a vast array of complex hybrid financial products, which allow risks to be isolated, but which, in many cases, seemingly challenge human understanding.'"[32]

This equivocal celebration of technologies and admission of cognitive overload illustrates ideological contradictions of the post-Vietnam economy and influenced many areas of American culture. The effort to think "at the edge" recalls, for example, the oracular utterances of Defense Secretary Rumsfeld. Before the invasion of Iraq, in the diplomatic shadow play over Saddam's fabled weapons of mass destruction, Rumsfeld famously intoned: "Reports that say that something hasn't happened are always interesting to me, because as we know, there are known knowns; there are things we know we know. We also know there are known unknowns; that is to say we know there are some things we do not know. But there are also unknown unknowns—the ones we don't know we don't know."[33] The "unknown unknowns" seemed to refer to the menace of a terrorist surprise and to possible weapons of mass destruction. The utterance seemed to say that policy-makers such as Sec. Rumsfeld were cognizant that a successful terrorist attack could be unlikely and unexpected—like creative disruption in markets—and therefore called for similarly radical thinking in response. The formulation sounded like a meta-theory but proved to be Delphic and wholly inadequate to the realities of the administration's war on terrorism. As that "war" was revealing its failings in Iraq and Afghanistan in 2008, the economic crisis was unfolding at home. When Sec. Rumsfeld mused on his "known unknowns" remark in an interview (2014), Erroll Morris reported that "the verbal exchanges that followed provide an excursion into a world no less irrational, no less absurd, than the worlds Lewis Carroll created in *Alice in Wonderland.*"34

The link between the financial world and the Pentagon is psychological but also structural. Both take in investments and promise forms of insurance or "securitization." Their stupendous budgets calculate risk in order to turn the threat of "unknown unknowns" into positive gains. Financial engineering expanded on Wall Street as explosively as private and governmental security forces did after the 9-11 attacks. Yet as historians of empire remind us, sooner or later wealth and superpower dominance lead to the overconfidence that this book associates with the berserker's godlike conviction. As with financial leverage, a drive for peak power can become overextended and hypercritical, with panic on the downside. In this instance, like an overextended Wall Street bank with inadequate reserves, Rumsfeld undertook the invasion of Iraq with a technologically leveraged, mobile, but grossly undersized force that proved catastrophically inadequate.

In a bank run or a market crash or a battlefield rout, panic is contagious. The "unknown unknowns" show up in feedback dynamics that overwhelm everyday expectations. For example, Wall Street devised "dynamic portfolio insurance" to preempt severe losses in investor portfolios. The scheme laid out a series of "stop loss" orders based on algorithms that would progressively sell off shares in a portfolio if the market declined, limiting the investor's losses. But this proved to be a two-dimensional map of a three-dimensional world in the Black Monday crash of 1987, when feedback loops spawned a cascade of selling. The cascade is a metaphor for the nervous system flooding in panic. And the creaturely motive involved is fear of being wiped out: the terror of death.

In this root fear, financial leverage reveals its kinship to the leverage of weapons. When crisis struck in 2008, some commentators invoked berserk combat as an explanation. There were analogies to General Custer and to Victory Culture: "With its decision last week to pump an additional $1 trillion into the financial crisis, the government eliminated any doubt that the nation is on a wartime footing in the battle to shore up the economy. The strategy now…is essentially the win-at-any-cost approach previously adopted only to wage a major war. And that means no hesitation in pledging to spend previously almost unimaginable sums of money and running up federal budget deficits on a scale not seen since World War II."35 A "win-at-any-cost" battle on an "almost unimaginable" scale: this is berserk style's familiar edge of abandon. The next paragraph shudders with survival panic: "analysts warn that the nation's next financial crisis could come from the staggering cost of battling the current one." It needs to be said that this emergency spending went to save banks, not to stimulate the domestic economy wrecked by the banks' excesses.

The "almost unimaginable sums of money" echoes Greenspan's description of financial instruments that "seemingly challenge human understanding." Like weapons, financial bubbles have momentum and grow bigger and more potent. Like the arsenal of Wall Street derivatives, nuclear weapons reach a point at which they become imponderable and impractical.[36] The weaponization of space through "Star Wars" is practically infinite. For Warren Buffett, derivatives are financial weapons of mass destruction; for former Federal Reserve chair Paul Volcker, they are hydrogen bombs. Two of the wiser heads in finance recognized the link between the signature atom bomb of victory culture and the financial devices magnifying American capital to epochal ends at a time when American hegemony was under stress and the Bush administration was hyping the nuclear peril of Saddam's WMDs to justify its wars.

In combat, berserk frenzy is the ultimate gamble: suicidal failure or survival. The economic analogue is do-or-die gambling. "Everybody wanted to bet," said Bill Bonner. "Wall Street took 50% to 80% of all the profits." Financial sector growth was a bubble promoting bubbles. "Before 1987, only about one of every 10 dollars of corporate profits made its way to the financial industry—in payment for arranging financing, banking and other services. By the end of the bubble years, the cost of 'finance' had grown to more than 3 out of every 10 dollars. Total profits in the United States reached about $6 trillion [in 2007]; about $2 trillion was Wall Street's share. What happened to this money? Other industries use profits to build factors and create jobs. But the financial industry paid it out in salaries and bonuses—as much as $10 trillion during the whole Bubble Period."[37]

With house prices exploding beyond the reach of ordinary salaries, mortgage originators and buyers moved with berserk daring. The mortgage company HCE, for example, touted "Ninja" loans—No income, no job (and) no assets. The name attributes uncanny force to the lender, but also tries to allay the fears of borrowers too. One mortgage company commercial crowed that "if you own a home, and have a pulse you can get a home equity loan." In the frenzy some banks fudged legal documentation, precipitating an echo bust when they tried to foreclose on distressed properties in 2010. The

Chicago Tribune's Mary Umberger warned that "Real-estate insanity is becoming the norm in Florida" (June 15, 2005). But of course if everyone is insane, then nobody is. And in any event, "insanity" here is a euphemism for predatory behavior. The outcome was an epic wave of foreclosures couched in berserk style. One headline asked, "As Foreclosure Nightmares Increase, Will More Homeowners Pay Off Their Bankers in Violence?" The news story itself opened with a form of threat display: "The economic crisis revealed late-capitalism's central offense: Human beings are being transparently treated if they were mere transactions. And they're going postal over it."[38]

MAKING A KILLING

The term "Ninja loan" conflates economic aggressiveness with combat and imagines leverage as an unorthodox heroic weapon. As berserk style, the term manages to be witty, satirical, and yet serious too. In one direction the Ninja fantasy looks to the culture of aggressive, underhanded entrepreneurs such as the junk finance buccaneers jailed in the 1980s or the Ponzi swindler Bernard Madoff. In the opposite direction the fantasy evokes the alienated employees, usually armed like Rambo, who have carried out the rash of workplace rampages that began in the 1980s.

The workplace rampages roared into the news just as the *New York Times* was openly deploring the "battlefield of business" strewn with "millions of casualties" in 1996.[39] The journalists' trope was an echo of the Vietnam War, which had left the nation in a decade-long slump after "capitalism's" costly clash with "Communism." The ideology that accompanied economic recovery celebrated combative "lean and mean" competition, creative destruction, outsourcing, and workforce triage. By the 1990s, labor faced relentless rustbelt triage and serious loss of union protection, while "captains of industry" were beginning to command record-breaking wealth. As Steven Greenhouse has shown, to reduce labor costs, more than a few businesses brazenly abused employees, deliberately subverting New Deal labor guarantees while shrinking health and retirement benefits.[40] By 2011, the campaign to maximize control over labor reached an unexpectedly heated showdown in Wisconsin when massive crowds protested Republican legislation designed to strip public workers of their historic right to a union.

On the "battlefield of business," stress began running amok as the new ideology took command in the 1980s. The Vietnam vet John

Rambo (Sylvester Stallone) naively dramatized the transition to the new era in 1982 by grieving that ""Back there [in Vietnam] I could fly a gunship. I could drive a tank. I was in charge of million-dollar equipment. Back here I can't even hold a job parkin' cars."[41] In Ted Kotcheff's *First Blood* the unemployed warrior and parking valet attendant faces social death. His best friend's death from the effects of Agent Orange leaves him the sole survivor of his unit. When local police bully him, Rambo resists with a sensational one-man guerrilla war against the town authorities, anticipating the fired workers and unemployed vets who made headlines in the 1980s and 1990s by "going postal."[42] His grief, alienation, and subjugation reproduced in civilian life the explosive disturbance that sent soldiers amok in Vietnam, and especially in attacks on their own officers (fragging). The screenwriters give Rambo post-traumatic flashbacks that continue the war on the American home front.

The *New York Times* study of rampage killing (April 8, 2000) found that while 26 percent of typical murderers were unemployed, the number rises to 57 percent among rampage killers.[43] In a culture that organizes identity around work and equates executive success with heroism, this is no surprise. Like Rambo, about half of rampage killers in the U. S. have had military training; many suffer symptoms of mental illness as he does. As in warfare, to be a loser means to face a form of death. Hence the pattern of wearing fatigues and hefting an arsenal of military-style weapons, as if anticipating the usual climactic battle with paramilitary SWAT police.

As John Kenneth Galbraith once remarked, American CEOs see themselves as generals commanding armies on the battlefield of business. In the 1980s business culture emphasized berserk style to repudiate postwar softness and glorify an uncompromising will to win. Management shelves featured books with titles such as *Leadership Secrets of Attila the Hun* (1987) and Robert Ringer's *Winning through Intimidation* (1973), which made threat display central in business and urged a gladiatorial recognition of "the certainty that you will die...so you might as well make the most of your one shot at life." Ringer formulated a classic berserk principle, his "Ice Ball Theory," according to which "it is ridiculous to take yourself too seriously because in the long run, nothing makes any difference; one day, the earth will be a lifeless ice ball."

The new generation of MBA slogans such as "no pain, no gain" and "lean and mean" fused martial ideas of purifying discipline and sacrifice with the implicit violence of "cutting," "shedding," "burning fat," or "downsizing" a bloated body. Just as eating disorders became a preoccupation in the 1980s and 90s, so downsizing became a form of corporate anorexia. In both behaviors, sacrifice and pain fuel convictions of perfectibility. Implicit is the economy of sacrificial killing, as in the Chicago School adage that "you can't make an omelet without breaking eggs." The complementary trope was body-building and the luxury fitness gym to service executive and corporate muscle. Business and the Pentagon shrank the workforce while looking to technology, rapid response, and pumped up morale to achieve exceptional results.

In squeezing labor through triage and givebacks, management was maximizing leverage to "get the most out of" workers. The core idea, as in berserk abandon, is that people have a reservoir of extra energy that can be tapped. Labor experienced the squeeze as stress. Like the speeded-up assembly line in Chaplin's *Modern Times* (1936), which leads the Tramp to run amok and shoot the boss with squirts of oil, the new workplace began to suffer episodes of rampage killing.

In ratcheting up survival anxiety to motivate the workforce in the 1980s, business culture praised Social Darwinism. In a glossy pamphlet called *New Work Habits for a Radically Changing World,* for example, the aptly named business guru Price Pritchett argues that business is war. "Examine the corporate body count over the last dozen years or so," he commands. "What you'll find is that 'slow' kills companies. And that, of course, means the death of many careers." Presumably including yours and mine. Mr. Pritchett tries to soften this death-threat by explaining that organizations *must* "travel light" and sacrifice anyone who can't keep up. "These are not casual moves or random acts dreamed up by bored or heartless top executives. What you're witnessing are raw survival instincts at work. Organizations *must* accelerate, or they will die" (p. 10).

Pritchett's pamphlet honors violence—"raw survival instincts"— and a hierarchy with the fittest—the most violent—at the top. There is no social contract in this business culture. The "bottom line" can take you out at any time, for any reason, with no recourse. If you can never feel safe and never trust others to behave in a rationally predictable way, then you are likely to experience what John Bowlby calls "disconfirmation" of your feelings, and to suffer symptoms that Bowlby associates with trauma.

As a trope, the battlefield of business established an atmosphere in which thwarted expectations of security created stress. If disconfirmation becomes too severe, the effect is alienation. To feel hopelessly misunderstood is to feel crazy as well as socially dead. The classic modern trope for this is the revolt of cyborgs. The speeded up assembly line, for instance, reduces Chaplin's tramp to a spastic mechanism: a robot. As the soldier is enslaved in the "war machine," so laborers are tacitly—and in American history literally—enslaved on the battlefield of business.[44] Today the cyborg mutiny is a staple of futuristic fiction. Robot or cyborg revolts routinely storm across the mental landscape of modernity, while masters aggrandize themselves by consuming the slave's will and vitality.

President Reagan's dissolution of the air traffic controllers' union (PATCO) in 1981 was the opening salvo in a new campaign to subdue labor. Forty-eight hours after issuing an ultimatum, he fired 11,350 controllers. AFL-CIO president Lane Kirkland saw berserk style in this "harsh and brutal overkill."[45] In years since, employers have seriously crippled organized labor. For a time *New Yorker* cartoons regularly satirized bosses who, like Sunbeam's "Chainsaw Al" Dunlap, "slashed" payrolls. The deep metaphor is eugenics: culling the weak from the herd. Often it has sadistic, paramilitary overtones, as in this analysis of "What Went Wrong with the Business-Process Reengineering Fad," which evokes a death march: "In re-engineering, we carry the wounded and shoot the stragglers."[46]

This is the atmosphere in which "going postal" emerged as a recognizable syndrome in 1983. In one *New Yorker* cartoon (January 27, 1997), an executive says to a manager: "We've got to get rid of some people, Cosgrove. Who are the least likely to come back and shoot us?" The cartoon's language ("get rid of some people") has mafia echoes, and the fear of retaliation implies gang warfare. While executive culture praised strategy and planning, the deep trope of survival violence rationalized anxiously aggressive responses to the specter of rising global competition. To maintain its standard of living in the 1980s, a typical U. S. household now required two wage earners. "Making a killing" began to look like a killing spree at the top, since income increased from 1997 to 2007 mostly for corporations and the very rich. For the average family, income stagnated and insecurity about health care, unemployment, and retirement intensified.[47]

THE EXECUTIVE DREAM

Some powerful trends came together in the bubble decades. Free market ideology reinforced belief in executive vision and rewards. Valuations seemed to be perpetually rising. Abundance seemed to be free for the taking, needing only entrepreneurial daring and disregard for petty inhibitions. Instead of tedious labor, the bubble celebrated force-multiplying derivatives and bonuses. In one direction the mentality is related to dreams of slavery, in which non-persons magnify the will of a master. In the bubble decades the executive will used cheap labor abroad to keep wages and workers' rights depressed at home. The vision of cheap labor coincided with the promise of breakthrough management theories and cybernetic innovations that gave new life to the utopian industrial dream of total automation.

As the nation deindustrialized in the 1980s, business culture wanted to abandon old prejudices and emulate new practices, from Japanese just-in-time management models to the latest incarnations of Taylorism. Total Quality Management (TQM) dressed up the older factory mentality while locking workers into a script the way command subsumes the combat soldier. While efficiency demands discipline and order, TQM dressed up venerable ideas such as interchangeable parts, making the controlling script more important than the individual worker. Despite its mockery of Soviet-style central planning, autocratic capitalism shared some of the same dynamics. In Warren Bennis's quip, "The factory of the future will have only two employees, a man and a dog. The man will be there to feed the dog. The dog will be there to keep the man from touching the equipment."

This factory is striking not for its automation, but as an elite immortality fantasy—a self-contained and bountiful entity with no human limitations: a perpetual motion machine. Yet the fantasy also embodies the seeds of workplace rampage. The working "man" exists only to serve the dog, who polices the man to prevent him from touching—taking a share in, "getting a feel for," or lashing out at—the exquisite machine. For management and owner, this is an *Atlas Shrugged* fantasy of total self-creation. No regulations, labor demands, or competition mar the dream. It is timely, too, since it reflects the sudden preeminence of the private security sector, and has an eerie echo of Alabama police dogs in Civil Rights protests and in the famous Abu Ghraib photos of guard dogs baring fangs at prisoners locked out of jobs and family.

Granted, Bennis's model is supposed to be witty, and most businesses do not station fangs at the office watercooler. Even so, the model takes for granted that a hostile, invisible autocracy owns and runs things. But after the meltdown of 2008, it can be applied to the financialization of the American economy. The factory that once relied on a workforce to manufacture goods such as cars became the unaccountable banking machine taking 40 percent of all profits. The banking machine facilitated the transfer of production to low-wage countries, the consumption of cheap imports, and the indebtedness of now-underemployed workers struggling with usurious credit card debt.

Like Bennis's machine, the financial complex is perversely autonomous insofar as it feeds on the resources that pass through it. The American worker is "there to feed the dog"—guarding the inaccessible machinery. In real life the dog is the hugely hungry corporate military and private security industry that protects the American financial factory around the world. The system that Bennis describes is "autocyclic" in economic terms: it feeds on itself, without oversight. In social terms it relies on threat (the dog) to subdue challenges. In Bennis's witticism what looks like a model of invincible stability is powered by berserk style.

America's great mythic factories rolled out cars. When Chrysler and General Motors suffered bankruptcy in 2009, it shook the nation's self-image. Critics blamed globalization, unionized labor and its legacy benefits, stultified planning, and out-of-touch executives who arrived in private jets to ask Congress for bailouts. Less often noted were characteristics of berserk style. In a parody of the Bennis factory, Detroit had long fixated on the beyond: on more cars, bigger cars, with grandiose tailfins and incalculable prestige. Ads placed the cars on a vast mesa, at a swanky resort, among the stars. The industry moved toward the model of a self-contained machine. When fuel prices spiked and the economy slumped in 2008, GM was still fixated on producing inappropriate new SUVs, the most profitable product in company history. As the industry sent production abroad, it shifted to finance. As the joke has it, Detroit only produced cars in order to collect interest on their sales.[48]

The joke identifies a complement to the autonomous factory: rentier economics. Like a bank, GM's financial arm GMAC would skim off interest and fees rather than manufacture things. Yet the fantasy of executive wealth depends on the continued decline of the median wage, and that creates an impoverished workforce and an economy starved for demand. In the slump that followed the 2008 crisis, the nation needed a tamed bubble to stimulate the demand necessary for recovery. In the U.S. as in Europe, however, cries for austerity reinforced executive visions rather than languishing demand.

These are cultural as well as systemic problems. In the Great Depression, Chaplin satirized them in *Modern Times* (1936), which defines the corporation as a machine amok. In the film the factory is always pushing the limits of control, striving for more product even as hunger oppresses the city outside. The Tramp is virtually enslaved on the job, and in one iconic scene devoured by the machinery. His boss is a Henry Ford lookalike who polices workers through an Orwellian telescreen, evoking Ford's company police spies and also the enthusiasm of American industrialists in the 1930s for Nazi controls on labor.[49] The boss personifies the corporation, but in the telescreen he is part of the machine, the more unaccountable because—like advertisements showing Henry Ford's face hovering in a sunburst above his plant—he is also godlike. Spying on the Tramp in the bathroom, the telescreen intrudes on his inner life like the voice of God, as if the Tramp suffers from PTSD.

The point is, the factory is so demanding that it is incipiently amok. When the boss tries to eliminate a lunch break by having a machine feed the Tramp on the job, the robot arm runs wild. It becomes a crazed parent cramming bolts down the throat of a helpless man. Later, as the assembly line accelerates, the Tramp's body goes into autonomic rebellion, perseverating as in the tics of shellshock. In his subsequent rampage the Tramp travesties beastlike and godlike fury as he swings over everyone's head like a monkey, "kills" the plant's power, and "shoots" fellow workers and the boss with squirts from an oil can. With bitter memories of the four demonstrators gunned down at the Ford Rouge plant several years before in 1932, played out in the clash of police and the unemployed in the film, the satire seethes with injustice. At one point during the Depression, Henry Ford's mansion had a machine gun emplacement for security. Then in 1937, following a riot described as "the Battle of the Running Bulls," auto workers occupied the GM factory in Flint Michigan and forced the negotiations that established the United Auto Workers.

Modern Times disenchants the self-serving assumption that the berserker goes crazy while the reasonable world looks on. Society itself is the "battlefield of business." Although elite management and workers are in conflict, they share a common fear of the ultimate enemy—deprivation, emptiness, and death—which fuels the frenzy of manufacture and policing in the first place. As Chaplin's plot illustrates, the chronic stress in society keeps the individual's symptoms from resolving. The tramp caroms from one disaster to another, with no time to recover his equilibrium.

There is a General Motors advertising film of 1936 entitled "Precisely So " which depicts the factory as a seemingly autonomous machine. At its climax a formation of animated tools marches into the camera. The tools—calipers, slide rules, and the like—are robots, more efficient and disciplined than human craftsmen. Precisely so. The tools replace human workers, anticipating the automation to come. The boss is a gauge that commands the march from an elevated dais like the Nuremburg rally filmed in Leni Reifenstahl's *Triumph of the Will* (1935). The tools parade to the triumphal march from Tchaikovsky's *Pathetique* Symphony, that most tragic—and inappropriate—of laments. The conversion of despair to a triumphal march is the 1930s fascist solution to the Depression. In its final moments the march cuts to an endless stream of identical new cars that rush out of the factory towards the consumer-viewer, cycled by trick photography in an endless, accelerating loop. As if self-created, the cars assault the viewer like robots, coming faster and faster, with berserk, orgasmic force.

Even as it pumped up morale during the Depression, promising greater personal freedom, the onslaught of cars in the advertisement signals an alarming loss of autonomy. The incarnations of consumer desire look and behave like military machines in a frontal assault. The factory shoves cars into the viewer's face like the feeding machine assaulting the Tramp.

Paradoxically, the production mania was self-defeating insofar as overproduction and underconsumption helped to bring on the Depression in the first place. With incomes skewed to the top, wages sinking, and consumers unable to buy the goods pouring into a glutted marketplace, the economy deflated. Henry Ford was able to give his son Edsel a million dollars in gold for a birthday present even as he was forcing down wages.

During World II the automakers prospered as defense contractors. And the ties persisted, as in Ford CEO Robert McNamara's service as secretary of defense during the Vietnam War. Thereafter, confronted by foreign competition, Detroit joined in the frenzy of deindustrialization: outsourcing, downsizing, concentrating on product lines such as the burly SUV. The strategy was corporate streamlining but also a kind of survival rage, and after the misery chronicled in Michael Moore's *Roger and Me* (1989), it climaxed in bankruptcy and government bailout.

Moore's film opens with archival footage of postwar parades and advertising that defined General Motors as a family. In effect, CEO

Roger Smith is the absentee father of the corporate family. Downsizing the company, he made many destitute orphans of GM's "children," shrugged off corporate responsibility, and rebuffed pleas for help.[50] Unemployed workers suddenly found themselves infantilized and helpless. Like Chaplin's Tramp, Moore's friend Ben suffered a breakdown in the factory and took refuge in a mental health center. In search of work, families migrated—fled—as they did during the Dust Bowl crisis and as the Tramp and the girl do at the close of *Modern Times.*

The corporation cultivated doublethink, exuding executive calm yet acting out survival panic, with minimal safeguards for the casualties. In the early stages the mass layoffs had the impact of a massacre. As Flint Michigan reeled in shock, squalor crippled the city. Abandoned housing fell to ruin. Sanitation and public services failed. Crime set records, and in a familiar mix of profit and panic, misallocated resources went into a new high tech prison in which former auto workers would guard their former line mates. In a telling incident a mentally disturbed black man in a Superman cape squats in the street with a shotgun, bent on rescuing the city until police marksmen shoot to disable him. He uses the form of a workplace rampage in a futile effort at heroism. Hauled off to an ambulance like the Tramp in *Modern Times,* the deranged Superman acts out the communal loss of control.

The counterattack against decay turned to public relations: psywar. Paternalistic government sponsored discount entertainment, celebrity pep talks, and consoling postwar nostalgia. On camera the singer Anita Bryant gushes Reagan and Thatcher nostrums about "a great new day" until she abruptly runs out of clichés, stammers, and the interview collapses. In time, the city tried to rebrand itself as a tourist destination, featuring a glitzy but doomed high-rise hotel and a new mall with a nostalgic museum depicting Flint in its automotive heyday and a GM version of Disneyworld featuring an animated mannequin auto worker singing "Me and my buddy" to the robot replacing him on the assembly line. The propaganda sought to manage morale by converting fight to flight—to migration and escapism.

For many audiences the definitive berserk trope in *Roger and Me* is the behavior of the unemployed Rhonda Britton, who sells rabbits for "pets or meat," and on camera kills one of the animals for sale by bludgeoning it with a pipe. "I was raised to be a survivor," she explains. The rabbits have to be slaughtered early in life, before overcrowding leads the males to gnaw one another's genitals. The animals' castrating survival competition and the woman's planned triage are a parable of the local effects of global capitalism. The trapped, determined survivor skins the rabbit before the camera, emptying out its organs as houses are being gutted, children evicted, and lives consumed around her.

The film's conclusion recapitulates the symbolic logic. As Roger Smith broadcasts a Christmas message to GM employees "around the world," a fatherly figure at a pulpit-like lectern, supported by a choir of children, the film cuts back and forth to an eviction in Flint in which bewildered toddlers watch their panicky young mother rage at Deputy Sheriff Fred Ross. Death-anxiety is in the air. The sheriff instructs a prison trusty moving out the family's belongings to lay the family Christmas tree down in the snow "or else the wind gon' blow it away." The soundtrack plays a novelty version of "Jingle Bells" featuring barking dogs that might evoke the guard dog policing the worker in Bennis's ideal factory.

Then Roger Smith recites a line from Dickens about Christmas as a time of unqualified generosity and love. Then with bizarre, unwitting irony the choir sings "Here Comes Santa Claus," whose lyrics depict menacing paternalism:

> You better watch out, you better not cry,
> You better not pout, I'm telling you why:
> Santa Claus is coming to town.
> He knows when you are sleeping,
> He knows when you're awake
> He knows when you are bad or good,
> So be good for goodness' sake.

The choral arrangement ends with a witty warning, a shouted "Watch out!" By association Santa Claus is the callous father Roger Smith and the kindly Deputy Sheriff Fred who executes evictions.[51] Spying on the sleeping and waking, Santa is also the all-seeing factory boss, the Big Brother who polices the Tramp via the telescreen as he sneaks a break in the men's room. The song reinforces the infantilization of those dependent on the company with a warning not to complain or misbehave. To be "good," the displaced workforce needed to abandon Flint and reinvent itself elsewhere; to be "bad," radically bad, would be to storm murderously through the workplace.[52]

During the 2008 smashup, the executive dream itself seemed to be amok. Jim Kingsdale turned to rampage imagery to describe the ambivalence aroused by the sight of auto executives flying in to

Washington in private jets to beg for corporate bailouts: "Cars cause America's 'oil addiction' which in turn has caused so much of America's balance of payments and foreign policy and military pains—with no end in sight." Government help would be a do-or-die gamble: "There's no currently discernable [sic] path to profitability for G.M. and Chrysler and thus no exit strategy for the bailout funds they need." At which point the critic makes a connection to the "war on terror": "So G.M. and Chrysler are like suicide terrorists wandering around the business community threatening to blow up both themselves and everyone else in the room. Nobody knows whether to feed them or shoot them."[53]

Who would pull the trigger? Berserk style attributed that role to Treasury Secretary Paulson, who "gets to decide who lives and who dies. The former investment banker from Goldman Sachs would be empowered as treasury secretary to be savior or grim reaper, the liquidator who essentially pulls the plug on some banks and financial firms or the man who rescues them from ruin."[54] Said Anatole Kaletsky: "Mr Paulson fired what he himself described as his financial 'bazooka'—and vaporised the shareholders of Fannie Mae."[55] The image sees the Treasury Secretary as a berserk soldier or a mafia executioner with the power of life or death. Feminists might rightly point out that this is implicitly a patriarchal fantasy.

In the event, bailouts did revitalize GM and Chrysler, though Flint and Detroit suffered epic squalor with no place to go.[56] Congressional demands for austerity during the weak and for a time jobless recovery wrangled over unemployment benefits and food stamps (SNAP) for the poor, as if the politicians couldn't decide whether to "feed them or shoot them." Santa Claus did fulfill the executive dream in some quarters. In "Meanwhile Back in the Wall St. Bonus Pool," Teresa Tritch writes: "A new report drives home just how excessive Wall Street bonuses are" (*NY Times*, March 14, 2015).

In berserk style the dream of executive heroism finds expression in radically ambivalent images from Santa to the warrior and the rampage killer amok. As berserk style, It looks back to the previous chapter on the "war on terror," but it also anticipates the next chapter's concern with crime, secrecy, and masks. "Psychologists concluded that, for a variety of reasons, the larger the number of observing bystanders, the lower the chances that the crime may be averted. We have just witnessed a similar phenomenon in the financial markets. A crime has been committed. Yes, we insist, a crime. There is a victim (the helpless retirees, taxpayers funding losses, perhaps even capitalism and free society). There were plenty of bystanders. And there was a robbery (overcompensated bankers who got fat bonuses hiding risks; overpaid quantitative risk managers selling patently bogus methods)."[57]

"A crime has been committed." There were individual criminals such as Attorney Marc S. Dreier and former Nasdaq chair Bernard Madoff, whose Ponzi scheme fleeced investors of $50 billion or so.[58] But the indictment above faces up to the crime's social and cultural frame. Although they never anticipated a Ponzi scheme, many of Madoff's more astute victims suspected him of crooked insider trading all along since his inexplicably superior returns implied something fishy.

But that's why they trusted their money to him.

CHAPTER 5

BOOTY AND THE BEAST

[The] American capital markets are a crime in progress.

　　　　　Matt Taibi, Rolling Stone, *October 14, 2009*

*Drugs money worth billions of dollars kept the financial
system afloat at the height of the global crisis, the United
Nations' drugs and crime tsar has told The Observer.*

　　　　　The Observer, *December 13, 2009*

*The hidden hand of the market will never
work without a hidden fist.*

　　　　　Thomas Friedman

Ordinarily we are disposed to see a naturally stable social order punctuated by crime. In the mania of a bubble economy, by contrast, berserk style naturalizes shady behavior. Rules stretch; inhibitions soften; the scale and pace of activity makes eyes water. In 2008, the Enron collapse betrayed what critics would come to call a "criminogenic environment" in business culture. Before long the FBI was warning of an "epidemic of mortgage fraud" (December 14, 2005). Three years later, *The Wall Street Examiner* reported on "Berserker

Funds in Commodities" that had been exploiting "a "'cash is trash' crack up boom speculative mentality," participating in "bubble blowing and crash cycles that have gone on for more than a decade."[1] In 2008. according to the Treasury Department's Financial Crimes Enforcement Network, over 730,000 "suspicious-activity reports" were recorded in America, roughly a tenfold increase from 1997. By then American banks were demanding taxpayer infusions to withstand implosion, and though prosecutors would eventually fine major institutions for criminal offenses, regulation would remain lax and nobody would go to prison. By 2014, Bank of America settled $16.65 billion in charges that it misled investors in its mortgage-backed securities: "the largest such settlement on record," according to the U.S. Attorney General, and part of at least $65 billion in outlays for faulty mortgage instruments.

This chapter examines that criminal contagion as an expression of cultural fantasies shaping behavior in and beyond the boardroom. Specifically, it reconsiders the antisocial character of some powerful post-Vietnam economic motives, and a competitive style of journalistic invective that reflects a generational change in business commentary.[2]

In boom times it is easy to overlook the role of survival concerns in economic behavior. But greed is greed for life, and can infect even euphoric success. The underlying survival rage stands out more clearly when prosperity falters, as in the violence that accompanied the banking crisis of 2008. "More and more experts attribute the rise in crime in recent months to the dire state of the economy. 'I've never seen such a large number [of killings] over such a short period of time involving so many victims,' Jack Levin, a professor of criminology at Northeastern University in Boston, told the *Washington Post*."[3] The number of stress-related workplace suicides also jumped.[4] As awareness of the downturn took hold, media shock jocks played up frightening stories about social unrest featuring stockpiled canned goods and guns.

The Enron fiasco dramatized how easily complexity could baffle and seduce auditors, ratings agencies, and government watchdogs. Wall Street banking executives operated behind banks of computers and esoteric math—who would have predicted that algorithms or "algos" would become routine jargon?—mystifying responsibility. William Black argues that the financial sector deliberately creates recurrent financial bubbles. The bubbles make possible what he calls accounting "control frauds," which "are seemingly-legitimate entities used by the people that control them as fraud 'weapons.' In the financial sector, accounting frauds are the weapons of choice. The financial industry's power and progressive corruption combined to produce the perfect white-collar crimes."[5]

A "bubble" sounds compact and integral, but the analogy is deceptive. In the housing "epidemic," the FBI was trying to cope with a "decentralized criminal conspiracy" that implicated "many with actual criminal records, whose entry into the mortgage industry was in no way hindered by the state regulatory agencies. They proceeded to amass fortunes large and small, using the same techniques familiar from previous financial scandals—pressurized sales techniques; targeting of the weak, elderly and insecure; outright fraud, forgery and deception."[6] In Florida, according to the Miami *Herald*, more than ten thousand convicted criminals entered the mortgage business, roughly four thousand of them as licensed brokers. "According to law enforcement experts, drug dealers often became [house] flippers, in order to launder money."[7] The subculture of cooperative deception is nicely exemplified by the mortgage industry's "liar loans."

In vain critics railed against "the unprecedented bingeing of the financial markets." They warned that "the global credit boom was nothing more than a massive pyramid scheme that is now toppling like a house of cards in a stiff breeze," outraged that profits "are being disgorged in a violently abrupt fashion [that] threatens the financial system as we know it" with "financial Armageddon."[8]

Decades of complaints reached a crescendo. As savings, pensions, and job security shriveled, public voices reached for images of radical violence. David Walker, the U. S. Comptroller General, saw terrorism in the nation's financial abandon: "I would argue that the most serious threat to the United States is not someone hiding in a cave in Afghanistan or Pakistan but our own fiscal irresponsibility."[9] He could have pointed out that just before the 9/11 attack unnamed players made a killing in options that bet the airlines' stocks would fall.

MAFIA BUSINESS

This chapter uses mafia with a lower case "m" to investigate ways in which berserk style shapes American fantasies about criminal business. Mafia is a particular historical entity, but also shorthand for the tendency of economic units to coalesce in gangs that use coercion and deception to do business. Used as a thought experiment, mafia foregrounds the atavistic roles of family, tribe, and warrior band that persist in modern business organization. Informal corruption such as cronyism is more likely than dedicated Mafia to rationalize unethical behavior, but both modes presuppose some "specialness" that excepts them from the rigors of law and fair play.

Mafia shows up regularly in business writing to indict shady behavior, as in this complaint: "The SEC has forgotten its investigation role, ever since ex-Wall Street heads have been in control of the commission. That is like hiring ex-Mafia dons to run a police force."[10] One journalist compared Wall Street's connivance at government bailouts in 2008 to the mafia practice of torching an asset for the insurance money.[11]

As loan sharks and surreptitious investors, mafias function as banks. Credit card issuers are infamous for usurious interest rates and their pressure on government to close off debtors' relief through bankruptcy. It could be argued that the speculative banking system and the Federal Reserve's nominal godfather "Easy Al" Greenspan invited the nation to go for broke with borrowed money. When the loans went bad, the broken bones and murders that mafia usually inflicts took the form of unemployment, bankruptcies, foreclosures, and social death. At the same time the bankers' collusion with government recouped the lost money from taxpayers in so-called bailouts, even as godfather CEOs scooped up obscene "bonuses."[12]

Before he was routed from office in a prostitution scandal reminiscent of a Hollywood movie, New York Governor Eliot Spitzer attacked "predatory lending" whose scale was "widely understood to present a looming national crisis" in which the Bush administration was allegedly colluding with the crooks.[13] As late as 2014, prosecutors were still fining banks for withholding critical information about the quality of the bonds they were selling. So many mortgages and bond packages were legally defective that futile attempts to foreclose when they failed resulted in a scandal dubbed "Foreclosuregate" after President ("I am not a crook") Nixon.

In the absence of meaningful regulation, hype ruled the airwaves. Speaking of Angelo Mozilo's Countrywide Financial in 2011, F.T.C. chairman Jon Leibowitz called it "astonishing that one single company could be responsible for overcharging more than 450,000 homeowners, which is more than 1 percent of all the mortgages in the United States." The company's business model was "based on deceit and corruption, and the harm they caused to American consumers is absolutely massive and extraordinary." In an interview with the Financial Crisis Inquiry Commission in 2010, however, Mr. Mozilo "described Countrywide as having prevented social unrest in the United States by extending loans to minorities, historically the victims of discrimination. 'Countrywide was one of the greatest companies in the history of this country,' Mr. Mozilo told the commission, 'and probably made more difference to society, to the integrity of our society, than any company in the history of America.'"[14] The audacity of the lie defied all grounds for criticism.

In a lawsuit against major banks the mayor of Cleveland contended that "the companies irresponsibly bought and sold high-interest home loans to people who had "no realistic means of keeping up with their loan payments," resulting in defaults that depleted the city's tax base and left entire neighborhoods in ruins, the *Cleveland Plain-Dealer* reported. The mayor compared the lenders' behavior to "organized crime....It has the same effect as drug activity in neighborhoods."[15]

The mayor sees the finance industry as a mode of organized crime enticing victims to gamble. Exorbitant rates allowed credit card companies to target customers whose interest charges kept them in debt peonage. In James Scurlock's documentary film *Maxed Out,* the manager of a debt collection agency brags that he "like[s] to make the analogy that you're like this pirate on this pirate ship, right? And you got this person and you're walking them out on the plank, and you walk them as far out as you can go without pushing them off. And then you bring them back to get what you want." This is classic mafia use of berserk style intimidation.

Operating on the edge, mafias are able to exploit creaturely ambivalence. Society's respectable Dr. Jekylls prowl the night as Edward Hyde. Mafias exploit that doublethink by devising an underworld whose drugs, sex, and gambling invert the virtues of Main Street. In effect, they market berserk play as a commodity, selling an experience of desperate conviction, making illicit ecstasy and rage available to customers toiling in the workaday grind. Mob playgrounds such as old Havana or Las Vegas mimic Cony Island or Disneyland.

"International affairs," says Noam Chomsky, "is very much run like the mafia. The godfather does not accept disobedience, even from a small storekeeper who doesn't pay his protection money. You have to have obedience otherwise the idea can spread that you don't have to listen to the orders and it can spread to important places."[16] After Venezuela nationalized assets of Exxon Mobil in 2007, President Hugo Chavez bristled. "The outlaws of Exxon Mobil will never again rob us," he vowed, claiming that the oil major colludes with "the imperialist government of the United States" as part of "worldwide mafias."[17] Similarly, Vice President Cheney asserted that control over energy pipelines is a mafia-style "tool of intimidation and blackmail."

Globalization moves business offshore, beyond national laws, into the traditional zone of piracy. Sociologist Zygmundt Bauman deems this an outbreak of berserking: "A most spectacular and potentially sinister consequence of the erratic globalizing processes, uncontrolled and running wild as they have been thus far, is...the progressive 'criminalization of the globe and globalization of crime.... Never before were the mafias so numerous, powerful, well-armed, and prosperous.'"[18] The central fact of globalization, says Richard Rorty, is that "[t]he economic situation of the citizens of a nation state has passed beyond the control of the laws of the state." No country's laws can any longer govern money flows because "we now have a global overclass which makes all the major economic decisions," beyond the reach of legislatures and voters. "The absence of a global polity means that the super-rich can operate without any thought of any interests save their own."[19] To this Bauman adds: "If this is...the 'central fact of globalization,' then the genuine issue is not so much the 'globalization of crime,' as deBernard says, but the annulment of the distinction between 'legal and illegal' which only an abiding and enforceable law may draw. There is no such global law to violate. There is no global law in operation that could permit the setting apart of mafia-style criminal pursuits from 'normal business activity'" (64–65).

Like the berserk state, then, mafia can be viewed as a trope for processes that annul the distinction between legal and illegal. From fraudulent contracts to money laundering involving major banks, mafia dissolves conventional boundaries or "firewalls." A federal prosecutor summed up a case involving Wachovia the bank's "blatant disregard for our banking laws gave international cocaine cartels a virtual carte blanche to finance their operations."[20] Yet the bank was allowed to settle out of court for a total fine of less than 2 percent of the bank's $12.3bn profit for 2009.[21] According to the *State of the Future* survey by the World Federation of United Nations Associations, international organized crime is a "$2 trillion threat to the world's security" since "Billions of dollars worth of bribes paid each year go into the pockets of public officials in rich countries."[22] Says the *Guardian*, "The annual taking of criminal gangs around the world are roughly equivalent to Britain's GDP, or twice the world's combined defence budgets. Half of that amount is paid as bribes, which tend to make the rich and powerful even wealthier. The 225 richest people on the planet now earn the same as the poorest 2.7bn, equivalent to 40% of humankind."[23]

Globalized scale, secrecy, and corporate penetration of government erode distinctions and frustrate accountability. What emerges is the hybrid corporate state and corporate military. As whistle-blowers keep signaling, revolving doors and collusion are everywhere in Washington. Intensifying J. P. Morgan's incestuous role in government, Goldman Sachs executives such as Robert Rubin and Hank Paulson have run the U.S. Treasury for many years.[24] Military officers regularly retire to the executive suites of defense contractors and hire out as expert news commentators, while defense contractors operate as government policy advisors. Journalist Bill Moyers, among others, has worried about a "Secret Government"—a tacit mafia within the constitutional government in Washington.[25]

With the help of the Supreme Court's "Citizens United" decision (2009), today's equivalent of Gilded Age robber barons can lawfully use unlimited corporate money to influence elections in perfect secrecy. In treating corporations as persons and stressing First Amendment protection of free speech, the Court blurred traditional definitions of political corruption.[26] For journalists, the idea of conspiratorial wealth in politics evokes pulp fiction. For the 2012 elections, the Koch Brothers convened a "Super-Secret Billionaires' Meeting… cloaked in secrecy. Helicopters, private security and police officers from neighboring cities patrolled the area constantly. In previous years, Supreme Court justices, some of the wealthiest businessmen in the country and Republican politicians like Congressman Paul Ryan have all gathered at these twice-annual events. The Esmerelda Renaissance, the conference venue this year, was guarded carefully with every entrance blocked and the entire 560-room resort rented out.[27] The magnates cooperate in this hyped-up security to inflate their stature and power in the eyes of the excluded public.[28]

Berserk style naturalizes the criminal coloration of society. As in an optical illusion, it makes figure-ground relationships unstable. In movies the bumpkin who blunders into crime and miraculously triumphs is a heroic stereotype. A number of cable television series present sympathetic ordinary folks pushed by circumstances into crime. In *Weeds* a widowed suburban soccer mom deals pot to make ends meet; in *Breaking Bad* a chemistry teacher cooks methamphetamine to pay for his cancer treatment and his family's security; in *Dexter* a police lab specialist moonlights as a homicidal vigilante; and *Nurse*

Jackie steals drugs from the hospital pharmacy to get through her heroic work day. The premise is that the stress of American life demands a touch of crime if underdogs are to maintain a decent life.

As a rule, mafia excess is background to "real" life. But let the mood change slightly, and crime appears dominant. As economies contracted in 2008 and Mexican drug cartels—classic mafia—escalated their chronic violence, U.S. media suddenly saw a nation consumed by crime. *Newsweek* gasped that Juarez Mexico was a "slaughterhouse." The magazine quoted "an acting special agent" who claimed that "the United States faced another lawless Waziristan—except this one happens to be right at the nation's doorstep."[29] To audiences resentful about immigration, broadcast media hyped the "nightmare scenario" of U.S. troops mobilized to defend the border against drug-crazed invaders.

BOOTY AND THE BEAST

There is more to the mafia analogy than the axiom that everybody has a touch of larceny. David Chase's HBO mafia epic (83 episodes) *The Sopranos*[30] opens a particular local window on fantasies of abandon and fears of cultural exhaustion in post-Vietnam America. The series presents crime as an integral part of everyday life, and ran from January 1999 to June 2007, the period that careened toward the crash of 2008.

"Sopranos" became shorthand for business crime on a personal scale. A Reuters story titled "Insider Trading Case As Much Sopranos as Wall Street" begins: "Zvi Goffer could have passed for Tony Soprano when he warned confederates in his alleged insider-trading ring that 'someone's going to jail.'"[31] In a familiar feedback loop screenwriters mimic criminals, who in turn emulate the models. In the insider trading case, "A criminal complaint naming Goffer [and others]... reads like a script for TV dramas like 'The Wire' or 'The Sopranos,' in which drug and Mafia criminals try to stay one step ahead of the law." Investigators had to use wiretaps and other methods "'traditionally reserved for the mob and narcotics traffickers' when the accused began 'taking a page from the drug dealers' playbook (and) deliberately used anonymous, hard-to-trace, pre-paid cellphones in order to avoid detection.' Calls recorded by law enforcement officials were littered with nicknames like 'the Greek' and 'the Rat.'" In making a killing Wall Street wise guys goosed up their morale by ripping off the prime example of berserk style on television.

The appetites and survival rage shaping the Soprano family and mafia "family" give distinctive, garish immediacy to inner life that helps to account for the show's power. In the opening episode Tony Soprano (James Gandolfini) worries that he "came in at the end. The best is over." Postwar America is vanishing; his father, the old boss, is dead; and his nominal successor, Tony's Uncle Junior (Dominic Chianese), is senile. Like the younger President Bush, Tony is a son trying to prove himself in a gap between the worlds of an iconic "greatest generation" and his own children, who want to be comfortably assimilated in respectable American life. For the family "business," reliable contracts and boundaries are fading, and rival families are a relentless menace. New immigrants and blacks have taken over old neighborhoods and the drug trade is flourishing where ethnic solidarity once prevailed. Meanwhile crime is sloppy, opportunistic, and shameful. Dogged by the FBI and paranoia, the mobsters are susceptible to panic and rage, and lamed by denial and regret.

In this environment the Soprano mafia family is an outmoded, failing local business. As scrappy underdogs, they attract audience sympathy. At one point Tony tries to adapt to the global scale by conspiring with Neapolitan mafia to smuggle a few luxury cars. But the tide is against him, and Tony the ostensible waste manager increasingly fears slipping into another sort of mob: the masses of wasted lives—to use Zygmundt Bauman's term—marginalized by globalization. To be sure, some new supermafias such as Enron, with its dummy global subsidiaries and price-fixing, may also die. Yet their impersonality and flimsiness only intensify the sense of instability and mistrust in business life. And on Tony's level, far down the food chain, stress leads to "wasting" lives as in killing.[32] But the problems are systemic: "Bankers and investors, especially global investors, abhor uncertainty in financial assets they hold. They treat it like toxic waste."[33]

The Sopranos and the series play to the insoluble ambivalence in us, by turns predator and underdog, infantile in appetite and desperate for self-disciplined honor. In a world fuddled by denial Tony can be bravely realistic. Yet the family spins self-serving myths as politicians do, so that it can play Santa Claus once a year. As in Wes Anderson's popular film *Fantastic Mr. Fox* (2009), in a tradition going back to peasant tales in re-revolutionary Europe,[34] a Robin Hood archetype justifies the outlaw life of the underdogs as a response to oppressive monopoly. The godfather fox and his extended family raid food stashes and narrowly escape to their underworld of burrows.

Tony Soprano suffers from affluenza: anxiety that in the midst of plenty, nothing has lasting value. "Civilian" life is a grind. Making a killing gives survival appetite ecstatic urgency but has poisonous, addictive side effects. Like other executives living on the edge such as Enron's drug-bedeviled Andy Fastow, Tony combats harrowing competition crippled by panic attacks and alcohol, drug, and gambling binges. He is fitfully honest enough to be a sympathetic character, but cannot get free of toxic lies. Like top American CEOs who have raised their pay from about 39 times that of the average employee in 1970 to nearly 1,000 times more in 2008, he skims everyone's earnings.

Chase's mafia is at once surreally violent and implacably banal. The Soprano families are defensively clannish. Tony pursues insatiable love affairs with opportunistic *comares*. His life abounds in raw, frenzied atrocity massively denied. Fitzgerald's Gatsby has Nick to make his story meaningful, whereas Tony uneasily confides in, and deceives, a therapist—and has to hide even that feint at authenticity from other mobsters. Fitzgerald gives Gatsby's life elegiac closure, whereas Tony's story ceases in a moment of humdrum randomness in the final episode, as the screen goes abruptly, unsatisfyingly, frighteningly blank. Rhapsodic desire and jeweled prose console for doom in *Gatsby*. Raw death-anxiety pervades Tony's milieu. The local godfather is not protected from turmoil below as GM executives are in *Roger and Me*. Making a killing leaves fingerprints on the psyche.

The profundity of the series lies in its atmosphere of complex cultural exhaustion. Tony's nominal business is "waste management." Mob rackets are decaying, yet insatiable expectations and exasperated discontent keep goading imagination to violence. Tony misses the ruthless conviction of his gangster father despite his crippling, half-conscious fear of him. Like his wife Carmela (Edie Falco) and their friends, he wants to believe in the American dream, yet they all fear, despise, and cheat on "big government." They watch their kids struggle for meaning, unable to accept that heroic values have hardened into consumer glitz—rings, watches, swanky cars—and stale rituals in church and on television.

Tony feels the exhaustion of a larger cultural transition. He sends his daughter to an overpriced prestige university to become a modern professional, yet mafia is atavistic. The godfather puts a plausible suburban face on a warlord subculture. He is the warrior-protector: priest, judge, and teacher. The poet Tasso trusted in his patron "as we trust in God. It appeared to me that, so long as I was under his protection, fortune and death had no power over me." As cruel and remote as his father was, Tony nevertheless mourns for that heroic faith.

This transference helps to explain audience fascination with the fantasy of the godfather. The Sopranos' post-Vietnam America celebrated individualism and weakened government guarantees while vastly enriching celebrity insiders. After 9/11, White House publicity tried to fashion a warrior president. Corporate CEOs make absurdly inflated incomes while commanding their underlings to be aggressive and to mistrust the "delusions" of loyalty and cooperation: "Don't fall into the trap of assuming that you're automatically 'entitled' to pay increases, promotions, or even your job...even if you perform well. [Never] con yourself into thinking that your employer is supposed to protect your future."[35] To expect a reasonable reward, personal loyalty, or "a future" is to "fall into the trap" or to "con yourself." Like marriage, mafia's oath of do-or-die loyalty is supposed to transcend that dog-eat-dog mentality, but mafia history shows otherwise. Overtaken by anxiety, individuals resort to berserk aggression—ultimately the cannibalism evoked when the mobsters cut up a corpse to dispose of it. In the large arc of the saga the family eventually consumes itself.

As a tribal or clan system, mafia generosity and rage are personal, grounded in kinship or tacit family, with little or no loyalty to abstractions such as the nation state or the human condition. Tony's New Jersey gang is closer to the social organization of Iraq than to modern democracy. As in Iraq, the propensity for dog-eat-dog violence increases when change undermines boundaries and hierarchies. After the American invasion, Iraqi mafia gangs were quick to exploit an orgy of looting and kidnapping, while sectarian militias and government agencies have conducted ongoing turf wars against religious and tribal rivals. The comparison could be extended in many directions, including the flood of money pumped into Iraq the way the banking system was pumping up the U.S. economy—paper money that would vanish in a squall of misallocation and malfeasance.

On a tribal scale Tony's mafia family is at once predatory and defensive—the ultimate guarantor of security. Tony considers himself a provider, an enforcer of local values, a protector, just as the United States appoints itself the global policeman. Yet the protection racket is elemental human behavior and can corrupt police as it does mafia. The high-minded global policeman does after all bomb civilians and force protection on some clients who happen to have valuable natural resources. In the process the world policeman takes advantage of his special leverage to speculate and incur stupefying debt with impunity. For better or worse, many oil customers and producers such as Japan and the Saudis tacitly pay for U.S. protection by buying U.S. Treasury debt. The corporate military budget is sacrosanct, with a shifting list of global clients and potential enemies to enforce funding demands.

Since 2001, in the same vein, Washington has pumped up a weakening economy with a vast Homeland Security industry, and bulked up private security companies in Iraq such as scandal-plagued Custer Battle and Blackwater. "The scale of the revenues at stake," says Naomi Klein, "is certainly enough to fuel an economic boom. Lockheed Martin, whose former vice-president chaired the Committee for the Liberation of Iraq, which loudly agitated for the invasion, received $25 billion in U.S. government contracts in 2005 alone. Democratic Congressman Henry Waxman noted that the sum 'exceeded the gross domestic product of 103 countries [and] was larger than the combined budgets of the Department of Commerce, the Department of the Interior, the Small Business Administration, and the entire legislative branch of government.' Lockheed itself deserved to be characterized as an emerging market"[36]

From the days of the Pinkertons private "security" agencies have operated to enforce discipline and to suppress labor activism as well as crime, with some famous rampages punctuating the historical record. After hurricane Katrina private security forces intervened in New Orleans as in a third world country. "'This vigilantism demonstrates the utter breakdown of the government,' says Michael Ratner, president of the Center for Constitutional Rights. 'These private security forces have behaved brutally, with impunity, in Iraq. To have them now on the streets of New Orleans is frightening and possibly illegal.'"[37] The alarm is akin to anxieties about mafia muscle.

Americans take the protection economy for granted. At the heart of the derivatives implosion in 2008 were financial instruments and agencies that advertised a fantastic new scale of "securitization" and guarantees. From the Brinks armored car to the Pentagon and the insurance and pharmaceutical industries, protection is a symbolically charged business, sublimating the ancient fantasy roles of warrior, priest, patriarch, and mother. Yet the demand for government protection at all costs is matched by fear of "big government" intrusiveness in personal lives.

The Sopranos painfully sharpens this ambivalence. Beneficiaries of government's guarantees and yet living under a constant threat

of surveillance and usurping governance whenever possible, the Soprano families are at once patriots, rebels, and outlaws. They resent
government intrusions, yet their protection racket is ruthlessly in-
trusive. Like a tax collector, Tony Soprano squeezes rewards from
vulnerable "civilians": sex from women, dinners from his restaurateur
friend Artie, and Rolex watches and other tribute from assorted clients. Like Fitzgerald's Gatsby stopped for speeding—"I was able to
do the commissioner a favor once, and he sends me a Christmas card
every year"—mafia and officialdom may cooperate.

As in mainstream American culture, the Soprano mob comple-
ments the anxiety and boredom of the protection economy with
investments in a thrilling shadow market that includes prostitution,
money lending, gambling, and drugs. The Bada Bing club and Tony's
exclusive high-stakes card games are the local mafia incarnation of the
national craze for casinos, lotteries, easy credit, and the pleasure palaces of Las Vegas. Tony's frantic gambling parallels the inflation of
the stock market bubble of the 1990s, which led intoxicated investors
to pitch money at stocks like chips on a roulette table.

In this context *The Sopranos* dramatizes the end of an era in which
immigrants were establishing families and local mafia could seem
heroically purposeful. Now that ethos is myth. Worse, as younger
generations discover its dark side, they try to deny or reinvent that
haunted myth of origins. This is what Tony does in therapy and his
daughter Meadow does in coming to resent law enforcement's "persecution." What finally count as heroism in the saga are the tragic
efforts of particular individuals to face up to demystification, the loss
of nostalgic consolations, the reality of their predatory greed and cruelty.

Tony's families are forced to grapple with creaturely motives in
themselves and others, and that can make them seem more significant
than humdrum, sheltered "civilians." To the extent that Tony's world
dies trying to turn its death-anxiety to account, the scripts are modeling heroic purpose for modern audiences the way gladiatorial combat
gripped spectators in the Roman amphitheater—but with the camera
now able to take spectators down into the subterranean dressing areas
where the abject and admired protagonists of death strap on their
armor struggling to master their terror.

With "casino" economics and failing wars in the background,
Tony's families mirror an America dangerously overconfident and
frightened of decline. The point is not that the United States is
equivalent to a New Jersey mob, but that in stressful historical mo-

ments group fantasies operate across unlikely boundaries. This is why Tony's inner turmoil and need for psychotherapy are such a useful vehicle for insight into the cultural moment.

Tony's sessions with Dr. Melfi (Lorraine Bracco) "may be the most realistic depiction of therapy ever depicted in a mainstream movie or television show."[38] His inner life comes to light in his unruly feelings toward her. He's attracted to her, grateful, humbled, resentful, and frightened. He wants to be noble and protective but helplessly bullies and lies to her. The sessions resolve nothing yet they humanize Tony and provide a lens on the culture that has shaped him.

Tony's distress crystallizes with his glimpse of a family of ducks abandoning his swimming pool at the end of summer. He's been feeding—parenting—them, and their flight panics him as an omen of old age, rejection, and death. He panics when showing his mother a nursing home. In fact death-anxiety has shadowed him since childhood. He remembers his father, the original family godfather, hacking off the finger of a butcher who failed to repay a gambling debt. Only when his father brought home "the bacon," Tony recalls, did his wife Livia (Nancy Marchand) ever reward him with sex.

In this psychic economy men pay for love—trust, nurture, conviction—with "bacon," by making a killing. The young strive for heroic patriarchal authority that turns out to be grounded in predation. Young Tony fainted in a panic attack at the sight of his father carving a roast at the dinner table. Livia's love of meat is a marker for cannibalistic appetite, borne out in her old age when in revenge for imagined offenses she plots with her brother-in-law Uncle Junior (Dominic Chianese) to have her son Tony killed.

The threat of cannibal frenzy is the toxic heart of the mafia mentality. In Ernest Becker's innocent-sounding premise: nobody ever gets enough life. In different ways Tony's parents dramatize the sinister greed for life that springs from survival-anxiety. Their appetites are the more frightening for being so fully naturalized in local mafia culture. The child fears that his own inadequacies, his inescapable failings, condemn him to punishment and death. In reaction he may lash out at scapegoats trying to identify with godfatherly invincibility. But he may also be overtaken by insoluble childhood dread, the terror that makes Tony's panic attacks also a berserk loss of control, but directed inward as well as at scapegoats around him. Mafia proves to be a theater of heroic cruelty and risk, and also of intensely rationalized punishment. In this way mafia epitomizes the hopes and terror of intimate life, since a god-"father" can turn a child into a "made man" or—like the ancient Roman patriarch empowered to kill disobedient children—destroy him.

Tony grew up in the force field of predatory appetites, feeling inadequate and ungrounded, with reason to fear real as well as social death. Having steeled himself to be tough, he complains of feeling "like a clown" inside. But that appreciation of life's absurdity never fully translates into letting go. In therapy he begins to recognize his mother's malice, but though he tries, he never really comes to terms with the survival rage aroused in childhood, and his capacity for empathy remains tragically impaired.

Dr. Melfi can probe the subject of death-anxiety, but for her it remains philosophically distanced, whereas for Tony it is close but numbed. When Tony is upset by Jackie Aprile's death from cancer, Dr. Melfi says, "That's the mystery, isn't it? God or whatever you want to call it? That we're given the questionable gift of knowing we're going to die?" But nothing comes of the question. They are never able to examine the terror and compensatory rage in Tony and a dog-eat-dog world. They come closest to the reality after Dr. Melfi has been raped. To Tony she pretends it was an auto accident, fearing he will go after her attacker. You can't control everything that happens to you, she argues. Tony objects: "But you can get pissed off."

> Dr. Melfi: "And then what? Lose control?" (That is, run amok?)
>
> Tony: "Who said anything about that? You can direct your anger where it belongs."
>
> Dr. Melfi replies that a panic attack "occurs when feelings of anger, revenge, or whatever overwhelm you.... Behavioral therapy can teach you to control these triggers." She speaks as if they agree that they are discussing berserk panic.
>
> Tony: "Then how do you get people to do what you want?" That is, how can you use berserk style's threat-displays to control others?

The exchange articulates two conflicting modes of coping with violence. While the psychiatrist recommends understanding and forbearance, Tony argues for strategic anger. One mode emphasizes self-control, negotiation, life as politics; the other dreams of masterful warrior force. It is the difference between diplomatic and military strategies. Both modes have limits. In the extreme, forbearance may lead to futile resignation, while in Tony's formula the equation of anger with desire, not to mention the tragic proximity of mastery and madness, opens the way to rage. Dr. Melfi fears running amok where Tony sees it as a tool for "getting what you want." The problem appears to be morale: the need for courage to overcome depressive fatalism in one direction, and self-control to forestall violence in the other.

But there is a cultural problem as well: both the therapist and the gangster see violence as purely personal. Neither has any faith in law as the will and guarantees of the community. After Dr. Melfi's boyfriend Randall is beaten up by a corrupt cop who is unbeknownst to her on Tony's payroll, she says to Tony, ruefully skipping over the failure of the law: "I guess I lead a sheltered life. I'm out of touch with the climate of rage in American society."

In a moment dizzy with ironies she proposes that American culture is governed by berserk style. And Tony, the suburban godfather, affirms mafia mentality as the sensible way to be American and get results. She speaks out of therapeutic culture, whereas the godfather defends a culture of macho confrontation. She underestimates the need for will—without which Tony would feel like an impotent child again. And in spite of therapy Tony cannot see the roots of the anger within him.

YOUR MONEY OR YOUR LIFE

Since the mob believes in a dog-eat-dog economy, survival greed is always eating away at inhibitions, threatening a war of all against all. As a result the group tries to police its motives though a paramilitary structure of "capos" and "soldiers" and a relentless threat of quasi-judicial killing for disobedience. Yet for all the macho cockiness, calculation, and paramilitary severity, gangs are susceptible to contagious panic, and much of Tony Soprano's torment originates in the conflict between dangerous appetite and a rage for order and security. To chop off a debtor's finger in front of your son is to demonstrate the berserker's godlike power but also the victim's terrified— castrated—insecurity. The moment is the more terrifying for flaunting the treacherous rationality of the gambler's contract.

Order becomes rage when carried beyond measure. His mother's whining passive aggression masks a potentially murderous demand for order. Less violent but nevertheless part of the underlying psychic economy is the demand for security made by mafia women. Like many Americans in the bubble years, Carmela frets about retirement. Insecurity disposes her to mistrust Tony as well as government Social

Security, and brings her to gamble on a crooked "spec house" so she can participate in the nationwide real estate mania that ran amok in 2008. In effect, women express fear that would unmake "made" men. Insofar as it allows the men to deny their own fears, the system is a form of dissociation.

The system comes apart as the Sopranos's marriage does. The burden of stress is plain enough today. Early immigrant families also labored under daunting stress, but they could find support in a heroic story of discovery and survival in addition to the patriarchal and clan bonds from the old world. In the myth-tinted heyday of La Cosa Nostra, Mario Puzo's *Godfather* epic (1969, 1972) portrayed the inheriting son Michael as soulless but triumphant. As the new godfather he is despicable yet queasily admirable: a figure as compelling as one of the great murderous dictators of the twentieth century.

By contrast, Tony Soprano lurches toward disorder and death. In anxious, sentimental moments his circle mourns for bygone days. Trying to reconnect with the Old World mafia of legend, he finds the Neapolitans he visits eerily cosmopolitan, with a woman godfather. His family is adrift in a tidal wash of exhausted narratives. The older generation decays in nursing homes. In the new world of brand names and industrial glitz, religious rituals and mawkish ethnic songs are empty gestures. Funerals and weddings are vacantly stereotypical. When Carmela breaks with Tony, she and her girlfriends gather to watch old movie "classics" on television in a wishful gesture at self-improvement, seeking consoling cultural authority in Hollywood's fading lowbrow heroism. Carmela knows women's roles are changing, and she can imagine rebellion but no story beyond that.

Alienated souls try to substitute loot for story. The behavior is poignantly childlike, as when Tony's face helplessly lights up at an underling's gift of a glitzy watch. More often it has the frightening force of addiction and triggers manic aggression. In this light mafia is a metaphor for what Dr. Peter Whybrow calls a "mania" for status and possessions: an "outbreak of greed" that drives Americans to live turbocharged lives at the expense of relationships with others.[39] Whybrow sees greed as biologically wired, implicated in the same brain chemistry as drugs such as cocaine and caffeine. But greed is also more difficult to manage in a depersonalized global economy no longer regulated by the neighborly market restraints envisioned in classical economics. In the credit crack-up of 2008 it was epitomized in the infantile self-indulgence of Wall Street executives buying corporate jets and Ali Baba office furnishings while begging for a government bailout.

Fetishistic frenzy is stressful and exhausting. Like addiction, it escalates, since berserk style tries to dispel or explode stress by concentrating the self in the furious moment, or by focusing on the beyond. Either way it moots reflection, depression, and self-doubt. As identities fray in *The Sopranos*, the families become more recklessly excessive. Tony increasingly abandons himself to gambling, intoxication, desperate sex, and paroxysms of aggression.

The younger, insecure mobsters try to emulate legendary mob exploits and end up amok and usually dead, the fate of Jackie Aprile Jr. (Jason Cerbone). As Tony's nephew Christopher (Michael Imperioli) tries to write screenplays, he becomes aware of his inner chaos. He complains to Big Pussy Bompensiero (Vincent Pastore) about unnerving murders he has committed: "I have no identity. I have bad dreams every night." The older man sympathizes: "The more you do [kill], the better you sleep." He recommends habituation and desensitization. But habituation kills stories. What's more, this is a recipe for addiction and berserk style: escalating violence ("the more you do") in search of stability that is perversely destroyed by the search and usually ends in a convulsion. Before long the "family" will destroy Big Pussy himself, along with Christopher and his fiancée Adriana (Drea DeMatteo).

The grisly film Christopher scripts reveals the death-anxiety that underlies so much aggression. Christopher grasps at the delusion that killing makes the self more secure. As a film within a film (The Sopranos), the metadramatic quality of his story becomes a way of showing the power of berserk style to control behavior. The gory torture in his film is at once real—a disguised "confession" of actual sadism Christopher has been involved in—and also a horror genre cliché that controls its audience by cueing applause. In effect, a subculture such as Hollywood or the Mafia projects genres that govern responses. The mobsters at the movie preview attend in order to see berserk style objectified on screen for thrills and thrilling profit. For Christopher, by contrast, the film is a means for the "made man" who is terrified of his own emptiness to inflate his life on screen, and use audience applause to substantiate himself. Given the outcome—Christopher's return to drugs—his Hollywood triumph demonstrates the way berserk lifestyle destroys character.

Christopher unwittingly arouses fatal suspicion in Tony by incorporating facets of Tony's story into his movie script. The irony is brutal: mafia mentality can make any contact with personal lives lethal. Yet the process of writing and listening to others in workshops makes Christopher and also his fiancée more aware of imaginative sympathy. And yet that opening weakens their capacity for denial and makes them fatally conflicted. This is a version of the dilemma Tony faces in seeing a therapist. Like fundamentalists, other mobsters refuse to see that the self is ultimately ungrounded and therefore depends on social bonds and self-examination for substantiation and coherence.

The pressure of death is electrifying in the series' violence, but it is most disturbing in the subtle markers that the scripts use to evoke the imprisoning and doomed human body. Tony always breathes noisily, as if running out of breath, struggling for air. After an auto accident leaves Christopher unconscious Tony, fearing his betrayal, pinches off his breathing to suffocate him. Tough guy godfathers Jackie Aprile (Michael Rispoli) and Johnny Sacks die of cancer, their machismo wasting away. Uncle Junior's senility leaves him finally marooned alone in the cavernous gloom of a state mental hospital. Outraged nerves call for alcohol and drug binges. More gruesomely, the corpses of murder victims are a chronic reminder of the body's persistence as macabre, guilty waste. From time to time they have to be dug up to avoid detection, and then moved or further destroyed.

The attempt to replenish vitality plays out in the trope of predation and specifically cannibalism, which in turn links the motives to popular culture's preoccupation with vampires and other monsters of survival greed. As in *Dracula,* the mafia predators are organized around an alpha leader who can transform himself and has enviable access to life. As boss, Tony Soprano takes in roles as he does food and blood money. The roles expand him. They give him access to sexual conquests, dominance displays, booze, bling, and other markers for fertility and vitality. He can be tender, amused, or sadistic: father, warlord, bandit, killer, gambler, judge, entrepreneur, and needy child, without end. Each change promises liberation, new life. The scripts shrewdly capture these efforts at self-creation. The gangsters try to emulate impressive fashions and vocabulary. Christopher would aggrandize himself in his screenplays.

What makes Tony poignant is his fitful ability to be wise enough to recognize the futility of his survival greed. It brings him to the verge of tragic insight. Living out multiple selves with criminal abandon, Tony half-perceives that his self-expansion subverts and vitiates identity even as it feeds his appetite, yet he keeps reaching for more.

At the point of abandon, the development of multiple incompatible selves is the Jekyll and Hyde paradigm. Tony is a regular guy but also a monster. The neighbors suspect—they "know"—that he is a criminal, but they're tantalized by the forbidden beyond: taboo power and appetite. Tony's compartmentalized identity—the orgiastic gambler in Las Vegas, the moralizing middle-class dad—evokes the larger cultural fantasy celebrated in the 1980s and 1990s as "multiple personality syndrome." Although debunked by research, the syndrome remains popular, presumably because it offers an explanatory tool for the conflicted motives people wrestle with, just as Victorian novels used Jekyll and Hyde to dramatize urgent questions about identity in the nineteenth century.

Tony's risk-taking and especially his binge gambling make sense as an attempt to break out of the chronic unfulfillment of affluenza and the strain of inner conflict. He invests in a racehorse to enjoy the "break neck" abandon of the race. His trips to Las Vegas are headlong lunges at fortune. He is an acute expression of the risk-taking that infected the national mood in the go-go 1990s. Many churches and state governments relaxed traditional strictures on gambling. Indian tribes erected gaming palaces. Investors called the stock market a casino. Tony's Las Vegas is more intoxicated than imaginative, an infantile Disneyland goosed up by winking sin. In Mike Figgis's *Leaving Las Vegas* (1995) the casino's glitter stands for exhausted sexual greed and suicidal compulsion. The mob's formative role in the gambling "industry" links making a killing to the tabloid "Murder Incorporated" associated with Vegas through Meyer Lansky and Bugsy Siegel. Martin Scorcese chronicled these mob exploits in *Casino* (1995), and now the city has a museum to enshrine its shopworn gangster mythology.

The corporate counterpart of the Vegas casino was the glitzy Enron tower in Houston, in which one trading floor was a stage set designed to fool visitors while executives gambled on future valuations and manipulated markets to favor the house. The trading floor was a "boiler room" operation of the sort mobsters use to peddle crooked securities. CEO Ken Lay infiltrated regulatory agencies, plying politicians up to the White House the way mafia pays off public officials. In the end speculation crowded out any semblance of productivity, and Ponzi dynamics took over. What Fortune magazine called "America's Most Innovative Company" turned out to be relying on frantic momentum and mafia deceit.

Enron's godfather and his inner circle projected godlike confidence. They could be suavely brutal as their millions of victims found out. Alex Gibney's documentary *The Smartest Guys in the Room* (2005) shows them verbally flogging their underlings to do-or-die exertions, while on private weekend retreats, like macho adolescents, they show off their daredevil bravado on dirt bikes. The biker play-acting suggests the unreal atmosphere surrounding their world-conquering ruthlessness. Abetted by unscrupulous accounting, the inner circle acted out a more elevated version of Tony Soprano's greed not just for loot, but for meaning. What we can glimpse of their inner lives is scripted by phony gentility and macho posturing, refining into banality the animal fury and anguish the scriptwriters attribute to Tony Soprano.

The firm's violence damaged millions of lives. Indicted on 98 counts of fraud, conspiracy, insider trading, money laundering, and more, Andrew Fastow received a "discounted" prison sentence from a judge who said that he had been "the subject of great persecution," including threats and religious slurs." The former executive could "shave" another year off his sentence by participating in a drug program "to help wean him from the undisclosed substances he used to mask his anxiety." He was sentenced on the same day that Bernie Ebbers, founder of World Com, reported to prison. One former Enron employee working three jobs to stay afloat commented, "I'm not guilty of anything, but my sentence will be longer than Fastow's."[40] Even behind bars the executive still had leverage and unspoken connections working for him.

The Enron chiefs' adolescent derring-do on dirt bikes illustrates the quality of play-acting that Robert Reich called "A Culture of Paper Tigers."[41] The fantasies resonate with the "bad boy" self-image of bejeweled, paunchy rap stars or a president being landed aboard an aircraft carrier dressed up as a fighter pilot. This is the romance of abandon, the executive magic so crisply summed up in *The Leadership Secrets of Attila the Hun* (1985), where recycled aphorisms come dressed up in barbarian warrior garb, prescribing loyalty, courage, decisiveness, and other virtues, but also fiery ambition and a sharp sword. The would-be leader could profit from Attila's example without fretting that the Hun's business plan was literally cut-throat, and that all empires eventually dissolve.

The Sopranos dramatizes the tragic absurdity of survival greed. The more the mobsters grasp at illicit immortality fantasies, the more terrifying the abyss that opens beneath their feet. It should not surprise us that as the neocon United States overreached in its quest for an American century, the doom of the Roman Empire began to haunt op-ed writers. In financial culture Wall Street bankers with nicknames like mafia chieftains chased magical profits and ended up in a vertiginous global credit collapse.

That queasy sense of the abyss creates the survival rage that drives even the striped-tie psychopaths in the executive suite. In the film *Wall Street,* Gordon Gecko is given to outbursts that turn mafia-style enforcement into berserk rage, "When I get a hold of the son of a bitch who leaked this," he screams, "I'm gonna tear his eyeballs out and I'm gonna suck his fucking skull." This is cannibalistic, vampire rage. The tantrum telegraphs creaturely motives ordinarily masked by the opaque windows of a limousine.

The social scientist Robert Hare concludes that many top executives "are callous, cold-blooded individuals....They have no sense of guilt or remorse...if I wasn't studying psychopaths in prison, I'd do it at the stock exchange." In a *New Yorker* cartoon (August 10 and 17, 2009) a personnel manager tells a Viking applying for a job: "Your resume is remarkably similar to our C.E.O.'s." In other *New Yorker* cartoons the boss's office usually commands the skyline with a window so huge that it evokes the "primary narcissism" of the young child who wants, as Ernest Becker says, to "swallow the world" (37). It may have a trapdoor that drops fired underlings into the abyss of social death.

Enron's magic factory was not just a flashy glass showplace. Like the rules and rites of "mafia" that turn a gang of appetites into the enabling fiction of Tony's "family," the Enron tower was above all manufacturing an illusion of heroic purpose desperately needed in a culture whose convictions and consolations cry out for renewal.

CHAPTER 6

THE LIVING END

Apocalypse has become banal.

     Anthony Giddens, Modernity and Self-Identity

Rampage killing is figuratively an apocalypse. Eric Harris wanted in caps to "Kill 'em AALL!!!" Rage that would empty the world also empties out reasons for living. All conflict gone, supreme righteousness, justice, or revenge have no future.

Still, total oblivion is a big order. We are cognitively disposed to see endings as change. In Christianity the end of the world is officially a conversion experience: translation from earthly to heavenly or infernal existence. Victory in warfare annihilates an enemy and inaugurates a new age or confirms a new compact with the gods. In the Bible, God sends the Israelites to exterminate the Canaanites. In nations nearby "which the Lord your God is giving you as a heritage, you shall not let a soul remain alive. No, you must proscribe them... as the Lord your God has commanded you" (Deut. 20:18).[1] In rationalizing ethnic cleansing and appetite for land, the rhetoric of the beyond substitutes "us" for "them." Life goes on, but under new auspices.

Ideas of the beyond frame consciousness. Within the boundaries of Eden, there was no death, anxiety, and alienation. Following our eviction, we have depended on symbolic materials to create a prosthetic beyond that can frame life and make it seem enduring and significant. [2] Medieval crusaders stormed out of Europe in manic sallies that amassed treasure in heaven as well as in pack trains. Conquest was theology. The spectacular rampage killings at the World Trade Center and at the Pentagon in 2001 were also framed by fantasies of the theological beyond.

For the purposes of this book, apocalypse is best understood as a tool. For all the insistence on the terrorists' alien fanaticism, for example, their behavior mixed religious and worldly motives in the cauldron of berserk style. Likewise, public responses summoned berserk style to manage morale and integrate the terrorist rupture into the familiar stories we live by. Globalization has shaken traditional verities around the world. China goes home with Walmart shoppers; Coca-Cola and the U.S. Army are familiar in countries around the planet. Subatomic science and radical advances in cosmology have dispelled traditional certainties and controls. Modernity disenchants even the possibility of ultimate frames.

Viewed as a form of rampage killing, the September 11th terrorism has some intriguing features. For one thing, it could have elicited an international police response rather than the opportunistic, berserk-style "war on terror. As an analog to workplace and school rampage, the attacks were a perverse solution to serious conflicts in the lives of relatively affluent young men under pressure to find heroic purpose in countries such as Saudi Arabia in which modernity and reactionary repression are maddeningly in conflict. Career plans, sex, and family were problematical for almost all of the hijackers. While none lacked for opportunities, they grew ever more obsessed with "what is right." The plot of cosmic jihad against the American Satan's front office, as it were, allowed them to feel right—and while the spell lasted, supremely important. As in most such attacks, suicide allowed them to escape any modern ironies and tragic post-mortem analysis.

The jihadis' pious exaltation can be understood as the berserker's seething sense of injustice, godlike transport, and cold fury. They plotted to go postal in the aisles of everyday life, yet they were also self-consciously amok as soldiers under the banner of God. Reminders of medieval crusaders infuriated them, though they were crusaders themselves. They were also self-anointed priests righteously carrying out holy duties. In "the most blood-curdling sentence of his final instructions to the hijackers, [the ringleader Mohammed] Atta commanded that "You must not discomfort your animal during the slaughter." This phrase "is well beyond anger or hatred. It is the utmost in disparagement.... By having mercy on one's animals, one is imitating God, who rules over death."[3]

Carrying out this human sacrifice, Atta emulated ancient priests, but he identified with God. For all his piety, he is also a judge like the Columbine killers sentencing everybody to death. Recall Eric Harris's "Philosophy" on his website: "My belief is that if I say something, it goes. I am the law, and if you don't like it, you die. If I don't like you or I don't like what you want me to do, you die....I'll just go to some downtown area in some big ass city and blow up and shoot everything I can. Feel no remorse, no sense of shame."[4]

As at Columbine, the execution is also a suicide, so the priest-judge is sacrificing all the "animal" bodies in the plane and in the twin towers. This is in keeping with the asceticism that progressively overtook Atta from his student days. Like Dylan Klebold, he told himself he was "going to a better place." As Ruth Stein concludes in her analysis of Atta's final letter, evidence points to a breakdown of reality-testing familiar in cult behavior and psychosis. "Being immersed in a state of intense focus on God in word and thought, not detaching from attending His presence for one minute, in a kind of numbed, awed adhesion, yet at the same time functioning with extraordinary vigilance and competence, may be likened to cold psychotic paranoia at its height. The subject adheres to the idealized persecutory inner object, while the world, become insignificant and contemptible, vanishes into derealization" (Stein 106).

The "contemptible world" we are trapped in is first of all the human body. And if it won't agreeably "vanish," then it can be starved or done away with. The purification of the self promises an escape from repulsive mortality. As in anorexia, the cruelty of this syndrome lies in its distortion of rewards and defenses, so that the individual's self-protective systems short-circuit, and instead of triggering alarm and disgust, physical self-destruction generates mental exaltation. Although research has yet to make clear the interplay of neurological and cultural influences, the self-intoxicating quality of anorexic behavior is psychocultural. The nervous system responds to repeated bouts of stress, and as Atta's history shows, the mind seeks out or imagines sympathizers who will support the belief system. The more you starve yourself toward perfection, the louder the applause and the fiercer your resolve.

Rage and self-aggrandizement can be just as self-intoxicating. Hatred of unworthiness and injustice fuels an urgent search for release, in this instance a world-shattering rampage meant to open the gates of paradise. The hijacker's obsessive prayers are the equivalent of the rampage killer's seething fixation. The climax is an addictive, terminal binge. As it gathers momentum, anorexic self-denial resembles suicidal berserking insofar as growing disgust at the real body heightens the panic of being trapped: trapped not only in the ugly body and the "fat," ugly world, but also trapped in feelings of disgust. Rage at the grotesque, affluent enemy can feed righteous self-regard.

For all his supposed foreignness and religiosity, Atta's fantasies are pitifully familiar. Strange to say, pulp- and science-fiction resonate with his narratives. In describing *The Matrix* (1999), Mervyn Bendle uncannily echoes Ruth Stein's clinical observation of disgust and messianism: "The idea that everyday life is a vacuous illusion is central" in the film. The critic's account of the plot catches echoes of the terrorists' inner life. The hero, Neo, is a nobody working in a corporate cubicle until he meets the rebel leader Morpheus, who reveals that everyday reality is in fact the Matrix: a computer-generated virtual reality engrossing the entire globe and powered by energy drained from infantilized humans immobilized in artificial wombs. This is industrial-scale vampirism.

At the end of the movie Neo, in a voice-over, contacts the sinister and hegemonic AI system, declares his status as the Messiah and his intention to reveal to the denizens of the Matrix an alternative world without rules and controls, borders or boundaries, and where anything is possible. The Matrix registers "system failure" and Neo steps forth into the hustle and bustle of a busy city, watching the masses hurry by in their mindless everyday toil, before he ascends into the heavens to await the outcome of his intervention....Contemporary cinema offers extremely misanthropic representations of the apocalyptic near future and communicates a fear and hatred of everyday people. The masses are depicted as mindless, barely functional vermin, ready to tear each other apart in a desperate rage for survival. Accompanying this is a depiction of the heroes and survivors being readily transformed into effective killers, capable of butchering large numbers of people who, perhaps only hours before, may have been their friends, allies, or even family members.[5]

From the "butchered" animal masses to the hero's ascent to the beyond, it is all there: the persecution, the derealization, the messianic rebellion. Even Atta's conviction that the industrial world is robbing Muslims of their vitality echoes in the fantasy of battery-farms and infantilization. The remedy is the cosmic heroism of the terrorist mastermind.

Media and officials depicted Atta and Bin Laden as criminal geniuses. But rampage killers can be strategic even in the throes of an inner storm. Consider Mark O. Barton, who kept a mask on his inner turmoil until the summer of 1999, when he murdered his second wife and two children, nine people in two Atlanta brokerage houses, and finally himself. Barton had quit his job as a chemist and suffered financial ruin as a day-trader. "I have been dying," he wrote just before the end. Like a soldier trapped and overwhelmed by death-anxiety, "I wake up at night so afraid, so terrified that I couldn't be that afraid while awake. It has taken its toll. I have come to hate this life and this system of things. I have come to have no hope." In his "hate [for] this system of things," he could be speaking out of a terrorist manifesto. Even as his character was disintegrating, he was systematic in his assault on the brokerage houses. Failing as a trader, he attacked fellow brokerage customers who "greedily sought my destruction."[6] Like the Islamists who reviled U.S. prosperity, Barton hated the "greed" that meant happiness for others and marked his failure.

Barton, too, matched acute persecutory feelings with a special sacrificial relationship to God. Generally journalists examine religious pathology with euphemistic discretion because the taboos are so explosive. But like Atta, Barton used the beyond to rationalize his murders. In the note he left behind, waking and dream life blurred for him. He repeated a ritualistic formula naming the wife and children he had just slaughtered, then offering them to God as in an ancient ceremonial sacrifice. "I give you my wife, Leigh Ann Vandiver Barton. My honey, my precious love. Please take care of her. I will love her forever." The children follow, one by one, as he repeats the formula. Through this sacrificial murder, talking to "Jehovah," Barton shed his failures and hatred by playing the benevolent priest-judge as Atta did, but in a script meant to be read by sympathetic posterity.

Killing your family, you destroy your intimate life space in a personal apocalypse. In his role-playing Barton is lover, priest, judge, and executioner, and about to be a terrorist wreaking vengeance on his enemies. Meanwhile he lovingly summons divine protection for the family he has slaughtered as they accompany him into death like the sacrificed dependents of an ancient warrior-king.

What the doomed warrior-king does not say is that the police had good reason to suspect him of murdering his first wife and her mother on a camping trip half a dozen years before. Nor does he connect those crimes to the shattering turmoil inside him.

After slaying his family, Barton visited his lawyer to change his will, appearing composed. In the berserk state of exalted, vicious calm—the psychiatrist's "flaming ice"—he then resumed his rampage. A witness reported that "His eyes had this enormous sadness; he was flat-out hopeless."[7] His emptiness recalls Anne Greaves' description of Mohamed Atta at the flight school in Florida training for death: "he had a terribly sad expression on his face. Totally emotionless cold eyes.... such a fixed purposeful expression on his face. Almost as though he was hypnotised in a way.... just this sort of almost dead expression. Just no life in him whatsoever. Robotic. Not a flicker of emotion or excitement or anything. Nothing at all."

These observations show both men withdrawing from life, "hypnotized" by the beyond: filling up the "vacuous illusion" of life with God and death. Ruth Stein's description of Atta's "cold psychotic paranoia" suggests an organic etiology. But that would by no means eliminate psychocultural influences. The seeds of the deadness resonate eerily in the phenomenon the Romans called "the demon of noontide"—the experience of peering out a doorway at noon and suddenly finding the world utterly meaningless. What we know for sure is that both killers fought this depressive void by coming "to hate this life and this system of things." Barton coped with the feeling that "I have been dying" by forcing his death, just as Atta undertook a slow-motion suicide that reached apotheosis in the twin towers funeral pyre.

RAMPAGE RELIGION

Hatred of "this life and this system of things" could scarcely be a more telling than in the career of the Rev. Jim Jones. In a cruel parody of the original Puritan settlement of New England, he herded his Peoples Temple faithful out of California, where the law was beginning to investigate the cult, to build a new city on a hill in the bush of Guyana, where he murdered almost every one of them with cyanide, in a drug-addled, absurd apocalypse.

Childhood friends say that as a schoolboy Jim Jones (1931-1978), like Jeffrey Dahmer, was fixated on death and funerals.[8] As an abused child of an alcoholic family in rural Indiana, he found shelter in a Pentecostal church group. As a young preacher of a social gospel, he cultivated marginalized minority followers. In time berserk style enabled him to act out a fantasy solution to his own tormented childhood by taking the role of "Father" rescuing "his" children. He used utopian sympathies and criminal guile to build a shaky cult empire that collapsed in a spasm of rage and self-pity. As he directed the murder-suicide of over 903 followers, many still thought of him as father and God.

From the start Jones embraced berserk themes in the cultural materials around him, especially Cold War ideology. Jeanne Mills, who defected in 1975, wrote one of the earliest first-hand accounts of the Peoples Temple (1979).[9] She first fell under Jones's spell in November 1969, when the nation was shuddering through antiwar and civil rights clashes, nearly three dozen urban riots in three years, and the Bobby Kennedy and Martin Luther King assassinations (1968). The Black Panthers were loudly arming in self-defense, and President Johnson had been pressured out of office.

In this queasy atmosphere Mills and her husband Al attended a service at Jones's church in Redwood Valley, California. At this early stage Jones brought together a few middle class and many marginal members, white and black, young and elderly. His sermon that day was "about political problems, the war in Vietnam, which he claimed to have prophesied, the government-supported drug racketeering in our country, the social injustices committed against the minorities," and religious hypocrisy. At the climax he announced that "I have seen by divine revelation the total annihilation of this country and many other parts of the world....The only survivors will be those people who are hidden in the cave that I have been shown in a vision. Those who go into this cave with me will be saved from the poisonous radioactive fallout that will follow the nuclear bomb attack....It will be up to our group to begin life anew on this continent" (122). In the ideation of race war, "poisonous" fallout, and mass death the end was already present.

Like Jones's healings, this doomsday sermon made fear of death a shared group experience, even as the cave and the dream of repopulating the earth countered terror with fantasies of invulnerability, fertility, and special destiny. Jones played on Cold War themes of nuclear holocaust and backyard bomb shelters. In Stanley Kubrick's *Dr Strangelove* (1964), the sinister Strangelove advises the government elite that they can survive an imminent nuclear strike underground and with a harem, godlike, repopulate the earth—a fantasy personally appealing to Jones. Jeannie Mills had been raised in a "deeply religious" Seventh Day Adventist family (111), so she was used to millennialist theology. But the story spoke to her fear of nuclear war, and she responded to the racial harmony in the congregation.

Jones preached makeshift messianic doctrines increasingly centered on his superhuman powers to rescue followers from death. Services came to focus on miraculous testimonials contrived with a suite of confidence tricks and cunning confederates. Impersonating a cripple, responding to a command from Jones, a church secretary stood up from her wheelchair and walked. An elderly black woman praised Jones for helping her "spit up" a stomach cancer. After his sermon his psychic powers identified another woman in the congregation with a stomach cancer, and he dispatched her with a nurse to the toilet to disgorge it. The deadly flesh produced for all to see and smell was in fact rotting chicken guts and a prop. The congregation exulted at this exorcism.

In time Jones's fantasies of apotheosis became less sublimated. All along he mocked conventional belief in a fraudulent "Skygod," projecting onto this religious deception his own sinister motives. By 1972 he was asking to be called "Father" and hinting that "he was none other than 'God Almighty'" (180), as in this Peoples Temple song:

> Father is God,
> And we are blessed,
> I know you're God, I know you're God,
> I know you're God, God, God, God, God. (203)

His followers learned that he had been incarnated before as Buddha, the Bab, Jesus, and Vladimir Lenin (181).

As a seminarian Jones had been obsessed with inequality and exploitation. But like that other seminarian Josef Stalin, Jones's communistic benevolence gradually transformed into predatory survival greed. He seduced prospective followers by making them feel loved, bombarding them with testimonials from his followers—in cult jargon, "love bombing"—and promising rescue. But the craving for love became obsessive for him as well. He jealously attacked any follower who held back from hero-worship or showed desire for others.

As in classic domestic abuse, "Father" professed love for his family even as he viciously "disciplined" them. Surrendering autonomy and worldly goods to the cause, working themselves into a state of befuddled sleep-deprivation, his followers became increasingly dependent. That made them less threatening to "Father," but also less profitable and more burdensome. Since his business dealings were often irresponsible or inept, with no real goal beyond endless self-expansion, the organization was bound to be self-disabling in the long run.

As the man's criminal ambitions ratcheted up his stress, his demands for veneration and dominance followed suit. With mainstream American culture as the enemy, he was implicitly in combat, a guerrilla leader or mafia godfather. In his accelerating rampage during the 1970s he extorted property, defrauded the state welfare department, used children as hostages, and instigated assaults on "traitors." As his fear of exposure and punishment mounted, so did his compulsion to punish others, especially "disobedient" children, with public beatings and humiliation. As his excesses threatened everyone's sense of stability, his demands for loyalty became fanatical. Defections left behind an increasingly infantilized core of believers. Week after week his punishment of children modeled the helplessness of his adult followers, even as it allowed him to feel mastery over his own terrors. As his tyrannical violence became increasingly self-intoxicating, it required ever more sadistic excess to maintain his godlike exaltation.

As Jones experimented with abandon, testing limits, promising supernatural protection while making outrageous demands on the faithful, he became more openly paranoid. In 1971-72, evoking the assassinations of the Kennedys and Martin Luther King, he began to stage fake attempts on his life in which he would feign gunshot injuries and miraculously "dissolve" the bullets. He built a watchtower in his backyard and armed the bodyguards who would be his enforcers during temple services and abet the murders in Jonestown.

By 1974, Jones was pushing berserk style toward abandon. He openly took the role of alpha male. "It was nauseating to listen to him tell a congregation of a thousand or more adults and children that he had the biggest penis of any man" (258). He humiliated rival males: "If you think you can fuck women, prove it here, in front of everyone. If you think you know how to make love, then show us. You fuck your wife and I'll fuck mine, and we'll see who is able to do it longer and better" (258). The emphasis on stamina, his terror that anyone should see his penis, his dyed graying hair, and his embarrassing pot belly enabled the once-transfixed Jeannie Mills to recognize the turmoil in the man. In 1975, several years before the mass murder in Guyana, he began to test his inner circle by pretending to poison them and watching to see who would die willingly for "the Cause"—for him. The messiah would not go alone into failure and death.

In the year or so before the move—or flight—to Jonestown, the Peoples Temple took on an air of saturnalia. Financially the empire was coming apart. Despite blackmail and death-threats, defectors were pressing for legal sanctions to recover family members held hostage. Jones openly cultivated the berserker's godlike and beastlike abandon. He fulminated against imaginary enemies and looked for excuses to punish. During services he bragged about sexually servicing his followers as if they were his harem, forbidding sexuality among themselves. Defying legal advice to mask his emergent homosexuality, he reveled in it and taught that everyone was basically homosexual, incoherently boasting of superhuman powers of procreation. At times he would mock his sexual partners in his sermons, ridiculing them for infecting him with venereal warts or failing to use an enema before he sodomized them, his self-hatred deflected onto the sexual acolytes.

Poignantly, Jones half-acknowledged his mental illness: "He explained that he had a sugar imbalance which caused people to go crazy. 'People who have this problem usually become murderers,' he said, 'but I am able to stay in control.' He explained to his bodyguards that there might be times when he would be unable to control his 'righteous indignation' because of this sugar imbalance. His instructions to them were, 'Watch me if I should begin to lunge toward someone. Pull me away from them so I don't harm an innocent person in my anger'" (272). And in fact there were occasions when he began to run amok and had to be restrained.

Jones's insanity played out the ambiguity in berserk style: at critical moments it was difficult to determine how in or out of control he was. For all his vehement iconoclasm, his "Apostolic socialism" shared many of the ideals of Vietnam era counterculture, its communes, and its frequently toxic gurus. His hodgepodge of doctrines borrowed from Communism but also from Cold War militarism, which like the Temple demanded a huge share of its citizens' wealth every year to protect them from demonized enemies who would eventually crumble with the Berlin Wall. According to Mills, in 1974 Jones confided to his inner circle that he was "negotiating the purchase of an atomic bomb for us" (277). Surrounded by armed guards, seeing traitors on all sides, he echoed the berserk rhetoric of groups as different as the Black Panthers, the John Birch Society, and the Manson family.

As a utopian project, the Peoples Temple espoused communitarian ideals. In its public image the group identified with the ethos of Lyndon Johnson's Great Society programs—the first national effort since the New Deal to bring all Americans into mainstream economic life—and with therapeutic culture. Economically, however, Jones pursued a boom-bust business model. While advertising self-sufficiency—planting crops in Guyana, for example—the group depended on Ponzi-style growth. The organization absorbed its members personal resources, taking houses and salaries in exchange for paternalistic guarantees, in some cases stealing social security and welfare payments. Jones ruthlessly exploited the labor of his followers in maintaining high-visibility public relations.

Working through an elite inner circle, "Father" was godfather in a tacit mafia that bled the largely black membership in a protection racket. With a plant in the state social services department he could divert benefit payments. The gang had its code of silence and a repertory of intimidation tactics. As a de facto aristocracy, Jones, his natural family, and his inner circle lived on the labors and resources of the ordinary members. As in mafia, with ritualized Orwellian doublethink, the leadership stressed love and loyalty even as it established a tacit prison system, with armed guards, work details, supervised social relationships, spies, and punishment for rebels.

As a spokesman for the poor, Jones was able to woo politicians by providing them with campaign workers and flattering endorsements. To parry criticism, he emulated corporate public relations blitzes, mounting letter-writing campaigns and stage-managed protests. Playing on public opinion, he was able to intimidate editors and silence reporters, quashing Lester Kinsolving's early expose in 1972.

By the time that disaffected followers, alarmed relatives, and investigators finally began closing in, Jones had good reasons for his persecution mania. Congressman Leo Ryan's fatal visit to Guyana eerily evoked the trips up river in search of a berserk renegade in Conrad's *Heart of Darkness* (1902) and Francis Ford Coppola's contemporaneous *Apocalypse Now* (1979). Jones's mental instability and drug use were by then well advanced. Having stockpiled cyanide, he was entertaining a homemade apocalypse of cosmic victimization and vindication.

Jeannie Mills was convinced that Jones planned to survive the mass poisoning of his followers, and it remains unclear how he came to be shot to death. In exhorting the followers to accept death because "we" were tired of life, he was confessing his own exhaustion and the futility of the Peoples Temple scheme. For a long time he had taken no pleasure in alpha male sex and triumphal fraud; investigations were cutting off his financial resources and any hope of expansion; and the group that remained with him, now wholly dependent, would be an insoluble burden to him. Expecting to be "terminated" like Coppola's renegade warlord and former colonel Kurtz (Marlon Brando), who has become a self-appointed god presiding over native warriors in the jungle, Jones was overcome by a form of combat stress. Using his guards and cyanide as his weapons, he launched the rampage that killed reporters, a U. S. congressman, and nearly a thousand followers.

Jones's paranoia was palpable, yet the clinical term flattens out the ambiguity of his actions. Given his predatory behavior, his fear of retaliation was realistic. Yet like the desire to be a god, the fear was also limitless. This is the miserable truth evident in the tape of Jones's final harangue as the faithful were swallowing the cyanide-laced fruit juice he called "the medication." Ordering the murder of Congressman Ryan and the journalists who had seen through his sham utopia, Jones behaved like a rampage killer slaying a boss and severing connections to the world. Now he faced certain punishment, taking out his guilt and numbed anger on his flock. Like Mark Barton killing his family, the warrior-king wanted company in death. "His" group death magnified his martyrdom even if he was holding out hope for his own magical last-minute rescue.

The tape begins with Jones at the microphone declaring his love for the group, defusing resistance from the group and his own fury and guilt from the murder of the congressman's party. As usual he mixes grandiosity, flattery, and self-pity. He—"we"—had been "born too soon" into a despicable world. We are revolutionary heroes but engulfed by enemies. Logically, some of his victims to propose carrying on the fight or escaping. The con man instantly counters that their deaths are not a spectacular suicide at all, but the routine practice by which every revolutionary group in history has "passed over" when finally cornered.

Pitching his plan for suicide, Jones is unctuous, emotionally dissociated. He rambles a little, lisping or slurring words as if under sedation. As resistance and turmoil circulate in the group, urgency begins to strain his crooning pleas for relaxation and peace: "Let's get gone. Let's get gone. Let's get gone. (Children crying.) We had nothing we could do. We can't—we can't separate ourselves from our own people. For twenty years laying in some old rotten nursing home. (Music.) Taking us through all these anguish years. They took us and put us in chains and that's nothing. This business—that business—there's no comparison to that, to this." [10]

The "rotten" nursing home and chains are the fears of the exhausted, aging criminal who in fact faces life in prison. Warning that "they" are coming to kill "our babies," he projects onto enemies the murders he is actually directing now, attested by the shrieks of poisoned children in the background. Babies stand for rebirth and immortality, but also for the hope of reintegrating personality splintered by lies and internal conflict, the hope of finding a coherent self: "They've robbed us of our land, and they've taken us and driven us and we tried to find ourselves. We tried to find a new beginning. But it's too late."

As he pretends that the decision is voluntary and democratic, Christine Miller, an articulate sixty-year-old black woman, brings up his past promise that the Russians have "given them a code" and in a crisis a plane would take them to Russia. The magician pulls more excuses from his hat. Maybe "next time," after reincarnation, she may go to Russia. And when she persists that she has a right to her own opinion and the babies have a right to their lives, Jones tops the lie without missing a beat: "Right now I'm making a call to Russia. What more can I give you?"

Grasping for arguments, he observes that the defectors who left with Ryan's party were white, playing on racial fears and animosity. When an elderly woman picks up on the theme, he interprets her feelings to her, crystallizing her vague sense of racial betrayal. "Broke my heart completely," she agrees. Her reasoning reveals the tremendous need for self-esteem and acceptance in so many of the followers: "All of this year the white people had been with us, and they're not a part of us. So we might as well end it now because I don't see...."

Jones replies by insisting on his own concerns: "It's all over. The congressman has been murdered. (Music and singing.) Well, it's all over, all over. What a legacy, what a legacy." In response to an inaudible comment soon after he reinforces the mixed confession-denial: "I didn't, but my people did. My people did. They're my people, and they've been provoked too much. They've been provoked too much." Presumably he means the guards who carried out his murders at the airstrip instead of restraining him as he'd once commanded in less desperate days.

When protests flicker, he cries to the nurses, "Can we hasten with that medication?" And to the victims, "You don't know what you've done"—as if the group, not he, killed the visitors. Later on he refers to defector Tim Stoen as if Stoen is murdering the group. The exhausted rage to punish scapegoats comes out in his vow that enemies "brought this upon us. And they'll pay for that." He becomes urgent as the group's mood wavers. "Please. For God's sake, let's get on with it. We've lived—we've lived as no other people lived and loved. We've had as much of this world as you're gonna get. Let's just be done with it. Let's be done with the agony of it." (Applause.) His own fear of death surfaces again: "It's far, far harder to have to walk through every day, die slowly--and from the time you're a child 'til the time you get gray, you're dying."

The supreme leader wants to merge with—to hide in—the group. So the group can share his burden of guilt he half-confesses that he has had the visitors murdered. "You can't separate yourself from your brother and your sister. No way I'm going to do it. I refuse. I don't know who fired the shot. I don't know who killed the congressman. But as far as I am concerned, I killed him. You understand what I'm saying? I killed him. He had no business coming. I told him not to come."

Unless the group "passes over," they will be tortured and killed. In reality of course Jones is killing them. And he cannot quite believe he too will die: "I want to see you go. They can take me and I don't care what they do with me." It is possible, as Jeannie Mills believed, that he was scheming to escape. The feint at martyrdom plays to the persistent hero-worship in the air. A handful of true believers come to the microphone and give testimonials as if this is just another temple service or an infomercial.

He tries to talk down the anguish before him. "Lay down your life with dignity," he coaxes. "Don't lay down with tears and agony. There's nothing to death. It's...it's just stepping over to another plane. Don't be this way. Stop this hysterics. This is not the way for people who are Socialists or Communists to die. No way for us to die. We must die with some dignity. We must die with some dignity. We will have no choice. Now we have some choice. Do you think they're gonna allow this to be done—allow us to get by with this? You must be insane." Not he is insane, but they. "Look children, it's just something to put you to rest. Oh, God." Children are crying. Jones begins to plead, and it is hard not to hear appeals to a fantasy mother akin to his sentimentality about his "seniors" even as he apparently scolds a woman trying to resist: "Mother, Mother, Mother, Mother, Mother, please. Mother, please, please, please. Don't—don't do this. Don't do this. Lay down your life with your child. But don't do this."

Like a dutiful child, a woman tells him, "We're doing all of this for you."

"Free at last," he replies evoking emancipation and Martin Luther King's civil rights rhetoric. "Keep--keep your emotions down. Keep your emotions down. Children, it will not hurt. If you'd be—if you'll be quiet. If you'll be quiet." With babies screaming in death throes and eddies of distress in the group he implores them all to "Stop this hysteria." At the evidence of their death agonies he is responding to the pressure of guilt and panic in himself as well. "So be patient. Be patient. Death is—I tell you, I don't care how many screams you hear. I don't care how many anguished cries. Death is a million times preferable to ten more days of this life. If you knew what was ahead of you—if you knew what was ahead of you, you'd be glad to be stepping over tonight." He can't resist some fatherly scolding: "Adults, I call on you to stop this nonsense. Stop exciting your children. Hurry, my children. Hurry…hurry." Quickly quickly quickly quickly."

In his effort to make rhetorical theater preempt fatal reality the rational mind snatches at fragments and formulas: "Death, death, death is common to people. And the Eskimos, they take death in their stride. Let's be digni—let's be dignified. If you quit tell them they're dying--if you adults would stop some of this nonsense. Adults, adults, adults. I call on you to stop this nonsense. I call on you to quit exciting your children when all they're doing is going to a quiet rest. I call on you to stop this now if you have any respect at all. Are we black, proud, and Socialist, or what are we? Now stop this nonsense. Don't carry this on anymore. You're exciting your children."

The children can't rationalize. They sense panic.

In the closing turmoil incoherence spreads. "No, no sorrow—that it's all over," he says. "I'm glad it's over. Hurry, hurry my children. Hurry. All I think (inaudible) from the hands of the enemy. Hurry, my children. Hurry. There are seniors out here that I'm concerned about. Hurry. I don't want to leave my seniors to this mess. Only quickly, quickly, quickly, quickly, quickly." There is a pause in which one of the victims apparently professes some sort of devotion, and with stupefying dissociation Jones replies in the scripted formula of everyday business, "Good knowing you."

Several true believers praise the Cause and Father's love. One woman brings out the infantile subtext: "Right. Yes, eh. Dad's love and nursing, goodness and kindness and bring us to this land of freedom. His love—his mother was the advance—the advance guard to socialism. And his love (inaudible) will go on forever unto the fields of—"

She runs out of clichés. But Jones is anxious to get on with his business plan, the final act of their play: "Where's the vat, the vat, the vat? Where's the vat with the Green C on it? The vat with the Green C in. Bring it so the adults can begin."[11]

That is, die.

As in Mohammed Atta's final instructions to his gang, Jones the God-priest was concerned that "You must not discomfort your animal during the slaughter." But like Atta, he had come too far to turn back to a world of self-doubt and guilt. There was nothing left now but sweaty bodies, needy dependents, and squalling babies. The glorious possibilities lay in the beyond, an illusion—what did it matter as long as no one was left to be happily rescued by others and to testify to his failure and criminal rage?

The final Jonestown tape shows not a cadre of suicidal fanatics or, despite the menace of Jones's armed guards, crushing force. On the contrary, the collapse gathered momentum among disoriented, conflicted followers marooned in a jungle, alienated from home and familiar landmarks. They had literally abandoned familiar cognitive boundaries. Now they depended on group solidarity, Jones, and a flattering ideology for coherence and willpower. The tape reveals only wavering resistance to abandon and death. The few true believers who take the microphone tell us that confused imaginations clung to Jones's grand themes—including martyrdom—to ground themselves. A few voices objected to death, but nobody proposed a realistic alternative or condemned the murder of Congressman Ryan and his party. The followers had surrendered much of their autonomy to Jones and to the nebulous community. Like Jones's euphemism of "passing over," the poisonous fruit juice made an apt metaphor for the pressure of conformity in the group. Under stress, berserk style disposed them to reach for purpose in the hallucinatory beyond.

STAR WARS

In the following decade evangelical ministries took to the airwaves as a route to expansion. They banished the sinister Jonestown themes with variety show entertainment and an upbeat message. After this sunny interlude berserk themes darkened again. Infuriated by the Federal government's incineration of David Koresh's band of Branch Davidians at their compound in Waco Texas, Timothy McVeigh blew up the McMurrah Federal Building in Oklahoma City (1995) in the deadliest terrorist attack in the U.S. before the World Trade Center inferno. Based on his interest in the white-supremacist novel *The Turner Diaries* (1978), McVeigh's racial convictions were the opposite of Jones's. Still, the novel fantasizes a doomsday nuclear race war of the sort that terrified Jones's followers. Where Jones fantasized about buying an atomic bomb, McVeigh actually built a five thousand pound ammonium nitrate bomb that killed nearly two hundred people and damaged more than 300 buildings in Oklahoma City.

The Christian right achieved new visibility in the post-Vietnam decades with its rousing attacks on social issues such as abortion, evolution, and homosexuality. While some of this militancy has been strategic—acquiring political influence and donors, for example—the core themes exercise a soft version of survival rage. On its website a "pro-life" organization called "Survivors," for example, directly inflames personal death-anxiety with ominous music, photographs of concentration camp corpses, and the warning that "If you were born after 1972, we challenge you to consider yourself a Survivor of the Abortion Holocaust. 1/3 of your generation has been killed by abortion in America! The Survivors are taking an active stand on behalf of those who have already been lost, and for those who are scheduled to die through abortion. We are empowered by the truth, enabled by extensive training, and unafraid of condemning the death of innocents." Although carefully inexplicit, this rhetoric is paramilitary and judicial. "You" are part of a special group, "your generation," and in a genocidal war. You need "training" to "rise up…willing to be used by God to 'defend those unjustly sentenced to death.'" This is the language of jihad, directed at a nation that "schedules" annihilation through "death sentences." It calls for a heroic battle for survival, with "you" enacting a version of "the greatest generation's" triumph over Nazism—the nation's last righteous war.

Circulating on the web is a video titled "Battle Cry." Prefaced by Christ's threat display, "I come not to bring peace, but a sword," the video uses crusader swords and portentous melodrama—Carmina Burana chant, cascading echo effects—to beef up this mantra for Christian "soldiers":

"I'm not an innocent bystander,
I am a threat to my enemies
I am powerful
I am strategic and bold
I will not sit idly by
I will take ground
I will advance
I will tear through my enemy
I will not avoid the difficult fight

I will fight
I will be wounded
I will be targeted & I will bleed
I will not tire
I will see tragedy I will feel pain
But I will be restored
My feet will not stumble
My hands will hold fast
I will not be intimidated
I cannot be stopped
I will stand by my brothers in arms
I will fight until my last breath
I will push the limits
I scale the mountains
My enemy will cower
For I serve a great king!"

This is not the Christianity of the Sermon on the Mount. The chant directs teenagers to role-play at berserk abandon: "I will bleed, I cannot be stopped, I will fight until my last breath." The mantra mixes adolescent narcissism, idealism, and a need to belong with suicidal self-sacrifice and the demonization of enemies.

The crusader chant honors the Christian story of the crucifixion less than the mystical group-bonding rituals of the Nazi SS and other paramilitary cults. The predominance of style and play-acting makes possible the nation's polite obliviousness to the literal meaning of the fantasies. The media paid little notice when vice-presidential candidate Sarah Palin's church, the Wasilla Assembly of God, handed out Samurai swords—the emblem of Japanese fascism—to young adults in the congregation, with the incitement to use "a double edged sword in their hands to inflict vengeance on the nations, and punishment on the peoples, and to bind their kings with fetters, their nobles with shackles of iron, and to carry out the sentence written against them" (Psalms 149 verses 6-9).[12]

Projection of berserk tropes onto the "enemy" has supported attacks on abortion clinics and the assassination of doctors. Scott Roeder, who allegedly murdered Dr. George Tiller in a Kansas church on May 31, 2009, fits a familiar profile: a man divorced, preoccupied with death-anxiety (abortion), and according to his brother David, mentally ill at various times of his life. But Roeder acted in an atmosphere that legitimized the murder. The son of clergyman Frank

Schaeffer posted an apology online explaining that his father had written the best-selling *A Christian Manifesto* (1981). "In certain passages he advocated force if all other methods for rolling back the abortion ruling of Roe v. Wade failed. He compared America and its legalized abortion to Hitler's Germany and said that whatever tactics would have been morally justified in removing Hitler would be justified in trying to stop abortion. I said the same thing in a book I wrote (*A Time For Anger*) that right wing evangelicals made into a best seller."[13]

Schaeffer apologizes for unintentionally contributing to a "climate" that could encourage murder. As a style, however, incendiary language paradoxically seems "natural" or normal, even as its furious zeal makes it hard to see that style takes on a life of its own in which motives may be unaccountable. At the time of Dr. Tiller's murder, for example, anti-abortion rage was formulaic in rant media. Bill O'Reilly was vilifying Dr. Tiller for "Nazi stuff" and "operating a death mill." Columnist Kathleen Parker referred to media-savvy activists such as Randall Terry as "fire-breathers.[14] As the genre desensitizes audiences and yesterday's fire-breathing becomes today's stale breath, rhetoric escalates toward abandon. During the health care debates of 2009-10, for example, survival anxiety glibly switched to the specter of "death panels" that would triage the elderly.

The teenagers' crusader vision has a counterpart in the fundamentalist subculture within the U. S. military, in which the "global war on terror" is commonly construed as "a spiritual battle." "The Source of Combat Readiness," an Officers' Christian Fellowship (OCF) Bible study text, proclaims that spiritual battle means "continually confronting an implacable, powerful foe who hates us and eagerly seeks to destroy us." Another study, unfortunately named "Mission Accomplished," draws on the logic of witch panic: "If Satan cannot succeed with threats from the outside, he will seek to destroy from within." The defense is to subsume secular America into a militant theocracy. "God was to be Lord of all or not Lord at all."[15]

This crude Manichaean language makes inner life a combat zone. It converts fear to wrath and invites group solidarity. People are always looking for ways to legitimize scapegoat psychology and make its arguments credible. Since it ultimately involves survival fears and killing, it always opens toward the beyond, as religion and politics repeatedly demonstrate. Senator John Ensign, for example, belongs to a Pentecostal denomination, the International Church of the Foursquare Gospel, that "promotes a new health care paradigm in which both physical and psychological maladies can be cured through the casting out of demons. In the new approach, individuals can even heal themselves by exorcising their own demons."[16]

The "new approach' is of course an ancient fantasy system given topical authority as a "movement." The "demon-deliverance movement" or "Theophostic Ministry" ignores its historical affinity with early modern witch-hunt hysteria. Its style of thinking risks inflaming paranoid symptoms by attributing supernatural powers to troubling thoughts and, given the plasticity of imagination, seeing infiltrating enemies everywhere. By reducing experience to a melodrama, favoring hypervigilance, it intensifies preoccupation with the self even as it closes off other explanations, inviting self-intoxication. In a word, this is berserk style opening into magical thinking. "One very distinctive characteristic of Third Wave Christianity is its emphasis that average Christians can perform the same magnitude of healing miracles described in the New Testament to have been performed by Jesus Christ—including raising the dead."[17]

The totalizing character of the ideation is classic berserk style, echoing the psychodynamics of Islam's radical jihadis who would dominate society by imposing their own versions of history and sharia law. The preacher-proprietors of aggressive new religions like to claim millions of adherents, but in the absence of reliable data, zeroes tend to be promiscuous. The "neo-Apostolic" empire builder C. Peter Wagner speaks in terms of "megablocks" and boasts that "post-denominational" and more radical movements number hundreds of millions and are growing faster than the earth's population and faster than Islam. His claim revisits the ancient appetite for life more plentiful than the stars in heaven, and in the process outdoing a sinister rival. Such is the power of survival greed.

SUPERNATURAL ABUSE

In the post-Vietnam decades witch-hunt ideation assumed many guises. The most unlikely exponents of berserk style proved to be a subculture of psychotherapists who used sexual abuse to explain a wide host of symptoms. They were especially excited about dissociative disorders such as multiple personality (M.P.D., now called dissociative identity disorder) and recovered memories (suddenly recalled but unsubstantiated sexual abuse). Before long a subset of clinicians and patients were entangled in a classic iatrogenic feedback loop. Encouraged by popular self-help books and media hype, credulous sufferers reinforced each other's beliefs and gave social reality to some wildly implausible theories.

Feelings of persecution by evil parent figures have venerable precedents, from fairy tales to witchcraft lore, in which crones and the "father" of lies Satan supposedly cannibalized babies, sickened children, practiced loathsome sterile sex, and worse. The fascination with multiple personality owed much to Flora Rheta Schrieber's *Sybil*, (book 1973, film 1976) and Dr. Lawrence Pazder and Michelle Smith's *Michelle Remembers* (1980), each presenting a case study with sensational symptoms, and each reliably debunked.[18] Michelle's story explicitly borrowed heavily from witchcraft lore. By the 1990s child sex abuse and M.P.D. featured in novels for adolescents and critics could shake their heads at "The Vogue of Childhood Misery." [19]

The clinicians' ignorance of history included the history of their profession, in particular the belated recognition of iatrogenic and transference phenomena in the days of Charcot and Freud.[20] If nothing else, the elasticity of the theories should have raised warning flags. One of the most unsavory variants of the abuse theme proved to be "Satanic ritual abuse syndrome," which held that patients were suffering the effects of programming by a shadowy global cult whose Satanic rituals called for the abduction, sacrifice, and prostitution of children. Like medieval panic about Jews feeding on Christian children, the theory imagined the cult to be a wealthy, clannish elite bent on consuming the vitality of innocents.[21]

The cult supposedly exercised mind control through brainwashing techniques that could induce amnesia, giving the perpetrators a totalitarian cast dramatized in John Frankenheimer's Cold War thriller *The Manchurian Candidate* (1962). Mind control is a deeply engrained human preoccupation, evident in ancient beliefs about possession, in the fascination with Satan, in the allure of "animal magnetism," and in the cult delusions generated around Hitler's personality.[22] In *The Shock Doctrine*, Naomi Klein traces the origins of that corporate-military ideology to the CIA and Cold Warriors' obsession—and experiments—with brainwashing techniques. The web of analogy is dense, and colors a wide political spectrum.

These improbable materials haunt—no other word will do—the two cases reported in Ofra Bikel and Rachel Dretzin's lucid PBS *Frontline* investigation "The Search for Satan" (October 24, 1995). While the patients, Patricia Burgus and Mary Shanley, eventually won lawsuits against their psychiatrist Bennett Braun and other therapists, they both suffered dangerously destabilizing treatment driven by berserk dynamics.

"Mary S" (Shanley), a young teacher, sought treatment for persistent anxiety symptoms after some painful setbacks in an otherwise healthy middle-class life. In a brief intake interview at Rush-Presbyterian-St. Luke's Medical Center in Chicago, psychiatrist Roberta Sachs diagnosed multiple personality disorder caused by membership in a Satanic cult that Mary had been "programmed" to forget. The diagnosis led to two years of heavily drugged hospitalization and a regimen of interrogation meant to force the patient to "abreact" the spectral horrors of the childhood that the therapists projected on her. By the time she won her release in a lawsuit, she had been transferred to clinic in Texas, was in seriously impaired health, and destined for a nursing home—and her insurance policy had topped out at a sum in the millions.

To be sure, the absurdities of the diagnosis were in plain view. Mary S's family, the doctors told her, had been "cult royalty." The cult encoded its brainwashing programs using letters of the Greek alphabet. Her young son was dragged into the net, also hospitalized, and held to be in mortal danger. Nevertheless, as the woman tells the filmmakers, the doctors "were the authorities, the experts." And crucially, berserk style in the culture around her seemed to corroborate their diagnosis. She had heard her local pastor warning about Satan's infiltration of their neighborhoods. The media thrilled to stories about Satanists.

The diagnosis had coercive features reminiscent of Soviet psychiatry. The healers isolated the patient in their hospitals, blocking ordinary reality-testing and dosing her with inappropriate psychotropic drugs. Tape of one of the therapy sessions records a pitiably distraught and helpless Mary S shrieking in anguish while a circle of therapists browbeat her to remember cult atrocities and confirm their narrative. The therapists form an accusing circle as a pack would. More than a sufferer to be healed, the patient is a presumed perpetrator. This is not a figure of speech, since the doctors accused Mary S of being an agent of cult malice, endangering the lives of her husband and son and by implication her doctors. As in witch hysteria, the accusers imagine an evil mother in the service of a Satanic regime with what amount to superhuman powers.

Like brainwashing, the treatment devised by Dr. Braun and others perversely undermined the patient's identity. Accused of harboring murderous motives beyond her control while simultaneously being a target of cult assassination, the patient was consumed by panic. Drugged, sometimes held in restraints, stripped of her own life story, bullied to substitute a nonexistent cult childhood, she was suffering on the edge of an abyss. If abuse is so damaging because it is traumatic, and trauma is an effect of overwhelming terror, then patients such as Mary S, who presented acute anxiety and depression, needed serenity, trust, and a renewed sense of life purpose, not an emergency crusade against a hallucinatory past injury with features that resembled post- 9/11 "harsh interrogation tactics." Relief from terror depends on restoring trust and social bonds, not on imaginary triumphs over "perpetrators" and the Ultimate Perpetrator, Satan.

At the same time, the ritual abuse narrative made the patient death-tainted and a threat not just to her family and self, but also to the doctors. They were caught in a cognitive trap of their own devising. If they believed in their own story and therapy, they faced a menacing woman beyond their control. If they admitted the failure of their story, they faced guilt as well as helplessness: in effect, an attack on their own ground of experience. In short, the situation readily generated berserk panic, and the cruel absurdity of the therapies followed.

The therapists' anxieties were fuel for their heroic roles. In the film Patty Burgus describes how Dr. Braun coached her hospitalized sons to "remember" cult atrocities, rewarding them with stickers for a good performance. Dr. Braun in turn used the fabulations to prove his theories. At one point, as an expert witness in court, he testifies about the child's report of a cult rite in which he had witnessed a man's abdomen cut open and entrails spilling out with a putrid smell. Dr. Braun knows the story is true, he vows, because he's done surgery where such an eruption is a concern. How, he demands, would a five year old boy come by such information if not through the cult?[23]

The answer, says Patty Burgus, is that as she tried to tell Dr. Braun, her son was recounting an episode from *Star Wars* in which Luke Skywalker cuts open the gut of a space creature and gags at the smell of the erupting entrails. The doctor evinces anxiety about death-tainted bodies while blindly seizing on the tale as proof of his heroic narrative as physician. Similar turmoil underlies the hostility of practitioners when challenged by skeptical nurses.

The Satanic abuse fad developed out of banal cultural materials provided by psychologist D. C. "Corey" Hammond, among others. Hammond was a clinician and consultant with degrees in counseling psychology, marital and sex therapy, and clinical hypnosis. His background in suggestive techniques is evident in his own dreamlike suppositions. Behind the Satanic cult, he argued, was a Jewish doctor who had survived the death camps by collaborating with the Nazis and surfaced in the U. S. as "Dr. Green"—a clone of criminal masterminds from pulp fiction. Exposure to traumatic death anxiety (the death camps) arouses berserk survival greed that gorges on children and forbidden sex. "Dr. Green" is the evil twin of the good therapist who happens to be profiting from engaging with the suffering and terror of mental illness.

Just this potent elixir of dread and heroic aggrandizement links berserk therapy to forms of making a killing discussed in earlier chapters. The abuse phenomenon coincided with increased Federal funding for child abuse research. Dr. Braun ran a multi-million dollar dissociative disorders clinic at Rush-Presbyterian that was, after all, a business depending on insurance plans. "Bennett Braun seems to be a promotional genius;" said John Hochman, a California psychiatrist who likens Braun's own professional following to a cult. "He started [The International Society for the Study of Dissociation] and a journal. There were the conferences.... They were just very excited about what they had and nobody challenged them in a very big way" (AP, March 7,1999).

What finally broke the self-confirming paradigm was the data analysis of clinical outcomes by independent auditors who noticed that patients' conditions worsened rather than improved, and a combination of patients' lawsuits and the formation of critical groups such as the False memory Syndrome Foundation. In the meantime the billing for care resembled the unchecked extravagance unfolding in Wall Street finance.

For a time recovered memory and mind-control themes pervaded many areas of American culture. Futuristic thrillers such as Kathryn Bigelow's *Strange Days* (1995) and Paul Verhoeven's *Total Recall* (1990) used fears of brainwashing technology. Like the Terminator saga, *Total Recall* is a digest of berserk themes. It envisions a criminal mastermind reminiscent of Antichrist using a cult-like regime to rule over a servile class (on Mars!) through mind-control and false memories. Like the Satanic abuse delusion, the film associates cognitive mischief with episodes of berserk rage.

During the 90s the courts finally barred recovered memory testimony as research exposed its unreliability and the damage it caused. Mary Shanley suffered terribly, but her induced "memories" could have put her, her supposedly Satanic parents, or others in prison. Or worse. The State of Texas put Cameron Todd Willingham to death in 2004 after a conviction based on "junk science" and influenced by community fantasies about Satanism. The prosecution concluded that the unemployed father had deliberately set the fire that killed his three small children one morning while his wife was at work. Once gripped by the popular idea that they had discovered what the prosecutor called a sociopathic "demon," neighborhood witnesses reinterpreted their recollections of Willingham's behavior while the house burned. A psychologist testified that Willingham's rock group posters revealed pathological motives: "There's a hooded skull with wings and a hatchet. And all of these are in fire—it reminds me of something like Hell. And there's a picture—a Led Zeppelin picture of a fallen angel.... I see there's an association many time with cultive-type of activities. A focus on death, dying. Many times individuals that have a lot of this type of art have interest in Satanic-type activities." Political culture in Texas militates against clemency, and the Board of Pardons and Paroles apparently ignored an appeal based on new scientific evidence. "A Texas appellate judge has called the clemency system 'a legal fiction.'"[24]

The "demonic" rock band imagery and the tattoo of a skull used to help convict Willingham are an ironic reminder of how explosively ambiguous death-anxiety can be. For adolescents, the "Satanic" posters presumably objectify, and create some mastery of, fears of death and social death. The posters mark teenage solidarity. At the same time the imagery is a marketing tool to sell industrial entertainment. Unluckily for Willingham, the terrifying deaths of small children, in a culture limited by ignorance and latent anger, turned the fantasy images into grounds for judicial killing of a "demon" parent.

The cluster of fantasies around dissociative disorders and Satanic abuse defied reality-testing as long as it did in part because it drew strength from a confluence of unlikely voices, from fundamentalist preachers and law enforcement to MS magazine. In a keynote address at a 1991 conference on MPD in Chicago, feminist Gloria Steinem praised Dr. Braun for his life-saving work. The demoralizing slump after the defeat in Vietnam saw anti-scientific fundamentalism expand its appeal, amplified by aggressive new religious broadcasting, demographic transformation in the Bible belt, and the official sanction of figures such as President Reagan, who pumped up crusading spirit by calling the Soviet Union "the evil empire," and alluded in public to Armageddon and his Millennialist beliefs.[25]

THE LIVING END

As Otto Rank understood, nothing is more exhilarating than survival, and there is no survival more ultimate than doomsday. In Judgment Day theologies the divine parent defines the meaning of everything once and for all, and the blessed join Him in heaven. We can only think about such finality as we do death, in tropes. The process can take astonishing forms. In *The Pursuit of the Millennium*, Norman Cohn showed that Nazi and Soviet ideologies drew on millenialist mythologies. The "thousand year" Reich used an eschatological climax in the distant, unreal future to rationalize a berserk drive for expansion. The suicidal, blow-off climax of Nazi millennialism was effectively built in.

American Protestants have intermittently cultivated apocalyptic themes from colonial times. By the close of the twentieth century some American fundamentalists were lobbying for policies toward the Middle East that they hoped would fulfill biblical prophecies loosely associated with Armageddon in the book of *Revelations*. While there have been some political benefits for the believers, "Many of them have an ecstatic belief in the cleansing power of apocalyptic violence."[26]

An item in *L'Express* (February 26, 2009) reported that in a telephone call meant to persuade French president Chirac to join in the invasion of Iraq, President Bush asserted that "Gog and Magog are at work in the Middle East" and that "the Biblical prophecies are about to be fulfilled." Chirac listened with puzzlement and apprehension ("effroi"). After some research he was not amused. The absurd apocalyptic prophecy that Bush was invoking to justify his war plans—or the war meant to fulfill a prophecy—alarmed him. ("Chirac, lui, ne rit pas. Cette parabole d'une apocalypse annoncée pour réaliser une prophétie l'inquiète et le tourmente").

For decades fundamentalist Christians have been developing a feedback loop in which middle eastern turbulence substantiates the book of *Revelations* and, reciprocally, *Revelations* accounts for the tumult in the middle east. If we can trust the account in *L'Express*, Bush imagined that such millenarian ideas could persuade his French counterpart to join in a war. In theory, apocalypse frames the uncertain future, resolving anxieties and boosting morale. In the real world, as Bush's misreading of Chirac indicates, prophetic inspiration is prescriptive and not always attuned to the feelings of others.

Modernity is a history of traumatic disenchantments. The Renaissance thrilled and quaked at the rediscovery of magnificent civilizations that had perished. With science came evidence that humans may go the way of dinosaurs, and that life on earth will die out with the exhausted sun in a few billion years. Cable television documentaries especially favor doomsday topics from asteroids and dinosaur extinctions to nuclear weapons and global climate change. Like religious apocalypse, the documentaries frame, disturbing information so that imagination can develop defenses and get used to it.

Since "end times" scenarios are pure speculation, criticism can only assess the work they do in the present. Like rightwing media rant, doomsday can be a vehicle for self-medication. Self-congratulating "end times" soap operas such as Tim LaHaye's entertaining multi-volume "rapture" epic *Left Behind* can impart an adrenalizing morale boost, no matter how backward they may be as theology. The reported multi-million sales of the twelve-volume *Left Behind* series appears to confirm the estimate that as many as a third of Americans believe the world is coming to an end soon. But the actual market share of such fantasies remains hazy. The quality of belief is always hard to measure, and there is a palpable quality of play about pop apocalypses akin to the pleasure in popular supermarket tabloids ("Woman Gives Birth to Martian Baby"). Belief in the imminent end of the world focuses many cults and can be a tormenting symptom of schizophrenia, but for many believers it is a tonic or a token safely tucked away, and nothing more.

The *Left Behind* story's Rapture domesticates the terrors of the end, translating the righteous to a heaven of abstract nouns with no more inconvenience than a change of wardrobe. Thanks to the Rapture, believers can participate vicariously in berserk rage against unbelievers. Here is an efficient summary of the fantasy:

In the 19th century, two immigrant preachers (Edward Irving and John Nelson Darby) cobbled together a series of unrelated passages from the Bible to create what appears to be a consistent narrative: Jesus will return to earth when certain preconditions have been met. The first of these was the establishment of a state of Israel. The next involves Israel's occupation of the rest of its "Biblical lands" (most of the Middle East), and the rebuilding of the Third Temple on the site now occupied by the Dome of the Rock and Al-Aqsa mosques. The legions of the Antichrist will then be deployed against Israel, and their war will lead to a final showdown in the valley of Armageddon.

The Jews will either burn or convert to Christianity, and the Messiah will return to earth.[27]

The cosmic battlefield ranges from the biblical Armageddon to the guidebook Israel of Tim LaHaye's propagandistic soap opera *Armageddon*, in which generic Christians and Jews slaughter minions of Antichrist with Uzis and comic book dialogue. Again Monbiot: "before the big battle begins, all 'true believers' (ie those who believe what THEY believe) will be lifted out of their clothes and wafted up to heaven during an event called the Rapture. Not only do the worthy get to sit at the right hand of God, but they will be able to watch, from the best seats, their political and religious opponents being devoured by boils, sores, locusts and frogs, during the seven years of Tribulation which follow." In this theology berserk style converts the sadistic horror of the "final showdown" to righteous joy, while sanitizing the killing frenzy with the bizarre amalgam of biblical torments (boils, locusts, and the like) and typical pulp fiction toys (Uzis, rockets).

"Most journalists find it difficult to take seriously that tens of millions of Americans, filled with fantasies of revenge and empowerment, long to leave a world they despise. These Armageddonites believe that they alone will get a quick, free pass when they are 'raptured' to paradise, no good deeds necessary, not even a day of judgment." John Basil Utley compares them to Islamic fundamentalist jihadis, then adds: "These end-timers have great influence over the U.S. government's foreign policy. They are thick with the Republican leadership. At a recent conference in Washington, congressional leader Roy Blunt, for example, has said that their work is 'part of God's plan.' At the same meeting, where speakers promoted attacking Iran, former House Majority Leader Tom DeLay glorified 'end times.'"[28]

In the run-up to the millennium Year 2000 the fear of apocalyptic extremism generated the FBI's Megiddo Report (1999), an inventory of groups such as the Christian Identity movement that blend racist and cosmic chauvinism with millenarian melodrama and a propensity for violence. "Megiddo" is another name for the biblical battleground of Armageddon. Although law enforcement did report the disruption of Y2K bomb plots aimed at targets as far-flung as Jerusalem and the Los Angeles airport, the anticlimactic outcome of the fateful day exposed the degree of berserk style at work.

In fact the "rapture racket," as Barbara R, Rossing calls it in *The Rapture Exposed* (2004) allows people to consider topical fears while keeping them safely unreal. The "rapture" website "leftbehind.com" hypes prophetic signs that read like a news index: "Political crisis, Economic crisis, Worldwide epidemics. Environmental catastrophe, Mass disappearances, [and] Military apocalypse." The September 11th terrorism popularized allusions to past and present religious crusades, Satanic schemes, and mystified conspiracy. Equally salient is anxiety about the boundless growth upon which modern capitalism depends, environmental degradation, global pandemic such as bird flu, and new fears of global climate change. Doomsday ideation appears in television documentaries and movies that depict iconic cities sinking beneath the waves as in the myth of Noah.

In *Ecology of Fear,* (1998), urban critic Mike Davis calculates that Los Angeles has been destroyed in fiction and film 138 times.[29] Davis's "central claim is that the citizens of Los Angeles have imagined disasters through a lens of fear and misunderstanding and that the result is a profoundly unequal society that is apocalyptically out of balance with its environment."[30] Just such a cosmic imbalance or incommensurability is crudely dramatized in thrillers that play out variations on catastrophism.[31] In films such as Steven Spielberg's *A. I.* (2001) and Roland Emmerich's *The Day after Tomorrow* (2004) the pulp repertory of berserk convulsion and exhaustion is blockbuster box office. In films of the 1990s such as *Independence Day* (1996) and *Deep Impact* (1998), aliens and a rogue comet menace the earth with extinction.

In these films the catastrophe is actually a collision of everyday reality with cosmic ultimates. An imponderable universe crashes into the human world of flimsy, inadequate meanings. Humankind's deeply rooted guilt at inadequacy struggles against narcissistic survival greed. The imagery plays out harmlessly for most audiences, allowing people to entertain safely the wonder of life's absurdity. But for some, including the thirty-nine members of Marshall Applewhite's Heaven's Gate cult, the crash can be unbearable. The aging, unwell guru taught that universal doom was imminent. Since the guilty earth was about to be wiped clean and renewed, he urged group suicide. His followers accordingly converted the threat of cosmic collision into a sci-fi narrative of escape through death into the paradise afforded by a passing comet. As in the conditioning evident in the Peoples Temple, the group had long been slowly building up to berserk abandon. And as with Jim Jones, the group death provided comfort and company for the ailing guru as he faced his own death.

Some versions of end times stress the idea of abreaction or purgation. The supreme battle is supposed to open the way to a spell of utopian peace something like the return to life after a harrowing illness and the expulsion of "germs"—a cognitive bias evident in the central role of exorcism and emetics in the history of medicine. In such scenarios the expulsion of demons, poisons, or germs corresponds to the divine judgment's banishment of the wicked to Hell.

Even in the realm of industrial entertainment we can only estimate the effect of paranoid fantasies on public attitudes, including the post-9/11 passions. This ambiguity is painfully evident in the military's quixotic, staggeringly expensive "Star Wars" visions of militarized space. Such a "theater" is boundless. Robert Jay Lifton identifies what is at stake: "The war on terrorism is apocalyptic, then, exactly because it is militarized and yet amorphous, without limits of time or place, and has no clear end. It therefore enters the realm of the infinite."[32]

This is the territory of abandon in which potentially bottomless terror fuels fantastic— superhuman—appetite for life.

CONCLUSION

THE ROMANCE OF ABANDON

Words ought to be a little wild, for they are the
assaults of thoughts on the unthinking.

John Maynard Keynes

To return to the beginning: "the concept of berserk abandon is far more pervasive than conventional wisdom recognizes." This proposition spurred a friend of mine to ask, "If the concept is so pervasive, how come it isn't immediately recognized?" An answer came to her in a flash: the berserk is hidden in plain view, like Poe's purloined letter. Since it shades into everyday behavior and ritual, and takes protean guises in berserk style, it is latent everywhere.

Every individual and every culture devises strategies for managing abandon. One such strategy is the idea of "the American dream,"[1] which packages the nation's aspirations and furies as a prize to be achieved by heroic ambition. Schools across the country teach the term through Fitzgerald's *The Great Gatsby* (1925) and its vision of the romantic crook who "makes it" and tragically dies in a berserk America. For the most part, the schools are respectfully vague about the dream—it's something about freedom, wish-fulfillment, romance, and getting to be somebody. The novel is safe to teach because it ends with the green light glowing on Daisy's dock as "the orgastic future…year by year recedes before us." At a time of economic slippage and record inequality, young Americans can find some consolation in the rueful abandon—romantic but also didactic—that sums up: "So we beat on, boats against the current, borne back ceaselessly into the past." Most of us, it seems to say, are going nowhere beautifully. But we want to believe. We enjoy the romance of abandon.

Yet the novel is also a scathing protest. From personal experience Fitzgerald was wise to infantile greed for "the fresh green breast of the new world," "the milk of wonder," booze, the vanished glory of football, and a beloved voice "full of money." Behind that appetite is the creaturely terror of futility and death: the valley of ashes, hit-and-run death, "what a grotesque thing a rose is."

The novel is astonishingly prescient. Gatsby has created himself through berserk style, at home among Madoffs and Enron smart-alecks: a celebrity impresario of thrilling bacchanals, exploiting the nation's windfall war on intoxicants. His pal Wolfsheim's fix of the World Series bespeaks epic gambling and corruption. Diddled by the wealthy Tom Buchanan and despised by his wife Myrtle, the mechanic Wilson faces social death. "He's so dumb," sneers Tom, "he doesn't know he's alive." Wilson's one authentic act, his berserk murder, destroys the fabulous mirage around him for all the wrong reasons. To Wilson, the billboard with T.J. Eckleberg's eyeglasses comes to stand for what's right, grounding it in a hallucinatory religious beyond.

In Gatsby's fatal obsession with Daisy and Myrtle Wilson's blind rush into traffic, appetite for life is amok. But in the emasculated husband's God-obsessed, suicidal rampage, the novel recognizes the compulsion to enforce "what's right." Aware of Tom Buchanan's role in Myrtle's death and Gatsby's murder, Nick Carraway recognizes the crazed moral aggression: "I saw that what [Tom] had done was, to him, entirely justified."

The scale of these ironies defies tidy summary, which is the novelist's way of reminding us that the world is bigger than we are. Among the ironies, beyond even Fitzgerald's ken, is the way "the colored empires" in Asia have risen in an economic whirlwind, and Gatsby's dubious military medal from "little Montenegro" nods toward the 1990s U.S. military intervention in the Balkans. Post-Vietnam America still advertises the goal of making the world safe for democracy, but in an unruly world the global policeman can sound like the self-serving Tom Buchanan, that harbinger of conniving media rant: "Flushed with his impassioned gibberish, he saw himself standing alone on the last barrier of civilization."

Carried away, Tom might remind us of the panicky alarum triggered by the September 11th terrorism. To the shocked nation, the attacks epitomized do-or-die abandon, and evoked rhetorical, and eventually military, overreactions. Hysterical voices imagined a global array of Islamic fanatics menacing "our" God as well as Main Street. Terrorist abandon incited abandon in the victims: a concatenation of emergency responses that led to the USA Patriot Act (2001) and a Homeland Security force (2002). The legislation authorized unprecedented surveillance and an atmosphere of hypervigilance that included color-coded terrorism alerts.

The national security state encroached on traditional American liberties in too many ways to enumerate them all here. But it needs to be said that the militarization of security reached alarming proportions, not only in the invasion of Iraq and the expanded global network of U.S. military bases, but also in the militarization of police forces at home. In the wave of protests aroused by the police shooting of young black males, especially Michael Brown in Ferguson Missouri (August 9, 2014), local police mustered full-scale military hardware donated by the Pentagon and in Ferguson blocked journalists with, among other things, a military-sounding "no fly zone." In the terms of this book, forces within Federal and local government were using the idea of abandon to justify an ominous ongoing escalation of authoritarian controls directed particularly at minorities and the poor.

In *Gatsby*, Nick points to the rhythm of rampage and retreat: "They were careless people, Tom and Daisy—they smashed up things and creatures and then retreated back into their money or their vast carelessness, or whatever it was that kept them together, and let other people clean up the mess they had made."

Or whatever it was that kept them together.

One of the things that has kept Americans together is berserk style. The nation interpreted the breakneck momentum of development and historical change as progress and opportunity. The "United" States has always had to struggle against fragmentation, subduing the Confederacy, the territories of the wild west, and client regimes abroad. In the 21st century, the political paralysis of the country masks the de facto control of democracy by corporations and the corporate military. Self-styled militias and a range of nominally conservative ideologies openly scorn "big government."

This hostility to cooperation matters because, in Nick's judgment, Tom and Daisy "let other people clean up the mess they had made." The valley of ashes cannot see, let alone reach, the green light on

Daisy's dock. As in the 1920s and today, the mess came from unaccountable financial excess: speculative, leveraged, predatory, and mystified. In the new century, berserk development is changing "the fresh green breast of the new world" into a valley of ashes. On every continent ecosystems are showing stress: deforestation, atmospheric and water pollution, carbon and nitrogen release, soil degradation, resource depletion and extinctions. Globalization widens awareness, but it is grounded in fantasies of unlimited expansion, and expansion drives toward the edge of control.

Reporting on energy scarcity and "resource wars," Michael Klare issued a forecast titled "A Planet on the Brink: Will Economic Brushfires Prove Too Virulent to Contain?" Raising prospects of berserk panic, he observed that "continued economic decline combined with a pervasive sense that existing systems and institutions are incapable of setting things right is already producing a potentially lethal brew of anxiety, fear, and rage. Popular explosions of one sort or another are inevitable."[2]

If anything can counter this "lethal brew," it would be the emerging paradigm of sustainability, which offers means of managing abandon, but requires science and criticism, self-restraint and cooperation. Sustainability emphasizes equilibrium and interrelatedness, systems rather than individual triumph. It requires a different way of thinking about creaturely motives: death-anxiety and the appetite for fertility. It also requires political will that is nowhere on the horizon.

The present model of economic growth can only become more fraught as resources are depleted and less developed countries strive to match the well-being of the affluent. As the economist Jeffrey Sachs reminds us, China has been achieving nearly a 10% growth rate, meaning that its economy will double every seven years. In thirty years, the exponential demand is staggering to contemplate. And China is by no means alone among aspirants.

It remains to be seen if our creaturely limits will allow us to respond to the danger. The powers of denial keep us short-sighted to protect us from overwhelming panic, and toiling humans adjust with a shrug to slow, fatal change. But emergency alarms can be tragically perverse too. Just as some people react to a rampage by demanding more guns and freedom to shoot on sight, so survival greed tempts us to reinforce the barriers between the gated community and squalor.

Currently the will to develop sustainable policies is nearly nonexistent. The corporate state and the corporate military have captured representative government. If corporations are persons, as the

Supreme Court thinks, they are frankly selfish persons, striving to dominate markets and maximize the bottom line. They misallocate capital because they have no social responsibilities. If they cannot see the good sense in paying a living wage and taxes, how can they be expected to think about cooperation on a scale that can provide fresh water for a toxic planet? How can they invest in equilibrium if to them population growth means only more consumers and cheaper labor? If they are too big to fail, why should they advocate reform and renewal? If they are multinationals and free to abscond with their profits to another venue, why can keep them from enjoying the impunity of outlaws?

At the heart of the puzzle is the tragic dilemma Becker recognized in *The Denial of Death:* we are animals uniquely aware of, and terrified by, our mortal futility, yet also able to dream eternity, immortality, perfection, and divinity in the beyond. We are insolubly ambivalent, and energized by elemental conflict, driven to absurd denial in our efforts to manage our contradictions, as in the motivational psychology summed up in the bumper sticker:

LESS MONEY MAKES THE POOR WORK HARDER
MORE MONEY MAKES THE RICH WORK HARDER

The conflict could scarcely be more comprehensive. When the rich run amok, it is overreaching or "irrational exuberance," even though such crises sap net worth, drive down wages, starve public investment, and foment inequality. When Wall Street smashes up things and people, they "let other people clean up the mess they've made." When the poor "lose it," their abandon is a rampage to be suppressed by phalanxes of police with battle gear.

The conflict drives the stories that culture generates too. Much of today's journalism and fiction exaggerates flight or fight physiology to attract attention. Much adult drama follows the pattern of children's cartoons in which small underdogs outwit massive, terrifying villains, with the emphasis not on character, not on adaptation and moral courage, but on escape, heroic rescue, or triumphalism. The paradigm fits the politics of paranoia about "big government" and indifference to reform. When plots introduce a past trauma to explain motivation, the mechanism sidesteps character, projecting sentimental victimization or magical supremacy. Such formulas leave character an empty husk.

In the new century the American dream is as supercharged as ever: globally ambitious, morally ambiguous, technologically enhanced, and complexly in trouble. Anxiety about decline is in the air. Certainly the scale of things has changed. Only a decade or two before *Gatsby*, the American president could still answer his own mail. The great Ponzi and traction scams of the day are proportionally smaller than the global corporate rampages of the Enron era. Today the earth itself is a casualty in the headlines, and finite resources challenge scientific wherewithal to cope in time.

And these days the American dream is also more evanescent: less like the magisterial Miss Liberty chaperoning ambitious immigrants than the NSA's fabulous databank that supposedly contains all the country's activity at a given moment. Whether or not that plasma of information makes sense to the spies or actually exists in one place, we can envision it. The task for criticism is to make it work for people.

NOTES

INTRODUCTION

1. Howard D. Fabing, "On Going Berserk: a Neurochemical Inquiry," *The Scientific Monthly*, November 1956, 232-37.

2. Jonathan Shay, *Achilles in Vietnam* (New York, 1997), 77, 217-18. "Bare sark" could also be taken to mean "without shirt = armor."

3. These themes can be *transcultural*. Consider Milton Blahyi, former rebel commander in Liberia's ghastly civil war, who "has admitted to taking part in human sacrifices as part of traditional ceremonies intended to ensure victory in battle. He said the sacrifices 'included the killing of an innocent child and plucking out the heart, which was divided into pieces for us to eat"—as a bear might. Blahyi literally stripped off his *armor*: he "is better known in Liberia as 'General Butt Naked' because he went into combat with no clothes on, to scare the enemy." Blahyi's ordination at age 11 as "the traditional priest of my tribe" may have prepared the ground for the godlike conviction berserkers report, while his current calling as an Evangelical preacher may be functioning to control that conviction. See Jonathan Paye-Layleh, "I ate children's hearts, ex-rebel says," BBC News, January 22, 2008, http://news.bbc.co.uk/2/hi/africa/7200101.stm.

4. Aaron Levin, "Experts Seek Explanations for Mass Killings," *Psychiatric News* (Sept. 07, 2012), http://psychnews.psychiatryonline.org/newsarticle.aspx?articleid=1356728.

5. Pew Research Center, "Gun Homicide Rate Down 49% Since 1993 Peak; Public Unaware" (May 7, 2013), http://www.pewsocialtrends.org/2013/05/07/gun-homicide-rate-down-49-since-1993-peak-public-unaware/.

6. According to E. L. Maguigad, *amok* derives from *amoq*, the Malay word for furious warfare. See "Psychiatry in the Philippines," *American Journal of Psychiatry* (121), 21-25.

7. Ezra Klein, "Twelve facts about guns and mass shootings in the United States," *Washington Post*, Dec. 12, 2014, http://www.washingtonpost.com/blogs/wonkblog/wp/2012/12/14/nine-facts-about-guns-and-mass-shootings-in-the-united-states/.

8. Ford Fessenden, "Rampage Killers, A Statistical Report," *New York Times*, April 8, 2000.

9. Amy P. Cohen et al, "Rate of Mass Shootings Has tripled Since 2011, Harvard Research Shows," *Mother Jones*, October 15, 2014.

10. Gary Rosen, e.g., criticizes developments "allowing George W. Bush and Dick Cheney to run amok," in "Constitutional Detour," *New York Times Book Review*, November 25, 2007, 31. Andrew Pollack reports "concerns that synthetic biology could be used to make pathogens, or that errors by well-intended scientists could produce organisms that run amok." In "Researchers Take Step Toward Synthetic Life," *New York Times*, January 25, 2008.

11. John Seabrook describes the scientific background in "Crush Point," *New Yorker*, February 7, 2011, 34.

12. Daniel Mendelsohn, "The Bacchae: Ecstasy and Terror," *New York Review of Books*, September 25, 2014, 82.

13. James Surowiecki, *New Yorker*, May 11, 2009, 38.

14. Nancy C. Andreasen, "Post-Traumatic Stress Disorder," in *The Comprehensive Textbook of Psychiatry*, edited by H. I.Kaplan and B. J. Sadock, (Baltimore,1985), 919.

15. Eric Tucker, "FBI Report: 160 Mass Shootings, 100 Dead Since 2000," Associated Press, 25 September 14.

16. July 6, 2000. William Pollack, an assistant clinical professor of psychiatry at the Harvard Medical School "said reports of assaults by parents at youth sports events ''have gotten much worse'' in the last 5 to 10 years, and statistics show that the number of injuries in youth sports is also sharply up during the same period, a result at least in part, he said, of parents' encouraging their children to play more aggressively." Fox Butterfield, "A Fatality, Parental Violence and Youth Sports," *New York Times*, July 11, 2000.

17. David Aldridge, "Gambling Violence, Beer," *Washington Post*, September 18, 2008.

CHAPTER 1

1. Kimberly Flemke and Katherine R. Allen, "Women's Experience of Rage: a Critical Feminist Analysis," *Journal of Marital and Family Therapy,* January 2008.

2. Dolf Zillmann, "Mental Control of Angry Aggression," in *Handbook of Mental Control,* ed. Wegner and Pennebaker. Cited by Daniel Goleman, *Emotional Intelligence* (New York, 1995), pp. 60-62.

3. Craig MacAndrew and Robert B. Edgerton, *Drunken Comportment: a social explanation* (Chicago, 1969),

4. As I noted in *Post-Traumatic Culture,* Kay H. Blacker and Joe P. Tupin, "Hysteria and Hysterical Structures: Developmental and Social Theories," in *The Hysterical Personality,* ed. Mardi J. Horowitz (New York, 1977), 113. See also H. B. M. Murphy, "History and the Evolution of Syndromes: the Striking Case of Lateh and Amok," in *Psychopathology: Contributions from the Social, Behavioral, and Biological Sciences,* ed. M. Hammer, et al (New York, 1973); and Lydia Temoshok and C. Clifford Attkisson, "Epidemiology of Hysterical Phenomena: Evidence for a Psychosocial Theory," in *Hysterical Personality,* ed. Horowitz (1977).

5. For a revealing analysis of the interpretive processes affecting drivers' management of frustration and anger, see "Pissed Off in L. A.," in Jack Katz, *How Emotions Work* (Chicago, 1999), 18-86.

6. See Diane Binson and William J. Woods, *Gay Bathhouses and Public Health Policy* (New York, 2003).

7. Sam Delaney, "TV Preview: True Blood," *Guardian,* July 11, 2009.

8. *World History of Warfare,* ed. Christian J. Archer et al (Lincoln, Neb., 2002), 169-71.

9. See, e.g., Millon, T., & R. D. Davis (1998). "Ten Subtypes of Psychopathy." In *Psychopathy: Antisocial, Criminal, and Violent Behavior,* ed. T. Millon, et al. (New York, 2003). 161-70.

10. Pat Aufderheide, "Good Soldiers," *Seeing through Movies,* ed. Mark Crispin Miller (New York, 1990), 108.

11. Mark Crispin Miller, "End of Story," in Miller's *Seeing* through *Movies,* 210.

12. Ernest Becker, *Denial of Death* (New York, 1973), 27.

13. I take the term from Orlando Patterson's *Slavery and Social Death: A Comparative Study* (Cambridge, MA, 1982).

14. Ernest Becker, *Escape from Evil,* (New York, 1975), 2.

15. Karen Horney, *Neurosis and Human Growth* (New York, 1950, 1991), p. 39.

16. This is a premise of Terror Management Theory. See Tom Pyszczynski, et al, *In the Wake of 911* (Washington, DC, 2003).

17. To appreciate how thoroughly the need for "rightness" organizes human life, see Norman Cohn's *Cosmos, Chaos, and the World to Come* (New Haven, 1993) and his account of the comprehensively embodied concept of "ma'at," which in ancient Egyptian culture meant "base," as in the base of a throne,

but came to mean "a principle of order so all-embracing that it governed every aspect of existence.…[Nature] and society were imagined as two sides of one and the same reality: whatever was harmonious and regular in either was an expression of *ma'at*" (9). That meant all that is lawful, life-giving, and right, and it demanded repudiation, punishment, and death of all that was not.

18. "Tankless Toilet Makes a Fashion Statement," Associated Press, March 29, 2005.

19. Jennifer Steinhauer, "Gunman Shoots 6 and Kills 1 in Fla.," *New York Times,* November 6, *2009.*

20. Donald Dutton, *The Psychology of Genocide, Massacre, and Extreme Violence* (Westport and London, 2007), 142. Dutton is referring to the theory put forward by V. Nell, in "Cruelty's Rewards: The gratification of perpetrators and spectators," *Behavioral and Brain Sciences,* 29 (2006), 211-57.

21. Richard Slotkin *Regeneration through Violence,*(Hanover, NH, 1973), 156.

22. Nick Turse, "UnFair Game: Targeting Iraqis as Big Game," TomDispatch. com, October 25, 2007.

23. Evan Wright, *Generation Kill: Devil Dogs, Iceman, Captain America, and the New Face of American War* (New York, 2007).

24. Dutton, *The Psychology of Genocide,* 102-03.

25. Elias Canetti, *Crowds and Power* (New York, 1978).

26. Wendell Berry, "Faustian Economics: Hell Hath No Limits," *Harper's Magazine* (May 2008), 15.

27. Mike Nizza, "The Heroes Among Us," *New York Times,* July 9, 2007.

28. Tim Shipman, "Sarah Palin Blamed by the U.S. Secret Service Over Death Threats Against Barack Obama," *The Telegraph, UK,* November 08, 2008.

29. Jonathan L. Friedman, *Media Violence and Its Effect on Aggression: Assessing the Scientific Evidence* (Toronto, 2002).

30. Bill Moyers, "NOW," PBS, September 12, 2008. The *New York Times* "reported that a mass email opposing the bill suggested that its supporters needed to be 'taken out by *any means*.' The bipartisan support collapsed, the bill died and right-wing talk-radio hosts took credit."

31. "Talk Show Host Calls for Murder," FAIR: Fairness and Accuracy in Media, June 24, 2008, http://fair.org/take-action/action-alerts/talk-show-host-calls-for-murder/.

32. Robert C. Elliott, *The Power of Satire* (Princeton, 1960).

33. De Becker, *The Gift of Fear,* (Boston, 1997), 92-102.

34. The trope is popular in rightwing rhetoric. An apparently straight-faced op-ed essay in the *Wall Street Journal* compares President George W. Bush to the superhero Batman, echoing Crusader religiosity in its demand that "Islamo-Fascists" must be "hounded to the gates of Hell." Andrew Klavan, "What Bush and Batman Have in Common," *Wall Street Journal,* July 25, 2008.

35. Jan Hoffman. "A Girl's Nude Photo and Altered Lives," *New York Times,* March 26, 2011.

36. See Francis Parkman's account in *The Jesuits in North America in the Seventeenth Century* (1867; Lincoln, Neb., 1997), 168-71.

37. Slotkin, 90. In Slotkin's reading Tompson's poems show the settlers caught up in the outrages, including cannibalism, that they attributed to the Indians.

38. See John Demos, *Entertaining Satan* (New York, 1983).

39. While Upton Sinclair's *The Jungle* (1906) dramatizes the stress that industrial workers experienced, Michael Lesy's *Wisconsin Death Trip* (1973) demonstrates the everyday presssure of mortality and madness in the newly settled west.

40. Herman Melville, *Moby Dick,* ed. Elizabeth Renker (New York, 1998), p. 157.

41. "Tropical rainforests are disappearing at a rate of 2 percent per year. Populations of most large fish are down to only 10 percent of what they were in 1950. Many primates and all the great apes—our closest relatives—are nearly gone from the wild." See Jerry Coyne and Hopi E. Hoekstra, "The Greatest Dying," *The New Republic* online, September 24, 2007.

CHAPTER 2

1. See, e.g., T. F. Denson, et al, "The angry brain: Neural correlates of anger, angry rumination, and aggressive personality," *Journal of Cognitive Neuroscience* 21, 734-44.

2. Tom Englehardt, *The End of Victory Culture* (New York, 1995).

3. Steven V. Roberts, "Ronald Reagan Is Giving 'Em Heck," *New York Times,* October 25, 1970.

4. N. Ben-Yehuda and E. Goode, *Moral Panics: The Social Construction of Deviance.* (Oxford: 1994); P. Jenkins, *Moral Panic: Changing Concepts of the Child Molester in Modern America.* New Haven, CT, (1998); Charles Krinsky, *The Ashgate Research Companion to moral Panics* (Burlington, VT, 2012); J. S. Victor, *Satanic Panic: The Creation of a Contemporary Legend* (Chicago, 1993).

5. See Richard Ofshe and Ethan Watters, *Making Monsters: False Memories, Psychotherapy, and Sexual Hysteria* (New York, 1994). For an analysis of a popular children's book that exploits this hysteria, see "Vampire Abuse" in my *Post-Traumatic Culture* (Baltimore, 1998), 199-211.

6. Susan P. Robbins, "The Social and Cultural Context of Satanic Abuse Allegations," *IPT Journal* 10 (1998).

7. "Kids recant abuse claim after dad jailed 20 years," AP, July 11, 2009.

8. *The Courage to Heal: A Guide for Women Survivors of Child Sexual Abuse,* ed. Ellen Bass and Louise Thornton (New York, 1988), 128. Frederick C. Crews offers a bracing overview of the MPD craze and responses in "The Revenge of the Repressed," Parts I and II, in *New York Review of Books,* November 17 and December 1, 1994.

9. Susan A. Clancy, *The Trauma Myth: the Truth about the Sexual Abuse of Children and Its Aftermath* (New York, 2009). See also Paul R. McHugh, *Try to*

Remember: Psychiatry's Clash over Meaning, Memory, and Mind (New York, 2008).

10. In "Clicking Their Way to Outrage On Social Media, Some Are Susceptible to Internet Outrage," *New York Times*, July 3, 2014, Teddy Wayne calls attention to some recent research.

11. Amy Pavuk, "Rebecca Sedwick's suicide highlights dagers of cyberbullying," *Orlando Sentinel* (Sept. 16, 2013) http://www.orlandosentinel.com/news/local/breakingnews/os-cyberbullying-victim-suicide-rebecca-sedwick-20130916,0,5554908.story

12. Jan Hoffman, "Poisoned Web: A Girl's Nude Photo and Altered Lives," *New York Times*, March 27, 2011.

13. Eva Illouz, *Hard-Core Romance:* Fifty Shades of Grey, *Best-Sellers, and Society* (Chicago, 2014), 73.

14. Janice Radway, *Reading the Romance* (Chapel Hill, 1984),

15. Whitford and Yates. *Presidential Rhetoric and the Public Agenda*: Constructing the War on Drugs (Baltimore: 2009), 58.

16. Anne-Marie Cusac, *Cruel and Unusual: the Culture of Punishment in America* (New Haven, 2009), 132.

17. David Cole, "Can Our Shameful Prisons Be Reformed?" *New York Review of Books*, November 19, 2009, 41.

18. *Time Magazine*, "The Youth Crime Plague," July 11, 1977.

19. Tom Hayden, "The Myth of the Super-Predator," *Los Angeles Times*, December 14, 2005.

20. Lois Beckett, "The Hidden Cost of Gun Violence," Pro Publica, September 5, 2014 ttp://www.propublica.org/article/meet-a-mother-and-her-seven-year-old-with-ptsd

21. Lisa Bloom, *Suspicion Nation* (New York, 2014)

22. "The number of people under supervision in the nation's criminal justice system rose to 7.2 million in 2006, the highest ever, costing states tens of billions of dollars.... The cost to taxpayers, about $45 billion, is causing states such as California to reconsider harsh criminal penalties. In an attempt to relieve overcrowding, California is now exporting some of its 170,000 inmates to privately run corrections facilities as far away as Tennessee." See Darryl Fears, "New Criminal Record: 7.2 Million: Nation's Justice System Strains to Keep Pace With Convictions," *Washington Post*, June 12, 2008. See also Anne-Marie Cusac, *Cruel and Unusual: The Culture of Punishment in America* (New Haven, 2009) and *The Real War on Crime: The Report of the National Criminal Justice Commission*, ed. Steven Donziger (New York, 1996).

23. Adam Liptak, "U.S. Prison Population Dwarfs That of Other Nations," *International Herald Tribune*, April 23, 2008. For an analysis of prison demography, see Glenn C. Loury et al, *Race, Incarceration, and American Values* (Cambridge, MA, 2009).

24. Proposal: Under the terms of Proposition 184, if a criminal has had one previous serious or violent felony conviction, the mandatory sentence for a second

such conviction is doubled. After two violent or serious felony convictions, any further felony, non violent or not, will trigger a third strike; the mandatory sentence will then be the greater of: 1) three times the term ordinarily required, 2) 25 years, or 3) a term determined by the court. Crimes committed by a minor of at least 16 years of age count as strikes. The amount of credit that a second or third strike felon can apply towards eventual release is reduced from one half to one fifth, and probation is not an alternative.

25. Daniel MacCallair and Mike A. Males, *Striking Out : the failure of California's "Three-Strikes and You're Out" Law.* (San Francisco, CA,[1999). Full version published by the *Stanford Law and Policy Review* (Fall 1999).

26. Systematic critiques of the law are Jerome H. Skolnick, "Wild pitch: 'Three-Strikes, You're Out' and other bad calls on crime," *The American prospect*, No. 17 (spring 1994). Twenty-six other states adopted "three strikes" statues, although none as severe as California's version.

27. John Nichols, "Bill O'Reilly's San Fran Rant," CBS News, http://www.cbsnews.com/stories/2005/11/15/opinion/main1044750.shtml Talk show celebrity Glenn Beck has openly toyed with murder on the air: "I'm thinking about killing Michael Moore and I'm wondering if I could kill him myself, or if I would need to hire somebody to do it. No, I think I could. I think he could be looking me in the eye, you know, and I could just be choking the life out of him. Is this wrong?"

28. Laura Sullivan, "Folsom Embodies California's Prison Blues," on "All Things Considered," NPR, August 13, 2009.

29. N.C. Aizenman, "New High In U.S. Prison Numbers," *The Washington Post*, February 29, 2008.

30. Solomon Moore, "California Prisons Must Cut Inmate Population," *New York Times, August* 4, 2009.

31. https://californiachoices.org/ballot-measures/proposition-36

32. Elaine Rapping, "Aliens, Nomads, Mad Dogs," *Mythologies of Violence in Postmodern Media*, ed. Christopher Sharrett (Detroit, 1999), 263.

33. See David Garland, *Peculiar Institution: America's Death Penalty in an Age of Abolition* (2010).

34. For an idea of how oppressive policing in black neighborhoods can be, see Alice Goffman's eyewitness account of Philadelphia, *On the Run: Fugitive life in an American City* (Chicago, 2014)

35. Ryan Gabrielson et al, "Deadly Force, in Black and White," *Pro Publica*, October 10, 2014. Brent Staples, "Race and Death in Police Shootings," *New York Times (Taking Note)*, October 10, 2014. "These data explain why the black and white communities generally have starkly different views of the police. They also show why African American parents warn their sons to remain perfectly still — and make no sudden moves — when they encounter the police. As the expression goes in the black world: 'Don't give them an excuse to kill you.'"

36. Rob Barry and Coulter Jones found that between 2007 and 2012, the FBI under-reported the tally of police homicides by 47%, as many as 550 victims. see "Hundreds of Police Killings Are Uncounted in Federal Stats," *Wall Street Journal,* December 2, 2014.

37. *Washington Post,* Dec. 21, 2012, "Remarks from the NRA press conference on Sandy Hook school shooting (Transcript)."

38. Grand Jury Testimony: https://www.documentcloud.org/documents/1370494-grand-jury-volume-5.html#document/p212/a189246

39. See the analysis of the Hulk in the Introduction.

40. Nonstop firing is a familiar symptom of berserk stress in combat, as in Lt. Calley's killing at My Lai. See the account of Kenneth Eastridge in Chapter 3.

41. Joan Walsh, "How Terrible Police Training Is Destroying America," *Salon,* September 27, 2014.

42. Patrik Johnsson, "Armed America: Behind a Broadening Run on Guns," *Christian Science Monitor,* April 13, 2009.

43. Eric Lichtblau and Mokoto Rich, "NRS Envisions 'a Good Guy With a Gun' in Every School," *New York Times,* Dec.21, 2012.

44. Robert S. Boyd, "Will robot killers be allowed to fire on their own?" McClatchy Newspapers, March 25, 2009.

45. Cf. the obsessions of real serial killer Jeffrey Dahmer as recounted in my *Post-Traumatic Culture* (Baltimore, MD, 1998), 334-36.

46. Becker, *Denial of Death,* 63.

47. See Marina Warner, *No Go the Bogeyman* (1998), republished as *Monsters of Our Own Making* (Louisville, KY, 2007), 132-33.

48. Stephanie Armour, "Managers Not Prepared for Workplace Violence," *USA Today* (July 15, 2004), http://www.usatoday.com/money/workplace/2004-07-15-workplace-violence2_x.htm

49. Goodstein and Glaberson, "Well-Marked Road to Homicidal Rage."

50. Stephanie Armour, "Inside the Minds of Workplace Killers." *USA Today* (July 14, 2004) http://www.usatoday.com/money/workplace/2004-07-14-workplace-killings_x.htm

51. Dave Cullen, "The Depressive and the Psychopath," *Slate,* April 20, 2004.

52. Quoted in Joel Achenbach and Dale Russakoff, "Teen Shooter's Life Paints Antisocial Portrait," *Washington Post* (April 29, 1999).

53. Achenbach and Russakoff.

54. Andrew Solomon expanded upon this report in his interviews with Adam's father Peter in "The Reckoning," *The New Yorker,* March 17, 2014, 36-45. References hereafter in parentheses.

55. Stephen J. Sedensky III, Stat's Attorney, "Report of the State's Attorney for the Judicial District of Danbury on the Shootings at Sandy Hook Elementary School and 36 Yogananda Street, Newtown, Connecticut on December 14, 2012," OFFICE OF THE STATE'S ATTORNEY JUDICIAL DISTRICT OF DANBURY, Nov. 25, 2013, 33. This is a useful collection of basic data on

Adam Lanza (cited here as SAR). http://www.ct.gov/csao/lib/csao/Sandy_
Hook_Final_Report.pdf

56. At the Yale Child Study Center, in 2006, Dr. Robert A. King concluded that
Adam "displayed a profound autism spectrum disorder with rigidity, isolation
and a lack of comprehension of ordinary social interaction and communications." (Griffin, Dec. 28, 2013).

57. Alaine Griffin and Josh Kovner, "Adam Lanza's PediatricRecords Reveal
Growing Anxiety," Hartford Courant, June 30, 2013.

58. James L. Knoll, "The 'Pseudocommando' *Mass* Murderer: Part I, The Psychology of Revenge and Obliteration" *Journal of American Academy of Psychiatry
and the Law*, March 2010, 38:1:87-94; and Part II, 38:2:263-72 (June 2010)

59. Alaine Griffin and Josh Kovner, "Lanza's Psychiatric Treatment Revealed in
Documents," *Hartford Courant*, Dec. 28, 2013. Adam's father suspected that
Adam's Asperger's could be masking schizophrenia (Solomon, 40), which
might accord with a symptom of schizophrenia described by Louis Sass: hy-
perrationality and an anxious preoccupation with the core or ground of identity. See "Introspection, Schizophrenia, and the Fragmentation of the Self," in
Representations 19 (Summer 1987) and Louis Sass and Josef Parnas, "Schizophrenia, Consciousness, and the Self," also *Schizophrenia Bulletin*, Vol. 29,
No. 3, (2003).

60. Judith Lewis Herman, *Trauma and Recovery* (New York, 1992), 33. Nancy.C.
Andreasen, "Post-traumatic Stress Disorder," in *The Comprehensive Textbook of
Psychiatry*, ed. H.I. Kaplan and B.J. Sadock (Baltimore, MD, 1985), pp.919.

61. Perpetrators of "autogenic" rampages, says P. E., Mullen, "tend to share common social and psychological disabilities. They are isolates, often bullied in
childhood, who have rarely established themselves in effective work roles as
adults. They have personalities marked by suspiciousness, obsessional traits,
and grandiosity. They often harbor persecutory beliefs, which may occasionally
verge on the delusional. The autogenic massacre is essentially murder suicide,
in which the perpetrators intend first to kill as many people as they can and
then kill themselves." (Mullen, 311). Cf. Katherine S. Newman, *Rampage:
The Social Roots of School Shootings* (also 2004), which emphasizes social forces
leading to isolation and infamy.

62. In her email exchanges with Marvin LaFontaine, Nancy Lanza humorously
(?) bragged that her Green Beret brother had taught her lethal self-defense
moves. See "Nancy Lanza in her own words," http://www.pbs.org/wgbh/
pages/frontline/social-issues/raising-adam-lanza/nancy-lanza-in-her-own-
words/ The clinician Adam saw at the Yale Child Study Center described her
as "non-compliant" because she refused to continue Adam's medication (Celexa) and terminated the sessions. (Griffin, Dec.28, 2013)

63. "Matricide is usually committed by overprotected boys—by a son who wishes,
as one study puts it, 'with his desperate act, to free himself from his state of dependency on her, a dependency that he believes has not allowed him to grow
up.' Another study proposes that, in each case examined, 'the mother-child

relationship became unusually intense and conflict-laden,' while the fathers 'were uniformly passive and remained relatively uninvolved.' The state's attorney's report says that when Nancy asked Adam whether he would feel sad if anything happened to her, he replied, 'No.' A Word document called 'Selfish,' which was found on Adam's computer, gives an explanation of why females are inherently selfish, written while one of them was accommodating him in every possible way" (Solomon, 43).

64. In email correspondence with Marvin LaFontaine, Nancy Lanza alluded to a potentially life-threatening inherited "time bomb" for which she underwent extensive medical tests, and about which she was secretive. It is unclear how this anxiety affected her behavior with her children. ("Nancy Lanza in her own words") http://www.pbs.org/wgbh/pages/frontline/social-issues/raising-adam-lanza/nancy-lanza-in-her-own-words/

65. Jonathan Shay, *Achilles in Vietnam*, 33.

66. *Washington Post*, Dec. 21, 2012, "Remarks from the NRA press conference on Sandy Hook school shooting (Transcript)."

67. Walsh, "How Terrible Police Training Is Destroying America."

68. Jennifer Medina, "Even in a State with Restrictive Gun Laws, Gunman Amassed Weapons," *New York Times*, May 25, 2014.

CHAPTER 3

1. Michael Barone, "Surge 101," *National Review Online*, December 29, 2007.

2. See Ernest Becker's account in *Escape from Evil*, 103. The link between blood and soil was less sentimental in the Napoleonic era. In *War is a Force That Gives Us Meaning*, Chris Hedges quotes *The London Observer* (November 18, 1822): "It is estimated that more than a million bushels of human and inhuman bones were imported last year from the continent of Europe into the port of Hull. The neighborhood of Leipzig, Austerlitz, Waterloo, and of all the places where, during the late bloody war, the principal battles were fought, have been swept alike of the bones of the hero and horse which he rode.... [They] have been...forwarded to the Yorkshire bone grinders [and] sold to the farmers to manure their lands."

3. Ken Jowitt , "Rage, Hubris, and Regime Change," *Hoover Institution Policy Review*, April & May, 2003, http://www.hoover.org/publications/policyreview/3449481.html.

4. A senior Bush advisor thought to be Karl Rove famously told journalist Ron Suskind that he and others were "'in what we call the reality-based community,' which he defined as people who 'believe that solutions emerge from your judicious study of discernible reality.'" When Suskind mentioned empiricism, the advisor "cut me off. 'That's not the way the world really works anymore. We're an empire now, and when we act, we create our own reality.'" See "Faith, Certainty, and the Presidency of George W. Bush," *New York Times Magazine*, October 17, 2004.

5. As counterterrorism director Richard A. Clarke, for one, reported in *Against All Enemies* (New York, 2004).

6. An estimated 500 deaths a month, according to Steve Coll in "The General's Dilemma," *New Yorker,* September 8, 2008, 36. The invasion created as many as 2.5 million refugees.

7. Joseph Siglitz and Linda Bilmes, "The Three Trillion Dollar War," *The Times,* February 23, 2008.

8. The editors were responding (July 16, 2009) to the Federal Report on the President's Surveillance Program (July 10, 2009).

9. Jowitt, "Rage, Hubris, and Regime Change."

10. Thom Shanker, "Despite Slump, U.S. role a Top Arms Supplier Grows," *New York Times,* September 6, 2009.

11. James Glanz and Andrew W. Lehren, "Use of Contractors Added to War's Chaos in Iraq," *New York Times,* September 6, 2009. They refer to the "Wild West chaos" of the war's early days.

12. Aaron Glantz, *Winter Soldier: Iraq and Afghanistan: Eyewitness Accounts of the Occupations* (Chicago, 2008).

13. Nick Turse, "A My Lai a Month," *The Nation,* November 13, 2008, and *Kill Anything That Moves: The Real American War in Vietnam* (New York, 2013)

14. Richard A. Oppel Jr., "Iraqi Assails U.S. for Strikes on Civilians," *New York Times,* June 2, 2006

15. Consider an Iraqi mother John Lee Anderson describes in "Inside The Surge," New Yorker, November 19, 2007. Her son Amar went on a systematic rampage to revenge his brother Jafaar, determined to kill ten Mahdi militiamen for every one of his brother's fingers. His mother, Um Jafaar, also fixated on this harvest of enemy life. She "took the body parts of Amar's victims, wrapped in cloth, to [Jafaar's] grave...and buried them there. 'I talk to my son, I tell him, "Here, this is from those who killed you, I take revenge....I put them around the grave. So far, I have taken one hand, one eye, an Adam's apple, toes, fingers, ears, and noses....But still my heart hurts. Even if we kill them all, I won't have comfort'" (66). Rage buffers her despair and sense of unbearable injustice. She is ritualistic in her magical thinking about the body parts, but also acts out creaturely motives. In effect, she feeds the butchered body parts to her dead son as if to replenish his spirit in a cannibal feast, not unlike the soldier described here who vowed to cut out enemy hearts for his dead friend.

16. See Deborah Nelson, *The War Behind Me: Vietnam Veterans Confront the Truth* (New York, 2008).

17. Quoted in *The Fresno Bee* October 10, 1965, when as governor of California, Reagan was working to suppress student unrest at Berkeley.

18. H. Bruce Franklin, *Vietnam and Other American Fantasies* (Amherst, MA, 2006), p. 73. The war in the Pacific was especially brutal on both sides, as Max Hastings recounts in *Retribution: the Battle for Japan, 1944-45* (New York, 2008). By the war's end, Allied bombs had killed no less than 1.8 million German civilians, whereas the official number of British civilian deaths is 100,297.

For an account of the victors' rage, see Giles McDonogh, *After the Reich: The Brutal History of the Allied Occupation* (New York, 2007).

19. As Franklin notes, many regarded the campaign as a form of genocide. See *In the Name of America: A Study Commissioned and Published by Clergy and Laymen Concerned about Vietnam, January 1968* (New York, 1968) and *Against the Crime of Silence*, ed. John Duffett (New York, 1968). For the role of racism in the war against Japan, see John Dower, *War without Mercy* (New York, 1993).

20. A trenchant analysis of the restructuring is Richard A. Gabriel and Paul L. Savage, *Crisis in Command: Mismanagement in the Army* (New York, 1978).

21. In Ricks, *Fiasco* (75-76) .

22. See P. W. Singer's wide-ranging overview, *Wired for War* (New York, 2009).

23. David Barstow, "Behind TV Analysts, Pentagon's Hidden Hand," *New York Times*, April 20, 2008

24. Paul Blustein, "Wolfowitz Strives to Quell Criticism," *Washington Post*, March 21, 2005.

25. Frank Rich detailed the process in *The Greatest Story Ever Sold* (New York, 2007). See also Michael isikoff and David Corn, *Hubris* (New York, 2006)

26. Tom Engelhardt, "Stuff Happens: the Pentagon's Argument of Last Resort on Iraq," *Mother Jones*, November 21, 2008.

27. Evan Wright, *Generation Kill: Devil Dogs, Iceman, Captain America, and the New Face of American War* (New York, 2007), in Michael Massing. "Iraq: The Hidden Human Costs," *New York Review of Books*, December 20, 2007.

28. Dropped from the *National Review Online*, Coulter was unrepentant in her book, *How to Talk to a Liberal If You Must: the World According to Ann Coulter* (New York, 2004), insisting she advocated the same position "Now more than ever." On her website (June 30, 2004), Coulter was heedlessly triumphal and malicious: "The Americanization of Iraq proceeds at an astonishing pace, the Iraqis are taking to freedom like fish to water, and the possibilities for this nation are endless."

29. See Jared Diamond's "Vengeance Is Ours," *New Yorker*, April 21, 2008, 74.

30. Jon Lee Anderson, "Inside the Surge," *New Yorker*, November 19, 2007, 66.

31. See "A Guide for the Perplexed: Intellectual Fallacies of the War on Terror," Chalmers Johnson's perceptive review of Stephen Holmes's invaluable study *The Matador's Cape, America's Reckless Response to Terror*, *TomDispatch.com* (October 22, 2007).

32. In *The Shock Doctrine: The Rise of Disaster Capitalism* (New York, 2007), Naomi Klein traces the shock doctrine to Washington's Cold War fascination with the possibility of "wiping clean" an adversary's personality, as in brainwashing, to induce total compliance.

33. Chalmers Johnson, *Blowback: the Costs and Consequences of American Empire* (New York, 2004).

34. Maj. Gen. John Batiste "Root Causes of Haditha," *The Salt Lake Tribune*, June 9, 2006. Though his title focused on Haditha, the general never men-

tioned that the scandal involved rampage killing. His heartfelt criticism understood the personal dimension lacking in the neocons' fantasies of leverage. including references to the Abu Ghraib and Haditha scandals.

35. Klein, *Shock Doctrine,* 323-40.

36. Thomas B. Edsall and Juliet Eilperin, "Lobbyists Set Sights on Money-Making Opportunities in Iraq," *Washington Post,* October 2, 2003.

37. Donald L. Barlett and James B. Steele reported the transfer in *Vanity Fair* (October 2007), yet it received virtually no mainstream media attention. In *Pay Any Price: Greed, Power, and Endless War* (2014), special investigator general Stuart W. Bowen recounts his thwarted efforts to account for the missing money under both the Bush and Obama administrations.

38. For background, see Pratap Chetterjee, *Halliburton's Army: How a Well-Connected Texas Oil Company Revolutionized the Way America Makes War* (New York, 2009).

39. Jane Corbin, "BBC Uncovers Lost Iraq Billions," BBC News, June 10, 2008.

40. "U.S.. Army: 'We will respond to contractor killings," CNN.com, April 1, 2004, quoting Brig. Gen. Mark Kimmitt.

41. Marjorie Cohn, "The Haditha Massacre," *Tr u t h o u t | Perspective* (May 30, 2006). http://www.truthout.org/article/the-haditha-massacre

42. Used against civilians it is an illegal chemical weapon, though Washington has not signed the international treaty restricting phosphorus munitions. BBC News (November 16, 2005) quoted an arms expert who said: "'It is not counted under the chemical weapons convention in its normal use but, although it is a matter of legal niceties, it probably does fall into the category of chemical weapons if it is used for this kind of purpose directly against people.'"

43. Dahr Jamail, "What I Saw in Fallujah," *New Statesman,* November 1, 2007.

44. Bill Van Auken, "Pentagon plans death squad terror in Iraq," *Newsweek,* January 13, 2005.

45. "Court Sentences 'Kill Team' Soldier to 24 Years in Prison," *Spiegel Online,* March 24, 2011. Lt. Col. David Grossman's *On Killing* (New York, 1996) estimates that about 3 percent of soldiers can kill without inhibition.

46. Zogby poll, February 28, 2006.

47. In "The Wounded Platoon," PBS *Frontine,* May 17, 2010.

48. Dave Philipps, Casualties of War, Part I: The hell of war comes home, *Colorado Springs Gazette* (gazette.com), July 25, 2009

49. Cohn, "The Haditha Massacre."

50. BBC News, 5.25.06 "Marines' Iraq conduct scrutinized"

51. Russell Carollo, "Suspect Soldiers: Did Crimes in U.S. Foretell Violence in Iraq?" *Sacramento Bee,* July 11, 2008.

52. Josh White, "No Murder Charges Filed in Haditha Case," *Washington Post,* January 4, 2008.

53. The account of Needham's PTSD is based on Philipps, "Casualties of War," July 28, 2009.

54. Chris Hedges, "Body Bagger in Iraq," March 21, 2011, reporting on a memoir by Jess Goodell, *Shade It Black: Death and After in Iraq:* http://www.truth-out.org/body-bagger-iraq68624.

55. Philipps, "Casualties of War."

56. Paul von Zielbauer, "Testimony in Court-Martial Describes a Sniper Squad Pressed to Raise Body Count," *New York Times*, September 28, 2007.

57. Michael Belfiore, *The Department of Mad Scientists: How DARPA Is Remaking Our World, From the Internet to Artificial Limbs* (New York 2010).

58. See Wilbur J. Scott's "PTSD in DSM-III: A Case in the Politics of Diagnosis and Disease," *Social Problems*, 37: 3. (Aug., 1990), esp. 295-99. http://links.jstor.org/sici?sici=0037-7791%28199008%29-37%3A3%3C294%3APIDACI%3E2.0.CO%3B2-I

59. "Invisible Wounds of War: Psychological and Cognitive Injuries, Their Consequences, and Services to Assist Recovery," ed. Terri Tanelian and Lisa H. Jaycox, Rand Corp. Monographs, April 18, 2008.

60. Harvard University psychiatrist Roger Pitman "sees post-traumatic stress disorder as a perfectly natural process gone amok," since ordinarily strong memories of a dangerous situation can make for precautions and future survival. See William J. Cromie, "Pill to calm traumatic memories," *Harvard University Gazette*, March 18, 2004.

61. Oliver Poole, "'Marines are good at killing. Nothing else. They like it,'" *Daily Telegraph, UK*, January 6, 2006. http://www.telegraph.co.uk/news/main.jhtml?xml=/news/2006/06/01/wbush101.xml.

62. Nick Turse, "(Un)fair Game: Targeting Iraqis as 'Big Game,'" Tomdispatch.com, October 25, 2007.

63. Nick Turse, "(Un)Fair Game." Fantasies of the hunt drove the massacre that closed the first Gulf War, when U. S. troops annihilated Iraqi convoys fleeing from Kuwait. "The slaughter continued after the cease fire. For example, on March 2, 1991, U.S. 24th Division Forces engaged in a four-hour assault against Iraqis just west of Basra. More than 750 vehicles were destroyed, thousands were killed without any U.S. casualties. A U.S. commander said, 'We really waxed them.' It was called a 'Turkey Shoot.'" *International War Crimes Tribunal* (10): http://deoxy.org/wc/warcrim2.htm.

64. http://combatarms.mu.nu/.

65. A detailed account, emphasizing traumatic stress, is Jim Frederick, *Black Hearts: One Platoon's Descent into Madness in Iraq's Triangle of Death* (New York, 2010).

66. FBI Affidavit in Support of an Arrest Warrant for Steven D. Green, June 30, 2006.

67. Josh White, Ex-Soldier Charged in Killing of Iraqi Family, *The Washington Post,* July 4, 2006. Green was convicted (May 8, 2009).

68. Brian Nicol, *Stalking* (London, 2006), p. 19.

69. In *Redacted* (2007), Brian DePalma loosely dramatized the murder of Abeer Qasim Hamza and her family. He tries to emphasize the repugnant criminal-

ity of the behavior, but he also reflexively criticizes berserk style-in-action by inventing within the film a soldier's homemade video diary and a terrorist Website, both of which bring out the problems of complicity latent in style. The film has been attacked and not allowed into full distribution.

70. Robert C. Elliot, *The Power of Satire* (Princeton, 1960).

71. Human Rights First has reported on the U.S. government's handling of the nearly 100 cases of detainees who have died in U.S. custody since 2002. http://www.humanrightsfirst.org/us_law/etn/dic/index.asp.

72. "A major focus of the Committee's investigation was the influence of Survival Evasion Resistance and Escape (SERE) training techniques on the interrogation of detainees in U.S. custody. SERE training is designed to teach our soldiers how to resist interrogation by enemies that refuse to follow the Geneva Conventions and international law. During SERE training, U.S. troops --- in a controlled environment with great protections and caution --- are exposed to harsh techniques such as stress positions, forced nudity, use of fear, sleep deprivation, and until recently, the waterboard. The SERE techniques were never intended to be used against detainees in U.S. custody. The Committee's investigation found, however, that senior officials in the U.S. government decided to use some of these harsh techniques against detainees based on deeply flawed interpretations of U.S. and international law." This was "a direct cause of detainee abuse and conveyed the message that it was okay to mistreat and degrade detainees in U.S. custody."

73. Seymour Hersh, "The General's Report," *New Yorker*, June 25, 2007.

74. Seymour Hersh, "The Gray Zone," *The New Yorker*, May 24, 2005.

75. Joan Walsh, "The Abu Ghraib Files: Introduction," *Salon:* http://www.salon.com/news/abu_ghraib/2006/03/14/introduction/

76. Kate Zernike, "Detainees Depict Abuses by Guard in Prison in Iraq", *New York Times*, 12 January 2005.

77. Lynddie England and others describe some of this background in Errol Morris's documentary "Standard Operating Procedure" (2008).

78. Seymour Hersh, "The General's Report."

79. "Other government agencies," in "The Abu Ghraib Files," *Salon* (Chapter 5 (Nov. 4-5, 2003): http://www.salon.com/news/abu_ghraib/2006/03/14/chapter_5/index.html.

80. See Andrew Sullivan, "Bush's torturers follow where the Nazis led," *Sunday Times*, October 7, 2007. Early in the war secretary Rumsfeld pressed for the adoption in Iraq of interrogation practices used in the prison at Guanatamo in Cuba and not sanctioned by the Geneva Conventions; and in a September 14, 2003 memo General Sanchez complied.

81. Janis Karpinski, *One Woman's Army: the Commanding General of Abu Ghraib Tells Her Story* (New York, 2005).

82. Philippe Sands, *The Torture Team* (New York, 2008)

83. Jane Mayer, "Whatever It Takes," *New Yorker*, February 19, 2007.

84. Thomas E. Ricks, "The Descent into Abuse," *Fiasco* (271-97).

85. David Bromwich, "Euphemism and American Violence," *New York Review of Books* (April 3, 2008), 30.

86. Repeated, trivializing treatment of torture in media desensitizes audiences. Polls show approval of torture increasing. See Amy Segart, "Torture Creep," *Foreign Policy,* September 25, 2012. http://www.foreignpolicy.com/articles/2012/09/25/torture_creep?page=full

87. Interview with John Cusack << *http://www.huffingtonpost.com/john-cusack/the-real-blackwater-scand_b_67741.html..*

88. Bryan Bender, "Pentagon Board Says Cuts Essential," *Boston Globe,* November 10, 2008.

89. Henry Kissinger, "Henry Kissinger on the Assembly of a New World Order," *Wall Street Journal,* August 29, 2014.

CHAPTER 4

1. Matt Egan, "2008: Worse than the great depression?" *CNN Money,* August 27, 2014. http://money.cnn.com/2014/08/27/news/economy/ben-bernanke-great-depression/

2. Roger Alcaly, "The Right Way to Control the Banks," *New York Review,* June 5, 2014, 58. Stiglitz was addressing a conference on banking regulation in Brussels, October 12, 2009.

3. Leo Cullum, *New Yorker,* December 15, 2008.

4. Matt Taibbi, "The Great American Bubble Machine," *Rolling Stone* (July 9-23, 2009), expanded in his *Griftopia: Bubble Machines, Vampire Squids, and the Long Con That Is Breaking America* (New York, 2010).

5. George A. Akerlof and Robert J. Schiller develop and critique Keynes in *Animal Spirits: How Human Psychology Drives the Economy and Why It Matters for Global Capitalism* (Princeton, 2008).

6. Richard Parker, "Government beyond Obama," *New York Review of Books,* Vol. 56, No. 4, March 12, 2009. He adds, "even after productivity growth returned in the mid-1990s, average wages—which had stagnated for twenty years—continued to stagnate. In fact, between 2001 and 2007, wages grew not at all, something unprecedented in any previous recorded business recovery."

7. Robert Kagan, "U.S. share is still about a quarter of global GDP," *The Financial Times,* February 7, 2012: http://www.ft.com/cms/s/0/d655dd52-4e9f-11e1-ada2-00144feabdc0.html#axzz2euUZAiCV Stephen D. King details the transformation in *Losing Control: The Emerging Threats to Western Prosperity* (New Haven, CT, 2010).

8. Bureau of Labor Statistics, Current Employment Statistics, Average Hourly Earnings in 1982 Dollars. Converted to 2008 dollars with CPI-U.

9. The calculations of economist Pavlina R. Tcherneva, based on data from Piketty/Saez and NBER. See Thomas Piketty, *Capital in the Twenty-First Century* (Cambridge, MA: 2014).

10. David Cay Johnston for Tax Analysts, "Scary New Wage Data," October 25, 2010, at http://www.tax.com.

11. Glenn Yago, "Junk Bonds," in *The Concise Encyclopedia of Economics*. http://www.econlib.org/LIBRARY/Enc/JunkBonds.html.

12. Michael Lewis has chronicled Wall Street's deceptions in the 1980s in *Liar's Poker* (New York, 1989).

13. John Kenneth Galbraith, *The Culture of Contentment* (New York, 1992).

14. In *The End of Easy Money and the Renewal of the American Economy* (New York, 2009), Peter S. Goodman sees the dominant motive as escapist magical thinking, underestimating the role of aggression and anxiety. The trope of binge gambling became a commonplace in the period. Vicky Ward incorporated the rampage killing trope of betrayal in *The Devil's Casino: Friendship, Betrayal, and the High Stake Game played Inside Lehman Brothers* (New York, 2010).

15. In Garry Marshall's *Pretty Woman* (1990), love for a hooker with a heart of gold (Julia Roberts) tames one such buccaneer. See my *Post-Traumatic Culture*, pp. 267-74.

16. For an incisive overview with data see Donald R. Barlett and James B. Steele, *America: What Went Wrong?* (Kansas City, 1992).

17. Savings were 8.9 percent of personal income in 1979, and reduced to 0.6 percent 2007.

18. The argument of Simon Johnson, former chief economist of the International Monetary Fund, in "The Quiet Coup," *The Atlantic,* May 2009.

19. Stephen Foley, "Paulson reveals U.S. concerns of breakdown in law and order," *Independent* (UK), July 17, 2009. Paulson gave a berserk-style title to his memoir of the meltdown *On the Brink: Inside the Race to Stop the Collapse of the Global Finance System* (New York, 2010).

20. Jill Lepore, "The Disruption Machine," *New Yorker* (June 23, 2014, 30-31), 35.

21. Nick Paumgarten, "The Death of Kings," *New Yorker,* May 18, 2009, 48. "Securitization" is the process of taking an illiquid asset, or group of assets, and through financial engineering, transforming them into a security. A typical example of securitization is a mortgage-backed security (MBS), which is a type of asset-backed security that is secured by a collection of mortgages" (Investopedia).

22. Kevin Phillips, "Numbers Racket: Why the economy is worse than we know," *Harper's Magazine,* May 2008.

23. Hanna Rosin, "Did Christianity Cause the Crash: How Preachers Are Spreading a Gospel of Debt," *Atlantic,* December 2009, 42.

24. Russ Winter, "Berserker Funds in Commodities," *The Wall Street Examiner,* May 21st, 2008 <<http://wallstreetexaminer.com/blogs/winter/?p=1664

25. William Greider, "Goldman Sachs Socialism," *The Nation,* October 6, 2008.

26. CNBC News (October 6, 2008).

27. Nouriel Roubini, "The world is at severe risk of a global systemic financial meltdown and a severe global depression," *Nouriel Roubini's Global EconoMonitor*, October 9, 2008, http://www.rgemonitor.com/index.php.

28. Jeremy Warner, "Mind-boggling growth in derivatives.," *The Independent,* Nov. 18, 2006. "The volume of over-the-counter derivatives traded rose by a quarter in the first half of this year to $370 trillion, driven primarily by rapid growth in credit default swaps and interest rate derivatives."

29. "In 1985, there were only $1.6 trillion in home mortgages. And only $500 billion worth of them were in pools used to back securities. Twenty years later, total mortgage debt approached $10 trillion, with $7.5 trillion of it securitized." Bill Bonner, "The Bottom Has Fallen Out," *Daily Reckoning,* 6.23.08.

30. Kenneth J. Gerbino, "Genève and Zurich Speech Notes ," Keynote Address, Academe Finance Conference, June 4-6, 2008, Posted Jun 19, 2008, http://www.gold-eagle.com/editorials_08/gerbino061808.html.

31. Anthony Faiola, et al., "What Went Wrong?" *Washington Post,* October 15, 2008.

32. Greenspan, "The Markets, Excerpts From Greenspan Speech on Global Turmoil," in *The New York Times,* November 6, 1998.

33. Department of Defense news briefing, February 12, 2002.

34. Erroll Morris, "The Certainty of Donald Rumsfeld (Part One)," *New York Times,* March 25, 2014. Morris had just filmed Rumsfeld in the biographical documentary *The Unknown Known* (2013).

35. Jim Puzzanghera, "Economic Rescue Could Cost $8.5 Trillion," *Los Angeles Times,* November 30, 2008.

36. A lucid overview is Steve Fraser, *Wall Street: America's Dream Palace* (New Haven, 2008)

37. Bill Bonner, "Inevitable and Disgraceful, but Still Unpredictable," *Daily Reckoning,* Nov 28, 2008. Bonner was already sounding an alarm when he published *Financial Reckoning Day* (Hoboken, NJ, 2003).

38. By Scott Thill, *AlterNet.* Posted November 9, 2009.

39. Louis Uchitelle and N.R. Kleinfield, "On the Battlefields of Business, Millions of Casualties," *New York Times,* March 3, 1996, sec. A.

40. Steven Greenhouse, *The Big Squeeze: Tough Times for the American Worker* (New York, 2008).

41. *First Blood*, dir. Ted Kotcheff (1982).

42. Postal employees are actually less likely to run amok than other workers. An independent commission in 1998 found 0.26 workplace homicides per 100,000 postal workers from 1992 to 1998. By comparison the rate was 2.10 per 100,000 for retail workers. The first post office rampage occurred on August 20, 1986 in Edmond, Oklahoma, when an ominously withdrawn and about to be fired letter carrier systematically shot to death fourteen fellow employees.

43. Ford Fessenden, "They Threaten, Seethe and Unhinge, Then Kill in Quantity: Rampage Killers / A Statistical Report," *New York Times* (April 8, 2000).

44. The Romans' specialized slave workshops were the first factories.

45. Bernard D. Meltzer, Cass R. Sunstein, "Public Employee Strikes, Executive Discretion, and the Air Traffic Controllers," *The University of Chicago Law Review*, Vol. 50, No. 2 (Spring, 1983), 731-99

46. Thomas H. Davenport and Laurence Prusak, "Re-engineering Revisited: What Went Wrong with the Business-Process Reengineering Fad, and Will It Come Back?" *Computerworld* (June 23, 2003).

47. Peter Gosselin, *High Wire: The Precarious Financial Lives of American Families* (New York, 2008).

48. "The automobile industry has been one of the losers in the new American economy. U.S. consumers spent less on new automobiles in 2007 than they spent on 'brokerage charges and investment counselling'; in 1979, they had spent ten times as much." Emma Rothschild, "Can We Transform the Auto-Industrial Society?" *New York Review of Books*, January 29, 2009, 8.

49. During the Depression, the editors of *Consumer Reports* complained that "Nazi pile-drivers [are] pounding the German workers into serfdom," while "in some of the large corporations of this country the techniques of Der Fuehrer and his cohorts are followed with avidity and approval and a feeling of 'why can't we get away with that too.'" *Consumer Reports* 2, No. 6 (1937), 32.

50. Today workers are often "orphaned" by being designated independent contractors for whom their employer bears no responsibility. See David Weil, *The Fissured Workplace: Why Work Became So Bad For So Many and What Can Be Done to Improve It* (Cambridge, MA: 2014).

51. At his retirement in 1990, GM's Roger Smith had his benefits gratuitously doubled. "The vote on what was once an obscure compensation issue has become something of an embarrassment for G.M.'s board. . . . The board adopted the change last fall, although some directors have indicated privately that they were unaware that it would almost double Mr. Smith's pension, from $700,000 to about $1.25 million a year, an official close to the board said yesterday." Anise C. Wallace, "G.M. Holders Likely to Back Rise in Executive Pensions," *New York Times*, May 24, 1990.

52. Cognitive linguist Anat Shenker-Osorio, author of *"Don't Buy It: The Trouble With Talking Nonsense About the Economy,"* finds that for conservatives, one idea "shaping perceptions of poverty, riches, inequality and desirable economic policy" is that "the economy exists for a specific purpose: to reward the good and punish the bad. It's a moral arbiter; simply having great riches indicates you deserve them because the economy loves you the best. Thus, it follows that poor people deserve to be poor and we can know this because they're poor." Paul Rosenberg, "Secrets of the right-wing brain: New study proves—conservatives see a different, hostile world," *Salon*, July 29, 2014.

http://www.salon.com/2014/07/29/secrets_of_the_right_wing_brain_new_study_proves_it_conservatives_see_a_different_hostile_world/.

53. "The Bright Side of the G.M. Disaster," Jim Kingsdale's Energy Investment Strategies, posted by Kingsdale on December 15, 2008 in *Energy Policy, The Economy:* http://www.energyinvestmentstrategies.com.

54. William Greider, "Bailout: What's Next?," Nation, September 29, 2008. Section 8 in the Treasury's three-page summary of Paulson's plan mandated that his supremacy was to be guaranteed: "Decisions by the Secretary pursuant to the authority of this Act are non-reviewable and committed to agency discretion, and may not be reviewed by any court of law or any administrative agency," http://dollarsandsense.org/blog/2008/09/political-and-financial-bedlam-william-greider.html.

55. Anatole Kaletsky, "We Must Have Confidence in Banks," *Times of London,* October 6, 2008.

56. See Yves Marchand and Romain Meffre, "The Ruins of Detroit," http://www.marchandmeffre.com/detroit/.

57. Nassim Taleb and Pablo Trian, "Bystanders to this financial crime were many," *Financial Times,* December 7, 2008. They add, "Listening to us, risk management practitioners would often agree on every point. But they elected to take part in the system and to play bystanders. They tried to explain away their decision to partake in the vast diffusion of responsibility . . . . Most poignantly, the police itself may have participated in the murder. The regulators were using the same arguments. They, too, were responsible."

58. A Ponzi scheme is a type of fraud based on fantasies of endless growth. The scheme pays off earlier investors with money raised from later victims until it runs out of new money and collapses.

CHAPTER 5

1. "Berserker Funds in Commodities," *The Wall Street Examiner: Winter (Economic & Market) Watch,* May 21, 2008, http://wallstreetexaminer.com/blogs/winter/?p=1664.

2. After describing CEO John Thain's extravagances, op-ed writer Maureen Dowd spluttered, "How are these ruthless, careless ghouls who murdered the economy still walking around (not to mention that sociopathic sadist Bernie Madoff?)—and not as perps?" in "Wall Street's Socialist Jet-Setters," *New York Times,* January 27, 2009.

3. Gregor Peter Schmitz and Gabor Steingart, "Crisis Plunges U.S. Middle Class into Poverty," *Spiegel Online,* April 23, 2009.

4. Andrew Clark, "Big Increase in U.S. Suicides at Work," *Guardian,* August 21, 2009. "The number of people who killed themselves at work in the U.S. rose 28% to an all-time high last year, in a grisly statistic that sparked speculation it was due to stress linked to the economic recession."

5. William K. Black, "How the Servant Became a Predator: Finance's Five Fatal Flaws," new deal 2.0, http://www.newdeal20.org/?p=5330. See also his *The Best Way to Rob a Bank Is to Own One.* (Austin, 2008). Black was an investigator of the 1980s Savings-and-Loan scandal.

6. Joe Conason, "Bring Wall Street Crooks to Justice," *New York Observer,* September 24, 2008.

7. George Packer, "The Ponzi State," *New Yorker* (February 9 & 16, 2009), 85.

8. Sprott Asset Management, "Welcome to the 2008 Meltdown," *Markets at a Glance,* January 2008, p. 1. See also Bonner and Wiggin, *Financial Reckoning Day.*

9. Dan Mitchell, "Walker, Fiscal Ranger," *New York Times,* March 10, 2007.

10. Bill Bonner, "The Dead Cat Bounce," *Daily Reckoning.* July 28, 2008.

11. Matt Taibi, "Wall Street's Bailout Hustle," *Rolling Stone,* February 17, 2010.

12. The title of George A. Akerlof and Paul M. Romer, *Looting: the Economic Underworld of Bankruptcy for Profit* (Toronto, 1993) draws on the trope of mafia and (institutional) killing for profit.

13. Eliot Spitzer, "Predatory Lenders' Partner in Crime: How the Bush Administration Stopped the States From Stepping In to Help Consumers," *Washington Post,* February 14, 2008.

14. Gretchen Morgenson, "An Unfinished Chapter at Countrywide," *New York Times,* August 23, 2014.

15. "Cleveland Mayor Frank G. Jackson Says Subprime Lending Practices No Different Than 'Organized Crime,'" UPI, January 11, 2008.

16. Michael Shank, "Chomsky on Iran, Iraq, and the Rest of the World," *Foreign Policy in Focus,* February 16, 2007, http://www.fpif.org/fpiftxt/3999.

17. "Chavez Threatens U.S. Oil Cutoff," Associated Press, February 10, 2008.

18. Zygmundt Bauman, *Wasted Lives: Modernity and Its Outcasts* (Cambridge, Eng., 2004), 63. Bauman quotes from Francois de Bernard, *La Pauvrete Durable* (Felin, 2002), 37-39. See also Richard Rubenstein, *The Age of Triage.*

19. Richard Rorty, "Globalization, the politics of identity and social hope," *Philosophy and Social Hope* (New York, 1999), 229-39.

20. Ed Vulliamy, The Observer, "How a big U.S. bank laundered billions from Mexico's murderous drug gangs," *Guardian,* April 2, 2011.

21. Jerome C. Glenn and Theodore J. Gordon, *2007 State of the Future.* The Millennium Project, 2007. See also Misha Glenny, *McMafia: A Journey through the Global Criminal Underworld* (New York, 2008).

22. Julian Borger, "Organised crime: the $2 trillion threat," *Guardian,* September 12 2007.

23. On the right, Austrian School economist Murray Rothbard, who regarded government as "a gang of thieves," held in his *World Market Perspective* (1984) that banks have been primary drivers of American policy.

24. In his 1987 PBS program "The Secret Government: The Constitution in Crisis," Moyers defines the secret government as "an interlocking network

of official functionaries, spies, mercenaries, ex-generals, profiteers and superpatriots, who for a variety of motives, operate outside the legitimate institutions of government." See, e.g., John Perkins, *The Secret History of the American Empire: Economic Hit Men, Jackals, and the Truth about Global Corruption* (New York, 2007).

25. Beatrice Edwards, *The Rise of the American Corporate Security State*. (New York, 2014).

26. Zephyr Teachout focuses on the Roberts' Supreme Court's decisions in *Corruption in America* (Cambridge, MA, 2014).

27. Lee Fang, "Koch Brothers Convene Super-Secret Billioniares' Meeting for 2012 Elections," *Alternet*, February 3, 2012.

28. Arian Campo-Flores and Monica Campbell, "Bloodshed on the Border," *Newsweek*, December 8, 2008.

29. Rucker, Allen and David Chase. *The Sopranos, A Family History*. New York, 2003.

30. Steve Eder, "Insider trading case as much Sopranos as Wall Street," Reuters, October 5, 2009.

31. Bosses of the Camorra, the Neapolitan mafia, watch their murders reported on TV news, and call killing "doing a piece," as in doing piecework or contract labor, and as if mob murder is a kind of manufacturing. See Roberto Saviano, *Gomorrah* (New York, 2007). Camorristi have gone global, selling toxic waste, money laundering, drug smuggling, etc. According to Saviano, the Camorra has no code or ideology beyond "the most aggressive neoliberalism."

32. F. William Engdahl, "The Financial Tsunami Part IV: Asset Securitzation," Financial Sense Editorial Archives (February 8, 2008), http://www.financialsensearchive.com/editorials/engdahl/2008/0208.html.

33. See Robert Darnton, "Peasants Tell Tales," in *The Great Cat Massacre* (New York, 1984).

34. Price Pritchett, *New Work Habits for a Radically Changing World*, 51.

35. Klein, *Shock Doctrine*, 424-25.

36. Klein, *Shock Doctrine*, 425.

37. Glen O. Gabbard, *The Psychology of the Sopranos : Love, Death, and Betrayal in America's Favorite Gangster Movie* (New York, 2002), xii.

38. Peter C. Whybrow, *American Mania: When More Is Not Enough* (New York, 2005).

39. Carrie Johnson, "Enron's Fastow Gets 6 Years," *Washington Post*, September 27, 2006.

40. In Nicholaus Mills, *Culture in an Age of Money: the Legacy of the 1980s in America* (Chicago, 1990).

41. Eric J. Fry, "Pinstriped Psychopaths," in "The Rude Awakening" blog, July 8, 2005. In their book *Snakes in Suits* (New York, 2006), Paul Babiak and Robert D. Hare argue that a surprising number of workplaces employ psychopaths. While psychopaths make up 1 percent of the general population, Babiak

and Hare found that 3.5 percent of the executives they worked with "fit the profile of the psychopath." Psychopathic employees are pathological liars who get away with doing little or no work. See also Robert Monk's bracing *A Traitor to His Class* (New York, 1999).

CHAPTER 6

1. "As he announces his plans for the ethnic cleansing of Canaan," says Jack Miles, "the Lord does not, to repeat, seem angry with the Canaanites, but the effect is genocidal all the same, and there is no escaping it." See Jack Miles, *God: a Biography* (New York, 1995, rpt. 1996), 117.

2. Reza Aslan surveys groups around the world that view their earthly struggles in cosmic terms. See *How to Win a Cosmic War* (New York, 2008). Like Samuel Huntington's *The Clash of Civilizations and the Remaking of World Order*, Aslan's book emphasizes the power of ideas to drive behavior.

3. Ruth Stein, "Evil as Love and Liberation," in *Terror and Apocalypse*, ed. Jerry S. Piven et al. (San Jose, CA, 2002), p. 107. See also her *For Love of the Father: A Psychoanalytic Study of Religious Terrorism* (Stanford, CA, 2010).

4. Quoted in Joel Achenbach and Dale Russakoff, "Teen Shooter's Life Paints Antisocial Portrait," *Washington Post* (April 29, 1999).

5. Mervyn Bendle, "The Apocalyptic Imagination and Popular Culture," *Journal of Religion and Popular* Culture, XI (Fall 2005).

6. "Gunman Wrote of Revenge," Springfield, MA, *Union-News*, July 31, 1999.

7. *People*, August 16, 1999, 121.

8. *Jonestown: The Life and Death of Peoples Temple*. American Experience, PBS.org.

9. Jeanne Mills, *Six Years with God* (New York, 1979).

10. Mary McCormick Maaga includes a transcript of the Jonestown tape in *Hearing the Voices of Jonestown* (Syracuse, NY, 1998).

11. "The suicides were so well organized that the potion for the children was prepared in a different container (at a lesser strength, I assume) than the potion

12. Bruce Wilson, 'Palin-Attended Church Event Featured Samurai Sword Ceremony," *Huffington Post*, July 17, 2009.

13. Frank Schaeffer, "How I (and other Pro-Life Leaders) Contributed to Dr. Tiller's Death," *Huffington Post*, June 1, 2009.

14. Gabriel Winant, "O'Reilly's Campaign against Murdered Doctor," *Salon*, May 31, 2009. Kathleen Parker, "Carnival of the Fire-Breathers," *Washington Post*, June 3, 2009.

15. Jeff Sharlet, "Jesus Killed Mohammed: the Crusade for a Christian Military," *Harper's*, May 2009, 34.

16. Bruce Wilson, " John Ensign Linked to 'Do-it-Yourself Exorcism Movement," *Huffington Post*, July 14, 2009.

17. Bruce Wilson, "Fighting Demons, Raising the Dead, Taking over the World," *Religion Dispatches*, April 1, 2009, http://www.religiondispatches.org/archive/politics/1273/fighting_demons,_raising_the_dead,_taking_over_the_world

18. The research debunking recovered memory and multiple personality is extensive. An incisive account of the craze is Joan Acocella, "The Politics of Hysteria," *New Yorker*, April 6, 1998. More comprehensive is Ian Hacking, *Rewriting the Soul* (Princeton, 1995). For MPD as a cultural fantasy, see my *Post-Traumatic Culture*, Ch. 7.

19. For details, see Ch. 7 of my *Post-Traumatic Culture, esp. 194-211.*

20. George Frederick Drinka, M.D. describes this process in *The Birth of Neurosis: Myth, Malady and the Victorians* (New York, 1984).

21. See D. Frankfurter, *Evil Incarnate: Rumors of Demonic Conspiracy and Ritual Abuse in History* (Princeton, 2006). In *Demon Lovers* (Chicago, 2002), Walter Stephens demonstrates that witchcraft fantasies can be understood as attempts to believe in supernatural religion. Fundamentalist Christians' professed horror at demonic influence in Halloween, Harry Potter, and Satanic ritual child abuse, says Stephens, is a case of "forlorn hope masquerading as morbid fear" (367).

22. Hitler's secretary Traudl Junge describes the trancelike apocalyptic atmosphere that engulfed her and the command bunker in *Until the Final Hour: Hitler's Last Secretary* (New York, 2004).

23. In "The Politics of Hysteria," Acocella reports that Dr. Braun came to believe that even florists were part of the Satanic cult, sending color-coded flowers to his hospitalized patients (76).

24. David Grann, "Trial by Fire: Did Texas Execute an Innocent Man?" *New Yorker*, September 7, 2009, 62.

25. For an overview of this development see Kevin Phillips, *American Theocracy: The Peril And Politics Of Radical Religion, Oil And Borrowed Money In The 21st Century* (New York, 2006).

26. Jon Basil Utley, "America's Amageddonites," Foreign Policy In Focus (October 10, 2007), www.fpif.org. See also Chris Hedges, *American Fascists: The Christian Right and the War on America* (Free Press, 2006).

27. George Monbiot, "U.S. policy towards the Middle East is driven by a rarefied form of madness. It's time we took it seriously," *The Guardian*, April 20, 2004.

28. Utley, "America's Armageddonites."

29. Mike Davis, *Ecology of Fear* (New York, 1998). In "The Irresistible Urge to Destroy New York on Screen," *New York Times*, December 26, 2007, Sewell Chan toted up eighteen films.

30. Jared Orsi, in *Humanities and Social Science Net Online*, September, 1998. http://www.h-net.msu.edu/reviews/showrev.cgi?path=11745907095636.

31. See, e.g., Ronald H. Fritze, *Invented Knowledge: False History, Fake Science and Pseudo-Religions* (London and Chicago, 2009), 168.

32. Robert Jay Lifton, "American Apocalypse," *The Nation*, December 22, 2003.

CONCLUSION

1. James Truslow Adams made the phrase popular with *The Epic of America* (New York, 1931).
2. Michael Klare, "A Planet on the Brink: Will Economic Brushfires Prove Too Virulent to Contain?" Posted at TomDispatch.com (February 24, 2009).

INDEX

ABOUT THE AUTHOR

Kirby Farrell is Professor of English at the University of Massachusetts in Amherst, and the author of *Post-Traumatic Culture: Injury
and Interpretation in the 90s,* and other literary and cultural studies.
He is also the author of several novels. For the Ernest Becker Foundation he has lectured and written on the psychology of violence, and
social justice. He is a regular contributor to *Psychology Today* online.
www.psychologytoday.com/blog/swim-in-denial